TREATISE
ON
MILITARY SMALL ARMS
AND
AMMUNITION,

WITH THEORY OF THE MOTION
OF A RIFLE BULLET.

A TEXT BOOK FOR THE ARMY

LIEUT.-COLONEL H. BOND, R.A.

The Naval & Military Press Ltd

Published by
The Naval & Military Press Ltd
Unit 10, Ridgewood Industrial Park,
Uckfield, East Sussex,
TN22 5QE England
Tel: +44 (0) 1825 749494
Fax: +44 (0) 1825 765701
www.naval-military-press.com

© The Naval & Military Press Ltd 2004

In reprinting in facsimile from the original, any imperfections are inevitably reproduced and the quality may fall short of modern type and cartographic standards.

THE COLOURED PLATES IN THIS REPRINT
ARE PLACED AT THE END.

PREFACE.

In writing and compiling the following "Treatise," the author begs to thank the Inspector-General of Musketry and the Staff at Hythe for their cordial co-operation. He gratefully acknowledges his obligations to his friend and late colleague, Major W. McClintock, R.A., to whom he is indebted for most of the tables, as well as much valuable information on other points. He also thanks Lieut.-Colonel Sladen for permission to use his "Principles of Gunnery," and his friends and brother officers who have kindly examined the proofs. He desires to acknowledge the courtesy of the Institution of Mechanical Engineers in allowing him to make use of an article on Breech-loaders by Mr. W. P. Marshall, in their Proceedings, and some excellent plates in connection with it. Chapter VII is taken from the original "Hythe Text Book," the matter only being re-arranged.

SUNDERLAND,
    March, 1884.

CONTENTS.

CHAPTER I.

PAGE

Definition of Terms and Expressions used in Connection with Small Arms, and the Motion of a Rifle Bullet .. 7

CHAPTER II.

Resistance of the Air to the Motion of a Projectile. The Trajectory of the Bullet. Penetration. Recoil .. 26

CHAPTER III.

Rifling. Breech-loading Military Rifles. Match Rifles. Repeating and Magazine Rifles. Revolvers. Tables of Military Rifles 47

CHAPTER IV.

Service Swords. Lances. Sword Bayonets and Bayonets .. 102

CHAPTER V.

Gunpowder. Composition of Gunpowder. Proportion of Ingredients. Force of Gunpowder, how Influenced. Outline of Manufacture. Ventilation of Magazines. Lead as a Material for Bullets 111

CHAPTER VI.

PAGE

Small Arm Ammunition. Cartridge Cases. Wads and Lubrication. Snider and Martini-Henry Cartridges. Professor Bashforth's General Tables, with Examples worked out by them 124

CHAPTER VII.

History of Small Arms to the Adoption of Breech-loaders. Early Arms. The Hand Gun. The Match Lock. The Flint Lock. The Percussion Musket. Rifles 156

Chapter I.

DEFINITION OF TERMS AND EXPRESSIONS USED IN CONNECTION WITH SMALL ARMS, AND THE MOTION OF A RIFLE BULLET.

EVERY cause tending to produce or change the motion of a body is called force. *Force.*

There are three forms of force to be taken into account in considering the motion of a bullet, viz.:— *Forces which act upon a bullet.*

1st. The pressure of the gas generated by the combustion of the charge of gunpowder which acts on the bullet until it leaves the muzzle of the rifle.

2nd. The resistance of the air, which acts upon the bullet during its flight, and gradually decreases as the velocity of the bullet becomes less.

3rd. The earth's attraction, which brings the bullet to the ground.

If the atmosphere is not supposed to be in a state of rest, the velocity and direction of the wind must also be considered as influencing the motion of a bullet.

The degree of rapidity with which a body moves is called its velocity. In this country the velocity of a bullet is estimated by the number of feet through which it would move in a second, and the muzzle velocity of the Martini-Henry bullet is spoken of as 1315 f.s., meaning that if it continued moving with this velocity it would pass through 1315 feet in a second. *Velocity.*

The velocity of a body may be either *uniform* or *variable*. It is uniform when it describes equal distances in equal times, and is variable when equal distances are not described in equal times. The speed of a bullet is an example of variable velocity, since it is constantly losing velocity from the time it leaves the muzzle of the rifle until it strikes. *Uniform and variable velocity.*

8

Uniform velocity, how measured. Uniform velocity is measured by the number of units of length passed over in a unit of time. Thus, suppose a body moving with a uniform velocity to pass over 100 feet in 4 seconds, its velocity is $\frac{100}{4} = 25$ feet per second.

Variable velocity, how measured. Variable velocity is measured by the number of units of length which would be described in a unit of time if at that moment the velocity were to cease to vary. Thus the velocity of a bullet at any point is said to be 1000 feet per second, not meaning that it passed through 1000 feet the second before or the second after it passed this point, but that if it continued with the velocity it had at that instant, it would go through 1000 feet in one second.

Accelerated and retarded velocity. When the velocity increases it is said to be accelerated; and when it diminishes it is said to be retarded.

Again, accelerated or retarded velocities may be either uniformly or variably accelerated or retarded.

Muzzle velocity. Muzzle velocity is the velocity with which the bullet leaves the muzzle of the barrel from which it is fired. It depends on the nature and amount of the powder charge, the quality of the powder, the weight of the bullet, and the amount of friction the bullet has to overcome when passing through the barrel, the length of the barrel, &c.

Remaining velocity. Remaining velocity is the velocity of a bullet at any given point in its trajectory.

Striking velocity. Striking velocity is the velocity of the bullet on impact.

Terminal velocity. If a bullet is fired at a high angle with the horizontal the velocity at the highest point of its path is almost nothing, in its fall downwards it is acted upon by the earth's attraction, and opposed by the resistance of the air, and the velocity continually increases, but should a certain point be reached where the weight of the bullet in pounds becomes exactly equal to the resistance of the air (the resistance increasing with the velocity of the moving body) the velocity of the bullet becomes uniform, when it is termed the Terminal Velocity.

Momentum. The momentum or quantity of motion of a body at any time is the weight* of the body multiplied by its velocity. In the case of a bullet, when it strikes it would be the weight of the bullet multiplied by its striking velocity.

The comparative momenta of moving bodies are in proportion to the products of their weights and velocities. A ball of 4 lbs., moving with a velocity of 18 feet per second, has twice the momentum of a ball of 3 lbs. moving with a velocity of 12 feet per second; because the 1st product, $4 \times 18 = 72$, is double the 2nd, $3 \times 12 = 36$.

Hence a comparatively light body, such as a bullet with a high velocity, may have as much momentum as a much heavier body with a low velocity.

The calibre is the diameter of the bore, and in the case of a rifle it is measured across the lands. Calibre.

Windage is the difference between the sectional area of the bore of the gun and that of the projectile. It is measured practically by the actual linear difference between the diameter of the bore and the diameter of the bullet. With muzzle-loading smooth-bore small arms the windage was the cause of great inaccuracy in shooting, but with rifles there is no windage, as on discharge the bullet is set up or expanded and completely fills the bore and grooves. Windage.

The axis of rotation is a line through the centre of gravity of a body about which the body revolves. Axis of rotation.

Grooves are spiral furrows cut in the surface of the bore, with the object of imparting a rotatory motion to the bullet as it passes from breech to muzzle. Grooves.

Grooves are said to be of progressive depth when they increase or diminish in depth from breech to muzzle. With the Snider and Martini-Henry the grooves are deeper at the breech than at the muzzle, the object being to ease the bullet at first and ensure its being gripped tightly on leaving the bore. Grooves of progressive depth.

Lands are the portions of the surface of the bore left between the grooves. Lands.

Rifling is the name given to the spiral grooves cut in the inside of the barrel of a firearm in order to give rota- Rifling.

---

* Weight and mass are used in ordinary language to mean the same thing.

tion to the bullet round that axis which coincides with the axis of the bore before the rifle is fired.

A spherical or an elongated bullet can be fired from a rifle, but only a spherical bullet can be used with advantage from a smooth-bore. If a conical bullet were fired from the latter arm, it would tumble over (or commence rotating round its shorter axis) immediately on leaving the muzzle, and range but a short distance, owing to the great resistance it would meet with in its passage through the air when thus rotating.

Uniform and increasing or gaining twist. In some cases the grooves of rifles are made with a uniform twist or spiral, others have what is called an increasing or gaining twist.

Grooves with a uniform twist make the same angle with a straight line drawn in the bore from the breech to the muzzle at all points, while with the increasing twist the angle is constantly varying.

With the increasing twist it is usual for the grooves to begin with a slight inclination at the breech, and the twist or spiral to increase regularly until it reaches the muzzle; then the twist towards the muzzle is said to be sharper or quicker.

Increasing twist unsuitable for military arm. An increasing twist is unsuitable for a military arm for the following reasons:—from want of care and other causes the grooves of rifles get rusty and require repair; to effect the removal of the rust a process called "lapping" is resorted to, which consists in taking a leaden cast of a portion of the bore with grooves; this plug of lead is then attached to a rod and worked up and down the barrel, and, with the aid of emery soon removes the rust; with an increasing twist the plug of lead could only fit the portion of the bore in which it was cast, and the process would be impossible. It is also evident that a bullet must alter its shape in conforming to the grooves of an increasing twist whil passing through the barrel, and in the case of dee grooves, this would certainly take away from the effective pressure of the powder gas.

The angle of spiral or twist of rifling. The twist of rifling in any rifle is so arranged that the bullet may have a sufficient velocity of rotation as it leaves the muzzle to ensure its rotating steadily round its longer axis during its flight.

No more twist should be given to the grooves than is necessary, for grooves with a quick twist foul more rapidly and are difficult to clean.

The twist of *uniform* rifling is estimated by the distance along the bore (expressed in calibres or inches) in which the spiral makes one turn; with the *increasing* twist it is estimated at any point by the distance in which the spiral would make one turn had the angle of the spiral remained uniform and the same as at the given point. *Twist of rifling, how estimated.*

The reader will see the similarity in the modes adopted for measuring an increasing twist, and a variable velocity.

The twist of rifling is often expressed in calibres, and that this is the best method for comparison will be made clearer by an example.

The grooves of the Martini-Henry rifle make one turn in 22 inches, and the diameter of the bore is 0·45 inch.

The twist of the Snider long rifle is one turn in 78 inches, and diameter of bore is 0·577 inch.

Were the latter rifle to have the same twist expressed in inches. viz., 1 turn in 22 inches, as the former, the actual twist of rifling of the two rifles, owing to the difference in their calibres, would not be identical. When, however, two rifles have grooves which make one turn in the same number of their calibres, then the actual twist of rifling in each is the same.

When the motion of bullets fired from rifles is considered, it is necessary to distinguish between the *motion of translation* and the *motion of rotation*. *The motion of translation and rotation of a bullet fired from a rifle.*

Motion of translation refers to the onward motion of a bullet through the air; the motion of rotation to its spinning round its longer axis.

Both these motions are combined in the motion of an elongated bullet fired from a rifle, but they are best considered separately.

The velocity of translation of a bullet is measured by its linear velocity in feet per second. *Velocity of translation.*

The velocity of rotation of a bullet may be obtained as follows:—If the bullet in the bore makes *one revolution* in n calibres. i.e., in nd inches, where d is the calibre in inches, and if V is the muzzle velocity of the bullet in *Velocity of rotation.*

12

feet per second (supposed uniform for a short space of time) then the number of revolutions of the bullet per second, S, as it leaves the muzzle of the rifle, or the velocity of rotation, is

$$S = \frac{12V}{nd} \quad \ldots\ldots\ldots\ldots\ldots (1).$$

Linear velocity of rotation. The linear velocity of rotation which for practical purposes is the most important, is the velocity with which a point on the surface of the bullet revolves round the axis of rotation. It may be found as follows:—as a point on the bullet describes a circle (the circumference of the bullet) each revolution, the number of revolutions in (1) must be multiplied by πd, d being the diameter of the bullet in inches, to get the number of inches per second through which the point travels, or the linear velocity of rotation.

When calculating the twist of rifling which a rifle must have in order that it should fire a bullet of a certain number of calibres in length, it is the linear velocity of rotation of the bullet which must be considered.

Examples:—

1. Find the linear velocity of rotation at the muzzle of a Martini-Henry bullet.

Muzzle velocity = 1315 feet per second.
Twist of rifling = 1 turn in 22 inches.
Diameter of bullet = 0·45 inch.

Number of revolutions per second at muzzle

$$= \frac{1315 \times 12}{22} = 717\cdot 28.$$

Linear velocity of rotation = $\pi d \times 717\cdot 28 = 0\cdot 45 \times 3\cdot 14159 \times 717\cdot 28 = 1014$ inches per second = 84·5 feet per second.

2. Find the linear velocity of rotation at the muzzle of a Snider bullet.

Muzzle velocity = 1240 feet per second.
Twist of rifling = 1 turn in 78 inches.
Diameter of bullet = 0·577 inch.

Number of revolutions per second at muzzle

$$= \frac{1240 \times 12}{78} = 190\cdot77.$$

Linear velocity of rotation $= \pi d \times 190\cdot77 = 0\cdot577 \times 3\cdot14159 \times 190\cdot77 = 345\cdot81$ inches per second $= 28\cdot82$ feet per second.

Mathematicians prefer measuring the velocity of rotation of a bullet by its *angular* velocity in units of circular measure per second. The angular velocity of a bullet making *one turn* in one second is 2π.

Another method.

Now, if ω be the angular velocity of a bullet per second, and S the *number of turns* it makes in a second, then

$$S = \frac{\omega}{2\pi}\dots\dots\dots\dots\dots\dots(2),$$

i.e., the number of revolutions per second is proportional to the *angular velocity*.

But by (1)—
$$S = \frac{12V}{nd}.$$

Equating (1) and (2),
$$\omega = \frac{24\pi V}{nd}\dots\dots\dots\dots\dots\dots(3),$$

whence it is seen that the angular velocity increases directly with the muzzle velocity, and decreases with an increase of calibre, or of n.

The linear velocity of rotation is the product ωr, where r is the distance in inches of the point considered from the axis of rotation, and ω the angular velocity.

From (3),

Linear velocity of rotation—

$$\omega r = \frac{24\pi V r}{nd} \text{ in inches per second,}$$

$$= \frac{2\pi V r}{nd} \text{ in feet per second,}$$

which is the same result obtained by the first method.

If bullets are fired from two rifles with the same twist in calibres but with bores of different diameters, and if the muzzle velocities are the same, then (1) the angular velocities of the bullets will be different; (2) the number of complete revolutions made per second will be different; (3) but the linear velocities of rotation will be the same.

(1) For $\omega = \dfrac{24\pi V}{nd}$ and d is different in each, therefore the bullet with largest diameter will have the least angular velocity.

(2) Again $S = \dfrac{12V}{nd}$, and d is different in each, therefore the bullet with largest diameter will make the fewest revolutions per second.

(3) Linear velocity $= \dfrac{2\pi Vr}{nd} = \dfrac{2\pi Vr}{n \cdot 2r} = \dfrac{\pi V}{n}$ a constant, therefore the linear velocity of rotation of the bullets will be the same.

It will also be seen that as the muzzle velocity and the diameter of the bullet influence the velocity of rotation, as well as the twist of rifling, before settling what twist of rifling a rifle is to have, it must be known what muzzle velocity, diameter, and length the bullet is to have.

Amount of twist. The exact amount of twist necessary for the grooves of any particular rifle can only be satisfactorily and definitely determined by careful experiments.

The longer the bullet in calibres the greater must be the velocity of rotation. The greater the length of the bullet in calibres the greater must be the velocity of rotation. Although the Martini-Henry and Snider bullets have the same weight, their length is different, the former being 2·82 calibres long, and the latter 1·806 calibres. It is for this reason that the Snider bullet can be fired with so much less velocity of rotation than the Martini-Henry bullet.

Drift. The drift is the deflection of a bullet due to the rotation imparted by the rifling. The greater the velocity of rotation the greater will be the drift of the bullet.

The deflection due to drift is found to increase in a greater proportion than that due to the range; this is because a bullet loses its onward motion quicker than its rotatory motion.

With our rifles, which have always a right-handed twist, the upper surface of the bullet rotates from left to right with reference to the firer, and the bullet deflects to the right.

The French Chassepôt and Gras, and some other foreign rifles, have a left-handed twist, and consequently their bullets deflect to the left.

A bullet is said to strip when it is driven out of the bore across the lands without following the grooves of the rifle; this seldom occurs. *Stripping.*

When a charge of gunpowder is ignited in a rifle barrel, a certain amount of residue will be found adhering to the surface of the bore and clogging the grooves of the rifling. This residue is called fouling and if it is deposited to any considerable amount good shooting with the barrel is impossible. With match rifles, when the bore was wiped out after every round, the fouling of the barrel was of no great importance; but with military rifles an efficient wad must be used to remove the fouling left by the previous round. Badly made gunpowder, or gunpowder which has been injured by damp, causes much fouling. *Fouling of the barrel.*

A rifle barrel is said to be leaded when particles of lead are detached from the bullet as it passes up the bore and adhere to the lands and fill up the grooves. If a barrel becomes very foul it is certain to become leaded, when the shooting at once becomes wild. Even a clean barrel is liable to become leaded, and it is to prevent this being the case that the Martini-Henry bullet is papered. The deeper and more angular the form of groove, and the quicker the twist, the greater the likelihood of the bore becoming foul and leaded. *Leading of the barrel.*

Arms are said to be interchangeable when the component parts of any one arm will exactly replace those of another of the same pattern. This important object is attained by machining the various parts, and subjecting them to a rigid examination at different stages of manufacture; they must also fit standard gauges, which ensures perfect coincidence in form and dimensions. *Interchangeable arms.*

Long and short butts are terms met with in descriptions of small arms. The Martini-Henry long butt is $14\frac{5}{16}$ inches, and the short butt $13\frac{13}{16}$ inches in length *Long and short butts.*

measured from the trigger to centre of the butt plate. Long and short butts are issued to the army in the proportions ⅔ long to ⅓ short. The Martini-Henry carbines have all long butts.

Axis of bore. The axis of the bore is an imaginary line passing down the centre of the bore.

Small bore. When the diameter of the bore of a rifle is less than 0·5 inch, it is usually described as a "small bore."

Line of sight. The line of sight is an imaginary line passing through the sights and the point aimed at.

Plane of sight. The plane of sight is the vertical plane passing through the line of sight.

Angle of elevation. The angle of elevation is the angle which the line of sight makes with the axis of the bore.

Line of fire. The line of fire is the direction in which the bullet is moving on leaving the rifle; or, in other words, a tangent to the trajectory at the muzzle.

Angle of descent. The angle of descent is the angle which a tangent to the trajectory at the first point of impact makes with the horizontal plane. It is always greater than the angle of elevation, slightly so at short ranges, but as the range increases the difference between the angles of elevation and descent becomes greater and greater. With the present military rifles at 1000 yards range the angle of descent is about one-third more than the angle of elevation.

Range. The range is the distance from the muzzle of the rifle to the intersection of the trajectory with the line of sight.

Point blank. A rifle is laid point blank if the line of sight is parallel to the axis of the bore.

Point blank range. Point blank range is a term sometimes met with; it was first used when the idea prevailed that the path of the bullet was a straight line for a certain distance from the muzzle; it is now used with different meanings, and it is questionable if it ought to be retained.

If the axis of the bore of a rifle was directed on a point at some distance from the muzzle, and if the bullet struck the point aimed at, that would be the point blank range of the rifle, but this can never occur unless the drop of the bullet due to gravity is counteracted by some extraneous cause, such as a jump up of the axis of the piece by recoil before the bullet has left the bore. In gunnery this jump is very marked, and artillery call the range due to the jump in any particular gun its point blank range. It is obtained as follows:—The gun is laid with the axis of the bore horizontal on a point on a target, at the same height as the axis, at a short distance from the muzzle. On firing it will be found that the projectile, owing to the jump, will strike above the point aimed at. If now the point aimed at is removed, still in the direction of the axis of the bore, to such a distance that the projectile will exactly strike it, this distance is called the point blank range of the gun.

The Martini-Henry rifle is found to shoot higher from a fixed rest where there can be no jump than from the shoulder. To account for this it is supposed that there is a buckling or springing of the barrel when unsupported, causing the muzzle to droop, and this is found to be increased when the fore end is removed. Expert riflemen also say they require less elevation when firing from the back position, where the barrel is supported further forward, than in the prone. It is evident from the above that the Martini-Henry rifle has no point blank range in the gunnery sense.

Experiments would most likely show that arms with short barrels, such as pistols, have a range due to the "jump."

Gunmakers are often asked for express rifles having a point blank range of say 150 yards. To meet the requirement they fix one back sight notch for all distances up to 150 yards, and use such a charge of powder as will give the bullet a muzzle velocity of 1800 or 2000 f.s., but even with these high velocities the bullet is found to drop 4 or 5 inches in 150 yards, and the firer is obliged to take a fine sight at short distances, and a fuller as the range increases.

The term "point blank range" is also sometimes applied to the range obtained by aiming the eye along the barrel where there is no back sight. It is evident that this range may be made to vary by altering the thickness of metal at either the breech or the muzzle, others apply it to the range given by the lowest notch on the back sight.

Lateral deviation.

The lateral deviation is the perpendicular distance of the point of impact of the bullet to the right or left of the plane of sight.

Resistance of the air.

The resistance of the air to a bullet during its flight is the force which tends to stop the bullet, and so continually diminishes its velocity. If the force of gravity did not exist, the resistance of the air would after a certain time cause a bullet when fired from a rifle to come to rest. The greater the velocity of a body, the greater the resistance of the air. The air consists of particles of matter in a gaseous condition, and on a bullet being projected with a high velocity into this medium, collision takes place between the particles of the air and the head of the bullet. Considerable force is expended in overcoming the inertia of these particles, and thus the velocity of the bullet is quickly diminished.

The muzzle velocity of the Martini-Henry bullet may be taken at 1315 feet per second (this being an average muzzle velocity), and the following remaining velocities at different ranges will show the loss of velocity due solely to the resistance of the air:—

Range.	Velocity.
0 yards.	1315 feet per second.
500 ,,	869 ,, ,,
1000 ,,	664 ,, ,,
1500 ,,	508 ,, ,,
2000 ,,	389 ,, ,,
2500 ,,	301 ,, ,,
3000 ,,	233 ,, ,,

Retardation.

Retardation is the rate at which the bullet loses velocity, owing to the resistance of the air.

This depends on—

1. The muzzle velocity of the bullet.
2. The density of the air.
3. The form of the head of the bullet.
4. The power of the bullet to overcome the resistance of the air due to its sectional density.

Sectional density.

Sectional density is a term used to express the relation which exists between the weight of a bullet and the area of its greatest cross section. This ratio may be expressed as

$$\text{Sectional density} = \frac{\text{Wt. of bullet}}{\text{Area of cross section}}.$$

In this country the weight of the bullet is expressed in pounds avoirdupois, and the cross section in square inches. Abroad it is expressed by the number of kilogrammes per square centimetre of section.

It has been deduced from careful experiments that the retardation a bullet meets with in its passage through any medium, such as the air, is directly proportional to its cross section, and inversely proportional to its weight. Thus—

(1.) Retardation is proportional to—

$$\frac{\text{Area of cross section}}{\text{Wt. of bullet}}.$$

Conversely, the power of the bullet to overcome resistance must be directly proportional to the weight, and inversely proportional to its cross section. Thus—

(2.) Ranging power is proportional to—

$$\frac{\text{Wt. of bullet}}{\text{Area of cross section}}.$$

This latter method is the one used on the Continent to compare bullets; it agrees with the definition of sectional density, and if the sectional densities of bullets are tabulated, their comparative powers of overcoming resistance are obtained.

In this country (1) is employed, and the comparative retardations the bullets would meet with are tabulated, and are called the $\frac{d^2}{W}$ of the bullets.

$\frac{d^2}{W}$ is thus obtained.

Retardation is proportional to—

$$\frac{\text{Section in square inches}}{\text{Weight in pounds}}.$$

is proportional to $\frac{\pi d^2}{4} \times \frac{1}{W}$,

(S.A.)

is proportional to $\dfrac{\pi}{4} \times \dfrac{d^2}{W}$,

where d = diameter of bullet in inches, and W = weight of bullet in pounds.

As $\dfrac{\pi}{4}$ is a constant, it may be neglected when comparing the powers of different bullets, and the value of their $\dfrac{d^2}{W}$ need only be calculated.

For example :—

Find the value of $\dfrac{d^2}{W}$ for the Martini-Henry and Snider bullets.

Diameter of the Martini-Henry bullet = 0·45 inch.
Weight   ,,   ,,   ,,   = 480 grains.
Number of grains in 1 lb. = 7000.

$$\therefore \dfrac{d^2}{W} = \dfrac{(0\cdot 45)^2}{\dfrac{480}{7000}} = 2\cdot 953.$$

Diameter of the Snider bullet = 0·577 inches.
Weight   ,,   ,,   ,,   = 480 grains.

$$\therefore \dfrac{d^2}{W} = \dfrac{(0\cdot 577)^2}{\dfrac{480}{7000}} = 4\cdot 855.$$

From this it will be seen that the retardation which the Snider bullet would meet with in its passage through the air is much greater than in the case of the Martini-Henry bullet moving with the same velocity, or in the proportion of 4·855 to 2·953.

If two bullets of the same form and dimensions, but of different material, are fired with the same muzzle velocity, the resistance of the air to each will be the same, but the retardations they will experience will be inversely as their weights.

It will be seen that by diminishing the calibre of a rifle and increasing the length of the bullet, a very favourable $\dfrac{d^2}{W}$ can be obtained, but there are limits which must not be exceeded in this direction.

1. The bullet must have sufficient diameter to cause destructive effect to men and horses.
2. There is a difficulty in burning a sufficient powder charge in a very small bore to give the necessary muzzle velocity.
3. By reducing the bore its surface is also reduced, and the deposit of fouling is increased.
4. The lengthening of the bullet makes it more sensitive to the action of a side wind.

The following table gives the value of $\frac{d^2}{W}$ for bullets fired from most of the military rifles of the present day.

TABLE COMPARING THE VALUES OF $\frac{d^2}{W}$.

Country.	Nature of rifle.	Calibre.	Weight of bullet.	Value of $\frac{d^2}{W}$.
		inches.	grains.	
America	Springfield	0·45	500	2·834
Austria	Werndl	0·433	370	3·547
Denmark	Remington	0·433	400	3·281
Egypt	Remington	0·433	400	3·281
France	Gras	0·433	386	3·416
Germany	Mauser	0·433	380	3·453
Great Britain	Snider	0·577	480	4·855
	Martini-Henry	0·45	480	2·953
Holland	Beaumont	0·433	378	3·472
Italy	Vetterli	0·408	310	3·759
Japan	Murata	0·432	420	3·110
Norway and Sweden	Remington	0·433	400	3·281
Russia	Berdan	0·42	370	3·336
Spain	Remington	0·433	400	3·281
Switzerland	Vetterli (Magazine)	0·409	310	3·777
Turkey	Peabody-Martini	0·45	480	2·953

The trajectory is the curve described by the bullet in passing from the muzzle of the rifle to the first point of impact. *Trajectory.*

It is of the greatest importance that the rifle bullet should, during its flight, have a trajectory approximating as much as possible to a straight line, and in order to attain this end, a large powder charge is now invariably used, which (the weight of the bullet remaining the same) gives a high muzzle velocity. It is chiefly to this high muzzle velocity that flatness of trajectory must be looked for at short ranges; at long *Flat trajectories.*

ranges a bullet must have in addition a favourable $\frac{d^2}{W}$.

It is known that the bullet must drop below the line of fire about 16 feet during the 1st second of its flight, 48 feet during the 2nd second, and so on, so that the object is to impel the bullet forward with a velocity as great as possible, and thus to get over the range before the force of gravity has had much time to act, bringing the bullet to the ground. The elevation (given by the back sight on the rifle) is for the purpose of giving *time* to the bullet to range, but the more elevation that is given in aiming at an object, the higher will be the trajectory.

Great object to obtain range with little elevation. The great object in rifle shooting is to get *range* with as *little elevation* as possible. This can be effected in three ways:—

1. By increasing the powder charge, without altering the weight of the bullet.
2. By decreasing the weight of the bullet, leaving the powder charge the same.
3. By increasing the weight of the powder charge and decreasing the weight of the bullet.

Of course it is to be understood that the same rifle is dealt with in each case, for if the calibre of the rifle is decreased using a suitable weight of bullet and charge of powder, it is possible to obtain a very high muzzle velocity, while the bullet has a low $\frac{d^2}{W}$, and therefore there is a fourth means of obtaining a low trajectory.

The objection to the first method is that the recoil will be increased, so that once the calibre of the rifle and the weight of the bullet have been fixed, the powder charge cannot be increased beyond a certain limit on account of recoil.

Methods 2 and 3 are those met with in sporting rifles of the Express class. For short ranges these rifles have very high muzzle velocities and low trajectories, but at long ranges the high $\frac{d^2}{W}$ of the bullets causes so much loss of velocity and consequent increase of elevation and height of trajectory, that as military arms they would be useless.

*The advantages of a flat trajectory are as follows:— <small>Advantages of flat trajectories.</small>
1. Greater accuracy, since the direction of the bullet is less oblique to the target with the flatter trajectory, consequently small errors in aiming or judging distance are of less importance.

2. Harder hitting, because the velocity being higher, and the bullets being of the same weight and fired out of similar rifles, the blow must be greater and the penetration increased.

3. Greater efficiency in covering the ground, because for the same range the bullet does not rise so high in the air.

Dangerous zones for cavalry and infantry are the <small>Dangerous zones for cavalry and infantry.</small> terms given to those portions of the range which are swept by the trajectory of the bullet at a height not greater than 8 feet 6 inches for cavalry and 6 feet for infantry.

Work.—When a bullet has been set in motion from <small>Work.</small> rest, some force or pressure must have been exerted upon it. This force or pressure is then said to have done *work*, and the amount of *work done* is measured by the product of the *pressure* into the *distance* through which the bullet has been moved. Work done is usually expressed in foot lbs.†

Thus, if P be the pressure in pounds exerted on a bullet through the space of S feet, then the work done on the bullet is

$$P \times S \text{ ft. lbs.}$$

But in practice the pressure exerted on a bullet during its passage through the bore of a rifle is not constant, but *variable*; so that to obtain the approximate amount

---

* *See* "Principles of Gunnery," by Major J. Sladen, R.A.

† It is necessary to have some means of estimating *work* numerically, and for this purpose the amount of work done in raising 1 lb. through 1 foot is called the unit of work, or foot lb.

If 1 lb. is raised through 1 foot, 1 unit of work is done.

If 1 lb. is raised through 2 feet, 2 units of work are done.

If 4 lbs. weight be taken in the hand and raised through 5 feet, 20 units of work will be performed.

of work done, the product of the *mean pressure* on the bullet into its *distance* moved through the bore of the rifle must be taken. Then

P = mean pressure on bullet.
  = mean pressure on the bore of the rifle.

Example.—If the total mean pressure on the base of a Martini-Henry bullet was 712·64 lbs., what would be the work done on the bullet at the muzzle?

The distance through which the pressure acts must be the difference between the length of the bore and the length of the powder charge.

Length of bore = 33 inches.
Length of powder charge = 2 ,,

The difference will be the distance passed over by the bullet from its seat to the muzzle, viz., 31 inches $= \frac{31}{12}$ feet; consequently, work done by the powder on the bullet $= \frac{31}{12} \times 712\cdot46 = 1841$ foot lbs.

Energy.

When a bullet is in motion, it is said to have *energy*, *i.e.*, it is capable of doing work, or overcoming resistance. The amount of energy is measured by the *product of the weight of the bullet into the height due to its velocity*, and is expressed in the same units as those of work done.

Thus, if W be the weight of the bullet in pounds, h the height, it would require *in vacuo* to attain a velocity v in feet per second, then the energy of the bullet is—

$$Wh = \frac{Wv^2}{2g} \text{ ft. lbs.}$$

Where $h = \frac{v^2}{2g}$.

Now, if V be the muzzle velocity of the bullet, its energy at the muzzle of the rifle is $\frac{WV^2}{2g}$; and since the energy of the bullet at the muzzle is equivalent to the work done on it in the bore:—

$$E = \frac{WV^2}{2g} = PS;$$

where E represents the energy at the muzzle.

It will therefore be seen that the energy of the bullet at the *muzzle* is equal to the work done by the pressure of the powder gas in the bore of the rifle.

Example.—Find the energy of a Martini-Henry bullet at the muzzle. Weight of bullet = 480 grains or $\frac{480}{7000}$ lbs., muzzle velocity = 1315 feet per second.

$$\text{Energy at muzzle} = \frac{\frac{480}{7000} \times (1315)^2}{2 \times 32\cdot 2} \text{ ft. lbs.,}$$
$$= 1841 \text{ ft. lbs.}$$

i.e., if a uniform resistance of 1841 lbs. were opposed to the bullet, it would penetrate *one foot* before it was brought to rest; or if the resistance were 712·64 lbs., it would penetrate $\frac{31}{12}$ feet, and so on.

In order to estimate the comparative power of rifles for piercing various substances, it is usual to express the energy of the bullet in terms of the number of inches in its circumference, *i.e.*, by dividing the energy by the number of inches in the circumference of the bullet. Thus, energy per inch of circumference

$$= \frac{Wv^2}{2g \times \pi d} \text{ ft. lbs.;}$$

where d is the diameter of the bullet in inches.

Also, energy per inch of circumference at muzzle

$$= \frac{E}{\pi d} = \frac{WV^2}{2g \times \pi d};$$

thus, muzzle energy per inch of circumference of a Martini-Henry bullet

$$= \frac{1841}{3\cdot 14159 \times 0\cdot 45} = 1302 \text{ ft. lbs.}$$

Energy per inch of circumference

CHAPTER II.

RESISTANCE OF THE AIR TO THE MOTION OF A PROJECTILE. THE TRAJECTORY OF THE BULLET. PENETRATION. RECOIL.

Resistance of the air.
THE resistance of the air to projectiles moving with high velocities and the form of the trajectories described, have long been subjects of interest to scientific men.

Some idea may be formed of the amount of this resistance by considering that wind blowing a gale has only a velocity of 60 miles an hour, whereas a bullet moving at the rate of 1300 feet per second has a velocity of 886 miles an hour.

It is easy to conceive from this with what force the particles of air must strike against the front of the bullet during its rapid flight.

Robins.
Robins, in 1742, was the first to demonstrate the immense effect of the resistance of the air. He considered it to vary as the square of the velocities up to 1100 feet per second, and for velocities above that to increase considerably.

Hutton.
Hutton carried out experiments in 1775, and found that even with velocities below 1100 f.s., the resistances were higher than those due to the squares of the velocities.

Hélie and Bashforth.
M. Hélie, in France, and the Reverend F. Bashforth, in England, arrived independently at results of great importance. They demonstrated that, although no simple law could be found to express the resistance of the air in the terms of the velocity, yet that such resistance could be accurately defined by the help of a *variable coefficient*, depending (1) upon the form of the projectile, (2) upon the velocity with which it moves.

Upon these assumptions, Mr. Bashforth states that it is a mere matter of convenience which *power* of the velocity is used, but he adopts the cubic law as giving the most simple formulæ for the calculation of remaining velocities, ranges, and times of flight. The expression he adopts is

$$R = kv^3$$

where k, instead of being a *fixed* multiplier, is a coefficient not only depending upon the form of the projectile, but also *varying* in amount for every 50 or 100 feet of velocity.

Mr. Bashforth carried out a very extensive series of experiments on the resistance of the air to elongated projectiles. By means of the electric chronograph invented by him, he was enabled to take the velocities at *several points* of the same trajectory, and thence he compiled tables of values for the variable coefficient k, corresponding to every 50 feet of velocity.

Although Mr. Bashforth has adopted the cubic law as his standard, it will prove of interest to point out the fluctuations in the resistances due to different velocities, the deductions being taken from his tables, these variations can be best shown by the ordinates of a curve, but the general results may be stated as follows in a popular form :— *Fluctuations in resistances.*

1. Between velocities of 430 and 830 f.s., the resistance of the air varies nearly as the square of the velocity.

2. Between the velocities of 830 and 1000 f.s., the resistance varies roughly as the cube of the velocity.

3. Above 1000 f.s., the resistance increases very suddenly and rapidly, varying between 1000 and 1100 f.s., roughly as the 6th power of the velocity.

4. The rate at which the resistance varies decreases above this point, until another point between 1200 and 1250 f.s. is reached, when the resistance again varies as the cube of the velocity.

5. The rate again decreases steadily, and between 1400 and 1500 f.s. it is about as the square of the velocity.

6. Between 1500 and 1900 f.s. the minimum is reached, the resistance between these limits varying roughly as the 1·7th power of the velocity.

7. Above 1900 f.s. the rate again increases steadily, until 2250 f.s., and then the resistance tends to become constant, and to vary as the cube of the velocity.

The cause of these fluctuations does not yet appear to have been satisfactorily explained.

Professor Bashforth also experimented on projectiles with different forms of head, to determine which form offered least resistance to motion through the air.

Four different forms of head were tried, viz.:—
1. Hemispherical. 2. Hemispheroidal. 3. Ogival head of 1 diameter. And 4. Ogival head of 2 diameters.

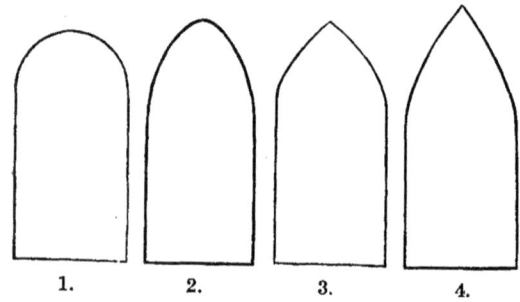

The resistances obtained under similar conditions of velocity, about 1200 f.s., were proportional to the numbers—

	Resistances.
Hemispherical	132·9
Hemispheroidal	104·3
Ogival (1 diameter)	109·7
Ogival (2 diameters)	104·2

Further experiments carried out with higher velocities, 1700 f.s., gave the following results:—

	Resistances.
Ogival head (1½ diameters)	83
Hemispherical head	113·6
Flat head	173·5

It appears that the resistance of the air to the flat

head was the greatest, and to the ogival head of 2 diameters the least. It was also considered that the resistance depended more on the form of the head near its junction with the cylindrical part of the projectile than on its having more or less a sharp point.

The resistance of the air is also probably affected by the shape of the hinder as well as the fore part of the bullet.

The next point to consider is the path described by the bullet. *Trajectory of the bullet.*

In early times it was thought—

1. That it went straight, and then fell perpendicularly.
2. That it went straight for some distance, then in a curve, and then fell perpendicularly.
3. That its flight was curved throughout but very slightly.
4. Galileo in the 17th century considered that it described a parabola, except insomuch as it was diverted by the resistance of the air, which he greatly underrated. *Galileo.*

It is now known that a bullet on leaving the muzzle of a rifle is under the influence of three forces, viz., the impressed pressure of the powder gas, the force of gravity, and the resistance of the air.

To commence the action of the first two forces only will be considered on the supposition that no atmosphere exists. From the impressed force of the powder the bullet will travel forward with uniform velocity, passing through equal distances in equal times; thus in the first second from A to B (Fig. 1), in the second from B to C, and in the third from C to D; but in obedience to the law of gravity, it will fall in the first second* 16 feet, B E, at the end of the second second it will have fallen 64 feet, C F, and at the end of the third second 144 feet,

---

* The vertical distance, S, a body free to move falls through under the action of gravity in any time t is given by the equation—

$$S = \tfrac{1}{2}gt^2.$$

Thus a bullet in 4 seconds will fall—

$$S = \frac{32 \times 4^2}{2} = 256 \text{ feet.}$$

D G, being at the end of these seconds at the points E, F, G, respectively, and describing in its path the trajectory A, E, F, G, which in this case would be a curve called the parabola.

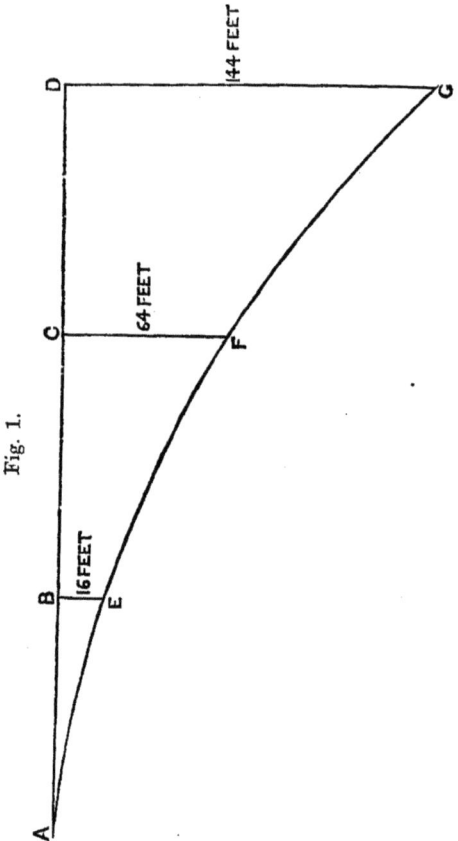

Fig. 1.

Having now established the general form of the trajectory, under the forces of gunpowder and gravity, the following conclusion is arrived at, that supposing a rifle is laid with its axis horizontal, it is immaterial with what charge it is loaded and with what velocity the bullet is projected, the latter will reach the ground in one second if 16 feet above it, and in two seconds if 64 feet, and so on; consequently if several rifles are laid above the level of the ground, with their axes in the same horizontal plane, the bullets projected from them at the same instant would reach the ground at the same moment irrespective of their velocities and height above the ground.

The resistance of the air will now be taken into account; owing to this resistance the flight of the bullet will be modified thus; it will not proceed equal distances in equal times, but the distances traversed will be successively less and less; instead of the bullet travelling forward a distance equal to A B (Fig. 2), in the first second of time, to B C in the second, and to C D in the third; the distances will be, say, A b, b c, and c d; and the action of gravity being the same as before, the bullet, at the termination of each second, will be respectively at e, f, g, the actual path of the bullet differing in a great degree from that of the parabolic curve, which is never approached except with projectiles moving with very low velocities.

It will be seen from the above that the force of gravity is the sole cause of the trajectory being a curved line, and that this curvature is increased by the resistance of the air, and it is due to these causes that elevation must be given to all arms, varying in an increasing ratio according to the distance. If gravity alone acted, elevation would be necessary, but when it acts in conjunction with the resistance of the air, an increased elevation is necessary.

The resistance of the air affects the time of flight of a bullet. In the air although the range would be shorter the time of flight would be rather longer.

In vacuo the greatest range would be obtained on a horizontal plane by firing at an angle of 45°. Owing to the resistance of the air, a bullet fired at about 33° is found to give the maximum range.

Whatever the form of a bullet may be, whether Trajectory

32

described by centre of gravity of the bullet. spherical or elongated, its trajectory is always described by its centre of gravity.

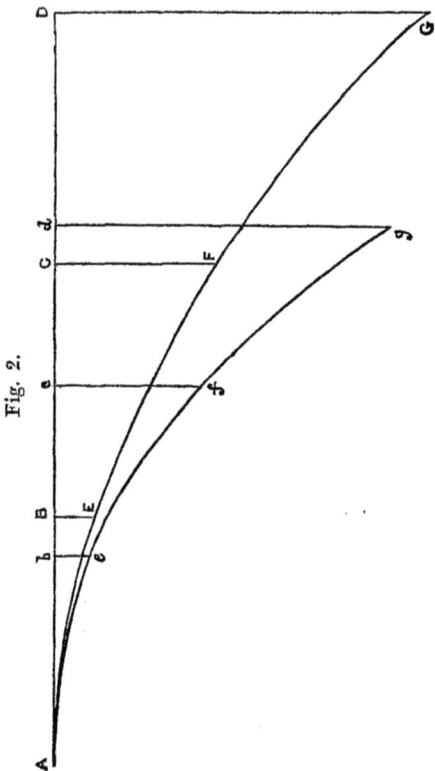

Fig. 2.

Position preserved by the axis of an elongated bullet in its flight. The position, with respect to the trajectory, which the axis of an elongated bullet preserves during its flight, has always been a matter of much dispute. It has been supposed by some that elongated bullets preserve their primary direction, or if they leave the rifle with a certain angle to the horizon, they maintain this angle during the whole of their flight. Again, it has been stated that under certain conditions the point of the bullet droops below the trajectory and the base is elevated; while other writers declare that the axis of the bullet is a tangent to the trajectory from beginning to end, and that the point goes first, resembling an arrow in its flight.

The last conclusion seems to be the correct one, still it is quite possible that an elongated bullet which has not a sufficient velocity of rotation to keep it spinning steadily round its longest axis, may not follow the trajectory point foremost, as there will naturally be some intermediate condition before it begins to revolve round its shortest axis; but when a bullet has that amount of velocity of rotation which is rendered necessary by its length, it invariably cleaves the air point first.

In order to satisfy himself of the correctness of this fact, the reader need only examine the portions of bullets which rebound from iron targets, when he will have ample evidence to convince him that (whatever be the range) the points of the bullets first struck the targets.

If the target be a wooden one, or of other soft material, the hole made by the bullet will always be found to be circular in form. It may be added that during the years 1878–80 a large number of rounds were fired at Shoeburyness in order to obtain data to enable Professor Bashforth to determine the resistance of the air to the motion of elongated projectiles when moving at high and low velocities. During these experiments some large 70 lb. shells were fired from a howitzer with such charges as to give velocities of from 130 to 140 feet per second, when the position of each shell could be clearly seen during the whole of its short trajectory, and also its rotatory motion round its axis. These shells went point foremost. *Hole made by bullet always circular in form.*

The deviation caused by the rotation of the earth is so slight in the range of small arms that it is not necessary to consider it. *Rotation of the earth.*

The effect of the density and hygrometric state (humidity) of the atmosphere on the flight of rifle bullets, more especially apparent at long ranges, is now universally recognized. Our first-rate rifle shots have *Effect of density and humidity of the atmosphere.*

(S.A.) C

their pocket barometers, compensated for temperature, for target shooting. The denser the atmosphere the greater the resistance and retardation, consequently the lower the bullet will strike; the rarer the atmosphere the less the resistance, and the higher the bullet will strike.

At considerable elevations above the sea level, the graduations on the back sight may be slightly lowered; this is due to the decreased density of the air.

Firing at objects at a high and low level. Military rifles are always sighted for horizontal distances, and it is sometimes asked if the graduations on the back-sights would be correct in firing at objects at the same distances, but at a much higher or lower level. The answer is not a simple one, as it can be shown that in a vacuum the sighting for certain angles, both above and below the horizontal, agrees with the horizontal sighting, while for other angles there is a difference: the question is further complicated by the resistance of the air. At moderate ranges the ordinary sighting may be taken as sufficiently accurate.

In vacuo no rotation would be necessary. In vacuo, no rotation to correct the flight of the bullet would be necessary; the existence of the air is the sole cause of their upsetting or deviating from their true path.

Tendency of bullet to rotate round its shortest axis. The tendency of an elongated bullet fired from a rifle with insufficient twist is to rotate round its shortest axis through the centre of gravity.

It was formerly considered that a rapid twist would be detrimental and decrease the muzzle velocity of the bullet; but this has practically been disproved; a high muzzle velocity and a rapid rotation can be given without causing any injurious effects, except an increase of fouling, and that the greater the velocity of rotation, with the same velocity of translation, the greater will be the drift, and the more the ricochet will deviate.

An elongated bullet is made heavier than a spherical one of the same diameter, and if each is fired from a rifle with the same charge, the spherical will have the greater muzzle velocity, but the power of the elongated to overcome will be greater, hence except at short ranges it will maintain its velocity better, range further, and have a flatter trajectory.

Lead being denser than iron, if bullets of identical shape

and dimensions were formed of these metals, and were fired with the same velocities, the leaden bullets would experience the least retardations inversely as the densities of the metals, or as 8 to 11.

To enable the reader to understand how the height of the trajectory of a bullet is affected by its muzzle velocity, section, and weight, diagrams of the trajectories of the Snider and Martini-Henry rifles and carbines are now given.

A knowledge of the exact form of the trajectory, and time of flight of the bullet, are points that should not be overlooked in the intelligent study of musketry. A hypothetical case would be an enemy formed up at some depth behind cover of a certain height, he might be perfectly safe from fire at short ranges, but if the attacking party retired, raised their back-sights, obtained a higher trajectory, the case might be different. *Knowledge of form of trajectory and time of flight of bullet important.*

Again, in firing at objects moving laterally, it is most important to know the time of flight of the bullet in estimating how much to aim in front. *Firing at moving objects.*

The following table gives the angles of elevation and times of flight of the Martini-Henry and Snider rifles and carbines:—

Range yards.	M.-H. Rifle.		Greatest height of trajectory of the M.H. rifle.	Snider Rifle.	
	Angle of elevation.	Time of flight.		Angle of elevation.	Time of flight.
100	0° 33′	0·24186 secs.	See diagram of trajectories.	0° 23′	0·26523 secs.
200	0 43	0·51372 ,,		0 29	0·56884 ,,
300	0 54	0·81114 ,,		0 43	0·90727 ,,
400	1 7	1·1262 ,,		1 6	1·2788 ,,
500	1 21	1·4609 ,,		1 30	1·6790 ,,
600	1 38	1·8212 ,,		1 55	2·1263 ,,
700	1 57	2·1959 ,,		2 20	2·6025 ,,
800	2 18	2·5906 ,,		2 51	3·0206 ,,
900	2 41	3·0100 ,,		..	3·6957 ,,
1000	3 6	3·449 ,,		..	4·3329 ,,
1500	5 15	6·045 ,,	147·1 ft.	..	..
2000	9 7	9·4287 ,,	357·8 ,,	..	..
2500	14 25	13·802 ,,	766·8 ,,	..	..

(S.A.)   c 2

Up to 1000 yards the angle of descent may be taken roughly as one-third more than the angle of elevation.

Range yards.	M.-H. Carbine.		Snider Carbine.	
	Angle of elevation.	Time of flight.	Angle of elevation.	Time of flight.
100	0° 22′	0·28071 secs.	0° 18′	0·28694 secs.
200	0 35	0·58600 ,,	0 40	0·61289 ,,
300	0 50	0·91649 ,,	1 2	0·96713 ,,
400	1 9	1·2658 ,,	1 24	1·3566 ,,
500	1 30	1·6455 ,,	1 46	1·7774 ,,
600	1 53	2·0412 ,,	2 14	2·2431 ,,
700	2 18	2·4715 ,,	..	2·7438 ,,
800	2 45	2·9236 ,,	..	3·2892 ,,
900	3 14	3·4084 ,,	..	3·8997 ,,
1000	3 45	3·9103 ,,	..	4·5516 ,,

From experiments carried out at Dungeness it was observed that the time of flight of the Martini-Henry rifle bullet at 3000 yards was 19·3 seconds. Angle of elevation, 23° 20′. Angle of descent, 46° 45′. This may be taken as the extreme effective range of the arm.

Penetration.

Velocity more important than weight.

From what has been said on the subject of Energy, Chap. I, it will be easily understood that an increase of velocity increases the penetration much more than an addition of weight; and that, therefore, the striking velocity of a bullet must be as great as possible in order to produce the maximum of penetration.

As has been previously noticed, an elongated bullet maintains its velocity better than a spherical one of the same diameter. Hence at long ranges the striking velocity of the elongated will be greater, and consequently it will have more penetrative power, due to both its velocity and extra weight.

Rotation of bullet increases the penetration.

The increased penetration of elongated rifle bullets is in a higher ratio than theory would assign them, and something further must be looked to than their superior

(3)
TABLE M.

TABLE of the Heights in feet, at every 50 yards of the Trajectories of the Martini-Henry Rifle at all ranges, for every 100 yards, from 200 to 1600 yards.

The rifle is supposed to be fired on a horizontal plane from the level of the plane.

Range in Yards.	0	50	100	150	200	250	300	350	400	450	500	550	600	650	700	750
200	0	0·7473	1·069	0·8351	0											
300	0	1·307	2·216	2·634	2·459	1·594	0									
400	0	1·901	3·446	4·544	5·071	4·958	4·124	2·135	0							
500	0	2·530	4·743	6·566	7·830	8·513	8·484	7·476	6·057	3·570	0					
600	0	3·208	6·151	8·750	10·81	12·37	13·20	13·25	12·61	11·06	8·492	4·782	0			
700	0	3·915	7·608	11·02	13·92	16·36	18·10	19·25	19·41	18·85	17·32	14·69	11·00	6·167	0	
800	0	4·657	9·148	13·41	17·18	20·55	23·25	25·56	26·56	27·02	26·59	25·09	22·56	18·89	13·93	7·805
900	0	5·446	10·77	15·94	20·65	25·01	28·72	32·25	34·16	35·72	36·43	36·16	34·85	32·42	28·76	23·92
1000	0	6·272	12·48	18·59	24·28	29·69	34·45	39·28	42·12	44·83	46·77	47·76	47·72	46·60	44·28	40·80
1100	0	7·144	14·29	21·39	28·09	34·61	40·50	46·68	50·52	54·44	57·66	59·99	61·31	61·86	60·64	58·59
1200	0	8·072	16·21	24·39	32·18	39·88	46·95	54·59	59·47	64·71	69·26	73·05	75·80	77·50	78·11	77·59
1300	0	9·042	18·21	27·51	36·45	45·36	53·67	62·82	68·82	75·37	81·39	86·66	90·93	94·12	96·34	97·38
1400	0	10·08	20·34	30·82	40·98	51·19	60·82	71·58	78·75	86·76	94·30	101·1	106·9	111·9	115·7	118·5
1500	0	11·15	22·57	34·29	45·71	57·31	68·31	80·76	89·15	98·65	107·7	116·2	123·7	130·3	136·0	140·5
1600	0	12·31	24·97	38·00	50·79	63·84	76·33	90·55	100·2	114·4	122·2	132·4	141·7	150·2	157·7	164·1

[To face page 36.

Yards.

800	850	900	950	1000	1050	1100	1150	1200	1250	1300	1350	1400	1450	1500	1550	1600
0																
17·48	9·632															
35·80	29·39	0														
56·11	50·23	21·27	11·63													
75·71	72·46	43·71	35·68	0												
97·21	95·63	67·66	61·34	25·71	13·96	0										
120·0	120·3	92·60	88·08	53·14	43·20	31·11	16·35	0								
144·0	146·1	119·2	116·5	81·74	73·67	63·52	50·86	36·54	19·01	0						
169·5	173·8	146·9	146·3	112·1	106·1	98·06	87·56	75·41	60·19	43·42	22·40	0				
		176·7	178·1	144·0	140·1	134·2	126·0	116·1	103·2	88·82	71·25	50·46	27·20	0		
				178·0	176·4	172·8	167·1	159·6	149·4	137·4	122·6	104·5	84·03	59·71	31·19	0

energy. This is furnished by their rotation on their longer axis, which appears to aid penetration.

With small arms, the great object being to incapacitate the enemy, pure lead is sufficiently hard for the ordinary purposes of penetration, but bullets hardened with tin or antimony have a greater penetrating power than bullets made of pure lead, and would be more useful against woodwork and defences in general; this is due to the increased hardness of the metal, which causes them to be less distorted, and not to the density, as the addition of tin or antimony reduces the density. Bullets of steel and iron cannot be used in the majority of rifles, which require bullets of an expanding character. *Hard and soft bullets.*

As has already been explained, the "work stored up in a bullet," or its "energy," is expressed by $\frac{WV^2}{2g}$. This gives the total blow in foot lbs. (W being the weight of the bullet in lbs.) which the bullet can strike. The power of the bullet to pierce any substance, or its "penetrative energy," differs however from its "total energy," and is for comparative purposes the number of foot lbs. *per inch of circumference* with which the bullet strikes the blow; or,

$$\text{The penetrative energy} = \frac{WV^2}{2g \cdot \pi d}$$

when $d =$ the diameter of the bullet in inches.

It will be easily understood that with bullets of equal weights (the Snider and Martini-Henry bullets both weigh 480 grains) and different diameters, that which has the lesser diameter will meet with less resistance to penetration when it strikes any substance.

If a Snider and a Martini-Henry bullet strike an object with the same velocity, they will have the same amount of work stored up in them, or the value of $\frac{WV^2}{2g}$ will be the same for each; but the Martini-Henry bullet will have the greater penetration as, owing to its smaller diameter, its penetrative energy will exceed that of the Snider bullet.

The following table will show how the total energies and penetrative energies of the Martini-Henry and Snider bullets vary for different striking velocities:—

38

TABLE SHOWING THE REMAINING VELOCITY, TOTAL ENERGY, AND ENERGY PER INCH OF CIRCUMFERENCE OF BULLET.

Range.	Martini-Henry rifle. Calibre, 0·45 inch.			Snider rifle. Calibre, 0·577 inch.			Martini-Henry carbine. Calibre, 0·45 inch.			Snider carbine. Calibre, 0·577 inch.		
	Velocity.	Total energy.	Energy per inch of circumference.	Velocity.	Total energy.	Energy per inch of circumference.	Velocity.	Total energy.	Energy per inch of circumference.	Velocity.	Total energy.	Energy per inch of circumference.
yards.	f.s.	ft. lbs.	ft. lbs.	f.s.	ft. lbs.	ft. lbs.	f.s.	ft. lbs.	ft. lbs.	f.s.	ft. lbs.	ft. lbs.
0	1315	1841	1302	1240	1637	903	1135	1172	829	1120	1336	737
100	1197	1451	1026	1043	1158	639	1021	948	671	982	1027	566
200	1053	1181	835	936	933	515	946	814	576	886	836	461
300	982	1027	726	849	768	423	881	706	499	808	695	384
400	922	905	640	776	641	354	825	619	438	740	583	322
500	869	804	569	711	540	298	774	545	385	679	491	271
600	821	718	508	652	453	250	728	482	341	622	412	227
700	778	645	456	598	381	210	684	426	301	570	346	191
800	738	580	410	547	319	176	643	376	266	522	290	160
900	700	522	369	501	267	147	604	333	235	477	242	134
1000	664	470	332	458	223	123	568	293	208	437	204	112

Experiments made to test the penetrative power of the Martini-Henry and Snider bullets furnish the following results :—

RESULT OF EXPERIMENTS TO TEST THE EFFECT OF RIFLE BULLETS FIRED AT UNBACKED PLATES AND OTHER SUBSTANCES.

Steel Plates.

Nature of rifle.	Range.	Thickness.	Steel Plates. Nature of plate.	Result on plate.
Martini-Henry rifle	yds. 20	in. $\frac{3}{16}$	Sharp steel	Plate broken in pieces.
,, ,,	,,	,,	Mild steel, not tempered.	Bulged, $\frac{7}{16}$ inch.
,, ,,	,,	,,	Mild steel, hardened in oil.	Bulged, $\frac{4}{16}$ inch.
,, ,,	100	,,	Mild steel, not tempered.	Bulged, $\frac{5}{16}$ inch.
,, ,,	,,	,,	Mild steel, hardened in oil.	Bulged, $\frac{1}{16}$ inch.
,, ,,	20	$\frac{1}{4}$	Mild steel, not tempered.	Bulged, $\frac{2}{16}$ inch.
,, ,,	,,	,,	Mild steel, hardened in oil.	Bulged, $\frac{1}{16}$ inch.
,, ,,	100	,,	Mild steel, not tempered.	Bulged, $\frac{2}{16}$ inch.
,, ,,	,,	,,	Mild steel, hardened in oil.	Very slight bulge.

Wrought-iron Plates.

Nature of rifle.	Plate.		Perforated plate at	Failed to perforate plate at
	Thickness.	Nature.		
	inch.		yards.	yards.
Snider carbine	⅛	Wrought-iron	300	400
Snider rifle	,,	,,	400	500
Martini-Henry carbine.	,,	,,	400	500
Martini-Henry rifle ..	,,	,,	600	700
Snider carbine	3/16	,,	100	200
Snider rifle	,,	,,	100	200
Martini-Henry carbine	,,	,,	200	300
Martini-Henry rifle ..	,,	,,	400	500
Snider carbine	¼	,,	—	20
Snider rifle	,,	,,	20	100
Martini-Henry carbine	,,	,,	—.	20
Martini-Henry rifle ..	,,	,,	100	200

Elm planks. When fired at ½-inch elm planks, placed one inch apart, the Martini-Henry bullet made an average penetration of 14½ planks; the Snider penetrated 8½ planks.

Fir timber. At 100 yards' range the Martini-Henry bullet perforated three balks of 3-inch dry fir timber, placed close together, while at 50 yards' range the Snider bullet was stopped by the second balk.

Rope mantlet. When fired at a rope mantlet (four thicknesses 3-inch rope), the Martini-Henry bullet penetrated at 350 yards and failed to penetrate at 400 yards' range; the Snider bullet failed to penetrate at 50 yards.

Ordinary gabion. An ordinary gabion, filled with earth from a clay soil, was penetrated by the Martini-Henry bullet at 25 yards, but not at a longer range; the Snider bullet failed to penetrate.

Jones's gabion. Neither bullet could penetrate the Jones' gabion (formed with iron hoops).

Sap roller. The Martini-Henry bullet penetrated a sap roller at 25 yards, and failed when the range was increased; the Snider bullet failed to penetrate.

Sand bag. A sand-bag containing one bushel of sand was penetrated by the Martini-Henry bullet up to 100 yards range; the Snider bullet failed to penetrate at 10 yards.

The average penetration of the Martini-Henry bullet into dry earth at 3000 yards is 8 inches.

The following thicknesses of material may be considered proof against rifle bullets at any range:—

Earth		2 ft.
Iron plate		$\frac{3}{8}$ in.
Steel plate		$\frac{1}{4}$ in.
Fir	In log	12 in.
	In 3-inch planks	6 planks
Oak	In log	6 in.
	In 2-inch planks	3 planks
Gabions filled with earth		1
Sandbags (filled)	Crossways	2
	Lengthways	1
Rope mantlet		6 in.
Loose cotton		4 ft.
Compressed cotton in bale		2 ft.
Brick wall		9 in.

As it is probable the military rifles of the future will have a muzzle velocity of 1600 or 1700 f.s., it is questionable if these thicknesses will afford then in all cases a sufficient protection at short ranges.

The length of bullets for rifled small arms varies generally from two to three calibres, which is found to be the most suitable length.

The following table gives the lengths of bullets fired from various military rifles:—

TABLE GIVING THE LENGTH OF BULLETS FIRED FROM VARIOUS MILITARY RIFLES.

Country.	Nature of rifle.	Calibre. Inches.	Length of bullet.	
			Inches.	Calibres.*
America	Springfield	0·45	1·322	2·94
Austria	Werndl	0·433	1·07	2·47
Denmark	Remington	0·433	1·073	2·48
Egypt	Remington	0·433	1·073	2·48
France	Gras	0·433	1·0625	2·44
Germany	Mauser	0·433	1·08	2·5
Great Britain	Snider	0·577	1·042	1·806
,, ,,	Martini-Henry	0·45	1·27	2·82
Holland	Beaumont	0·433	1·004	2·32
Italy	Vetterli	0·408	1·03	2·52
Japan	Murata	0·432	1·253	2·9
Norway and Sweden	Remington	0·433	1·073	2·48
Russia	Berdan No. 2	0·42	1·05	2·5
Spain	Remington	0·433	1·073	2·48
Switzerland	Vetterli (magazine)	0·409	1·00	2·44
Turkey	Peabody-Martini	0·45	1·27	2·82

* When calibres are mentioned reference is always made to the diameter of the bore.

Recoil.

Recoil depends on:—

1. The weight of the rifle.
2. The muzzle velocity of the bullet.
3. The weight of the bullet.
4. On the fouling of the barrel.

On the powder charge being ignited, the gas is only able to act with effect in two directions, viz., to force the bullet out of the muzzle, and to drive the rifle in the opposite direction. The lighter the bullet the greater is its muzzle velocity (with the same powder charge), and in the same way, the lighter the rifle the greater is its velocity of recoil.

If a rifle could be made as light as the bullet it fired, the energy of recoil of this rifle would be equal to the energy of its bullet at the muzzle; for on the powder-

43

charge being ignited, the rifle and bullet would be propelled with equal velocities, but in opposite directions.

Match rifles are generally made heavier than military arms, in order to lessen the recoil; for as the weight of the rifle is increased so is its recoil reduced. *Match rifles generally heavier than military.*

The friction between the bullet and the bore, as the bullet passes up the barrel is not considerable, so long as the rifle is clean, but increases rapidly when it becomes fouled, causing a great addition to the recoil; this is probably due to the increased resistance to motion of the bullet, and the charge exerting its pressure for a longer time.

The velocity of recoil and the energy of recoil are thus obtained:— *Velocity and energy of recoil how obtained.*

Let W = weight of rifle in lbs.
V = velocity of recoil.
w = weight of bullet in lbs.
v = muzzle velocity of bullet.

Then on firing the momentum of the rifle is equal to the momentum of the bullet.

$$WV = wv$$
$$\text{and} \quad V = \frac{wv}{W},$$

which gives the velocity of recoil.

We can then obtain the energy of recoil—

$$E = \frac{WV^2}{2g} \text{ ft. lbs.}$$

The following table gives the energy of recoil of various military rifles. In the calculations the weight of the powder charge has been taken into account; with small arms this does not much affect the results:—

Table showing Recoil of Military Rifles.

Country.	Nature of rifle.	Calibre.	Weight of rifle.	Weight of bullet.	Weight of powder.	Muzzle velocity.	Energy of Recoil.
		inch.	lbs. oz.	grains.	grains.	feet per second.	ft. lbs.
America	Springfield	0·45	9 5¼	500	70	1301	16·44
Austria	Werndl	0·433	9 14	370	75	1439	11·11
Denmark	Remington	0·433	9 5¼	400	75	1340	11·65
Egypt	Remington	0·433	9 5¼	400	75	1340	11·65
France	Gras	0·433	9 11	386	80	1489	13·14
Germany	Mauser	0·433	10 4	380	75	1430	11·01
Great Britain	Snider	0·577	9 0¾	480	70	1240	14·343
,, ,,	Martini-Henry*	0·45	9 0	480	85	1315	16·60
Holland	Beaumont	0·433	9 11	378	77	1332	10·07
Italy	Vetterli	0·408	9 9	310	62	1430	7·877
Japan	Murata	0·432	9 10	420	83	1487	15·486
Norway and Sweden	Remington	0·433	9 5½	400	75	1340	11·65
Russia	Berdan No. 2	0·42	9 12½	370	77	1444	11·27
Spain	Remington	0·433	9 5½	400	75	1340	11·65
Switzerland	Vetterli (magazine)	0·409	10 6	310	55	1314	6·003
Turkey	Peabody-Martini	0·45	9 10	480	85	1380	16·86

* Mark III.

The amount of recoil given in the above table in foot lbs. is the energy of recoil, as found by calculation, due to the weight of the arm, and the weight and muzzle velocity of the bullet.

The energy of recoil may be reduced (1) by decreasing the weight of the bullet; (2) by decreasing the muzzle velocity, in reducing the powder charge; (3) by increasing the weight of the rifle. *Energy of recoil, how reduced.*

When there is much recoil, accuracy in shooting is impossible, especially if the rifle is in the hands of young soldiers.

It is not to be supposed that every man firing a rifle experiences the same amount of recoil, as if the arm is held firmly to the shoulder, the recoil is merely felt as a push; while if the rifle be loosely held, the recoil acquires the character of a blow. *Manner of holding the rifle, its influence on recoil.*

The greatest velocity of recoil is said to be attained at the instant the bullet leaves the muzzle. *Greatest velocity of recoil.*

Many instruments have been devised for registering the amount of recoil, such as a system of springs which are compressed, an arrangement of levers, or by allowing the rifle to swing through an arc on being fired; the recoil being shown on a dial in connection with the apparatus, but none of these contrivances are to be relied on. *Other methods of registering amount of recoil.*

It has also been stated that the form of cartridge case had much to do with the recoil; but this is clearly incorrect, as exhaustive experiments have proved that the form of the cartridge case does not affect the amount of muzzle velocity of the bullet, and therefore it cannot alter the amount of recoil. *Effect of form of cartridge case on recoil.*

Schultz and E.C. powders are said to give as high a muzzle velocity as black powder, without so much recoil; it is difficult to conceive how this can be the case, for if the bullet attains a certain muzzle energy, it ought to have a corresponding energy of recoil with the same rifle. It is possible with a quick explosive some of the recoil is absorbed in compressing the wood of the butt, which is always more or less elastic. *Schultz and E.C. Powders.*

It would appear from all the considerations which have been advanced, that the great object of the present day is to obtain arms from which the bullet *Conclusions.*

can be projected with the greatest muzzle velocity, combined with the greatest possible power of overcoming the air's resistance, thus producing the lowest trajectory, and the greatest destructive effect at all distances.

CHAPTER III.

RIFLING. BREECH-LOADING MILITARY RIFLES. MATCH RIFLES. REPEATING AND MAGAZINE RIFLES. REVOLVERS. TABLES OF MILITARY RIFLES.

BEFORE entering on the subject of military breech-loading rifles, it is desirable to give some description of different systems of rifling, the object aimed at in all being to give the necessary rotation to the bullet round its longer axis, and to effect this grooves varying in form, depth, number, and twist have from time to time been adopted.

1. Enfield rifling, 1853, consists of three spiral grooves making one turn in 78 inches; the twist is right-handed, uniform, and of progressive depth from breech to muzzle (Fig. 1).

Fig. 1.

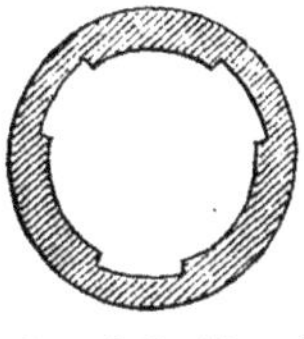

Section of the Barrel.

This form is found in the long Snider rifles, pattern 53, with which the Volunteers are at present armed.

The Snider short rifle and the cavalry and artillery Snider carbines have the same form of rifling, but are generally made with five grooves and a uniform twist of one turn in 48 inches.

2. The Lancaster or Elliptical (Fig. 2). The barrel is cut in the interior in the form of an ellipse, the difference

between the major and minor axes being ·012 inch; the twist is an increasing one from breech to muzzle.

Fig. 2.

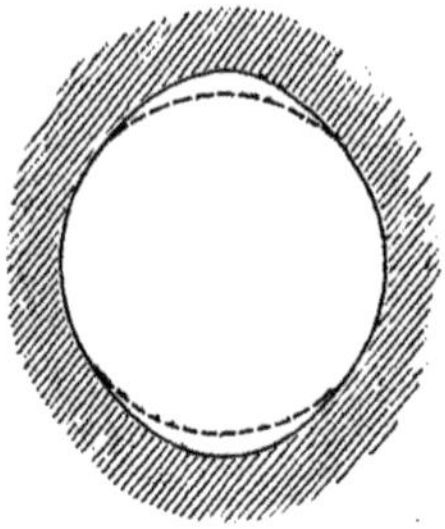

Section of the Barrel.

This form of rifling was used in the Snider rifles with which the Royal Engineers were armed; the ordinary Snider cartridge was used with these arms.

3. The polygonal (Fig. 3), as used by Mr. Whitworth. The bore is cut hexagonal in section with the angles rounded off. The twist is uniform, right-handed, one turn in 20 inches.

Fig. 3.

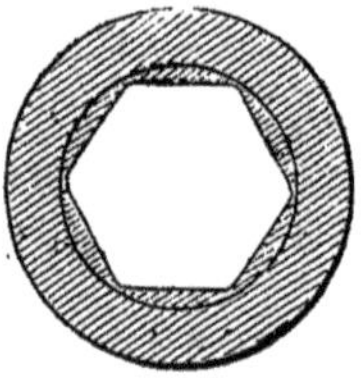

4. Henry rifling (Fig. 4) resembles the polygonal. It has seven grooves, ·03 inch of the original bore being left between each as lands. It will be seen by the figure that the lands and the centres of the grooves are contained in the same circle. Twist right-handed, uniform, one turn in 22 inches.

Fig. 4.

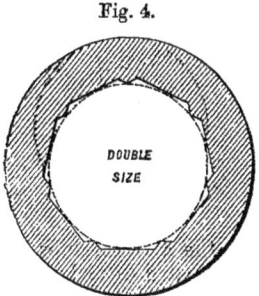

Section of Henry Barrel.

5. Ratchet rifling (Fig. 5) is an old form now coming into much favour. It will be seen that each groove runs out to nothing at one side. The figure is a section of the barrel looking from the breech, and with a right-handed twist the left or upright edge will be the one that resists, and causes the bullet to rotate to the right. Some advocate having the groove reversed, when with the right-handed twist the shallow sides of the grooves would be the resisting ones.

Fig. 5.

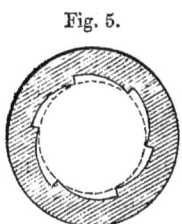

6. Many of the Continental military rifles are now rifled with four grooves (Fig. 6) of about the same width as the lands; the twist is uniform, the grooves of the same depth throughout, and concentric with the axis of the bore.

Fig. 6.

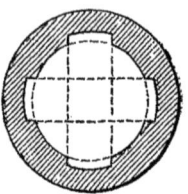

The drawing in the above figures, with the exception of Fig. 4. is exaggerated to make the form of grooves more clear. This may be understood from the consideration that grooves of modern rifles are seldom more than ·007 inch in depth.

In considering which is the right or left edge of a groove, it is best to imagine the observer as lying in the axis of the bore, with his head towards the breech; if he then looks at any groove, the right or left edge will correspond respectively with his right or left hand.

It seems to be now pretty well accepted that the simpler the form of the rifling the better; plain shallow grooves with an uniform twist appear to give as good results as those of a more complicated nature, which are more difficult to manufacture, to repair, and to keep clean.

It is probable that the ratchet form of rifling, with the edges rounded off, will supersede the Henry in our future military rifles; it is simple in form and construction, and easily kept clean.

BREECH-LOADERS.

Breech-loaders.

The invention of breech-loaders can be traced back to the 15th century, but from want of mechanical knowledge and the failure to adapt a proper cartridge, little success attended this nature of arms till towards the middle of the present century.

The chief advantages obtained with breech-loaders may be summed up as follows:—

1. Rapidity of fire.
2. Facility of loading in any position.

3. Certainty of employing the entire charge.
4. Impossibility of inserting a double charge.
5. Facility to inspect and keep the arm clean.

The invention of a reliable and thoroughly efficient military breech-loading action was a problem requiring considerable mechanical skill; the objects to be effected are as follows:—

1st. To open the breech of the arm and close it again rapidly and securely by simple and convenient movements without removing the hand far from the trigger, and without shifting the hold of the arm by the other hand.

2nd. To extract the cartridge case of the previous charge by the same movement as that which opens the breech, so as to present the open barrel ready for instant reloading.

3rd. To have the whole mechanism of a simple, strong, and durable character, free from risk of derangement, either by accident, long wear and tear, rough usage on active service, exposure to wet or sand, or fouling from long-continued firing. In the case of military arms the latter requirements are of special importance, as the value of a breech-loading arm in increased rapidity of fire would be outweighed by any increased liability to failure in action.

To meet the above requirements many plans have been devised for securely closing the breech; at present they may be classified under two heads—

          1st. Bolt systems.
          2nd. Block systems.

With the first the breech is closed by a bolt resembling an ordinary door bolt with handle, and contains within it the lock or striking arrangement to effect the explosion of the cartridge. To this class belongs—

1. Prussian needle gun.
2. Chassepôt .. .. France.
3. Vetterli .. .. Italy.
4. Beaumont .. .. Holland.
5. Mauser .. .. Germany.
6. Berdan No. 2 .. .. Russia.
7. Gras .. .. .. France.

The six latter are improvements and modifications of the needle gun.

With the needle gun and Chassepôt paper consumable cartridges were used, and no extractor was required; with the Vetterli, Beaumont, Mauser, Berdan, and Gras a metal cartridge case is employed, and an extractor becomes necessary, and this entails an extra piece at the front of the bolt except with the Vetterli.

The bolt system of military breech-loaders is most in favour on the Continent, and it appears to lend itself more readily to the adaptation of a magazine arrangement than the block.

Our objections are—

1. That the handle of the bolt is liable to catch in objects, and that it takes away from the symmetry of the arm.

2. A considerable length of the arm is taken up by the bolt action, and it is not suitable for short barrels such as carbine.

3. In the event of a cartridge case jamming, there is no leverage to effect the extraction.

4. Should the breech action fail owing to a defective cartridge or other causes, the bolt, being in a line with the firer's eye, would be more likely to cause him injury, and several accidents of this kind have occurred.

5. In the event of a projecting cap from the base of the cartridge, or an over sensitive one, the bolt, from the direction of its motion, would be more likely to explode it in closing the breech than with the block system.

The block system has more varied forms, depending on the position of the pivot on which the block for closing the breech hinges. In the Peabody, Martini-Henry, Werder, Field (military), and others, the block hinges on a pivot at right angles and above the axis of the barrel. In the Snider it hinges laterally on a pivot parallel with this axis. With the Remington the pivot is below and at right angles to the axis, and in the Werndl the pivot is in line with the axis. With the American Sharp action the block, sliding in a vertical slot, is lowered and the action opened by depressing a lever. In the Springfield and Albini Braendlin the block is pivoted above on the rear end of the barrel.

The Prussians were the first to foresee the great advantages to be gained by the introduction of breechloaders, and the needle gun, afterwards so celebrated in the Danish war of 1864, against the Austrians in 1866, and against the French in 1870, was adopted by them 30 years ago.

It is desirable to describe this arm fully, being the parent of the bolt system.

BOLT SYSTEMS.

Needle Gun.

The breech of the needle gun is closed by a bolt Needle gun. resembling an ordinary door bolt passing between guides and containing within it the lock or striking arrangement, to effect the explosion of the cartridge. To open the breech, strike up the handle K to the left till rather more than vertical, then draw back the bolt B in a line with the barrel. To close the breech, reverse this operation. The front end of the bolt forms a conical cup, which closes the breech when pressed home by the turning down of the handle to the right into an inclined catch. The explosion of the cartridge C is effected by a steel needle N, Fig. 1, which is driven forwards by a spiral spring, and, piercing the base of the paper cartridge, passes through the powder and strikes the fulminate inside a cap situated within the cartridge, and immediately behind the bullet as shown in Fig. 4. The base of the bullet is fitted into a sabot made of compressed paper, which is forced into the grooves of the rifle by the discharge, and causes the bullet to rotate with it. The spiral spring and needle carrier A are contained in a tube D, which slides within another longitudinal tube B, and this outer tube has also an independent longitudinal sliding movement, and forms a long bolt with a knob handle K, projecting at the side as in Fig. 1.

The 1st motion in loading is to withdraw the needle from the barrel by means of the thumb piece E at the rear of the bolt, pressing down at the same time on the spring catch F, which requires releasing to allow of the withdrawal.

2nd. To strike up the bolt handle K, and draw back the bolt B, carrying the needle and spring within it, and thus opening the breech.

3rd. Insert a fresh cartridge through the open breech as in Fig. 1.

4th. Close the breech again by pushing the bolt forwards into its first position as in Fig. 2, and turning the handle to the right to lock the bolt.

5th. Is cocking the gun by pushing in the end thumb piece E to its original position as in Fig. 3, where it is retained by the spring catch F; this compresses the spiral spring, as the shoulder on the needle holder A is held fast by the trigger nose I, which allows it to pass backwards when the sliding bolt B is withdrawn as in Fig. 1, but catches and detains the needle holder when the bolt is pushed forward again as in Figs. 2 and 3. The end thumb piece E, when pushed forward for cocking the gun, enters a slot in the rear end of the sliding bolt as in Fig. 3, and holds it from turning; thus preventing any possibility of the breech being opened while the gun remains cocked.

6th. Is firing the gun by pulling the trigger T, which lowers the trigger nose and releases the needle holder A, and allows it to be driven forward by the compressed spring as in Fig. 4.

In the needle gun the means of closing the breech, so as to prevent the escape of gas backwards from the barrel at the moment of firing, is by a conical cup at the front end of the sliding bolt, which fits over a corresponding conical end of the barrel as shown at G in Figs. 2 and 4, and is forced into close contact by the slightly inclined face of the catch into which the handle of the bolt is pressed when turned down sideways. In practice, however, it was found that this joint was not sufficiently tight to prevent the occurrence of a spitting or escape of gas into the face of the firer.

The cartridge case for this arm is of paper and consumed by the discharge, so no extractor is necessary. The bore is ·61 inch, and a bullet of 480 grains was fired with a charge of 70 grains of powder; it had a low muzzle velocity and short effective range.

To face page 54.

PRUSSIAN NEEDLE GUN.
1848.

Fig. 1. *Loading.*

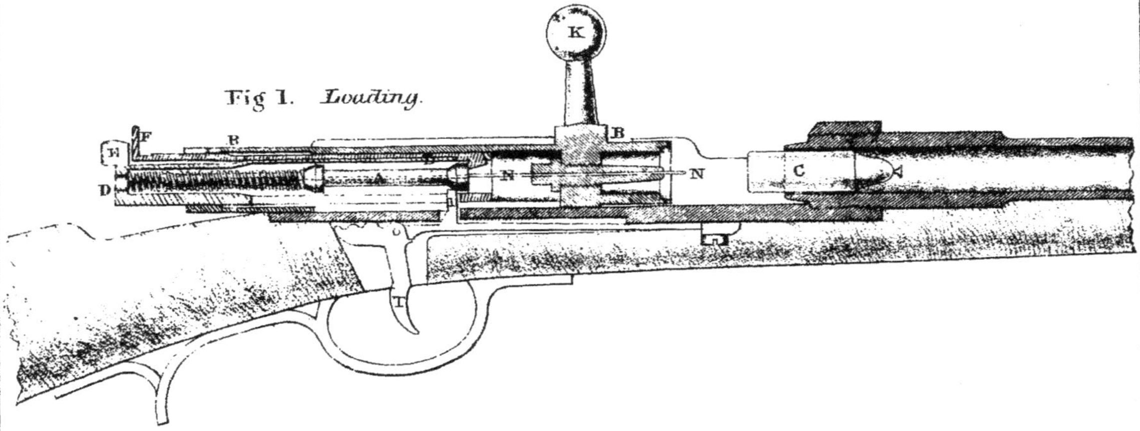

Dangerfield Lith 22 Bedford St Covent Garden.

To face page 54.

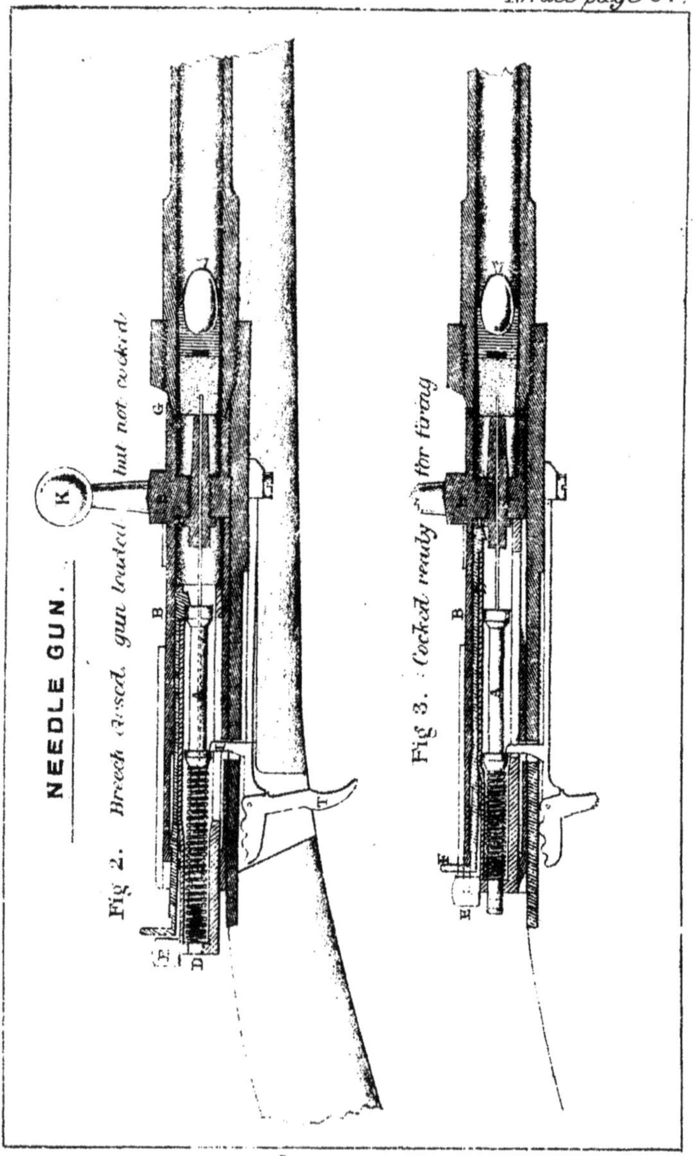

NEEDLE GUN.

Fig 2. Breech closed, gun loaded but not cocked.

Fig 3. Cocked ready for firing

DANGERFIELD, LITH 22 BEDFORD S^T COVENT GARDEN 6464

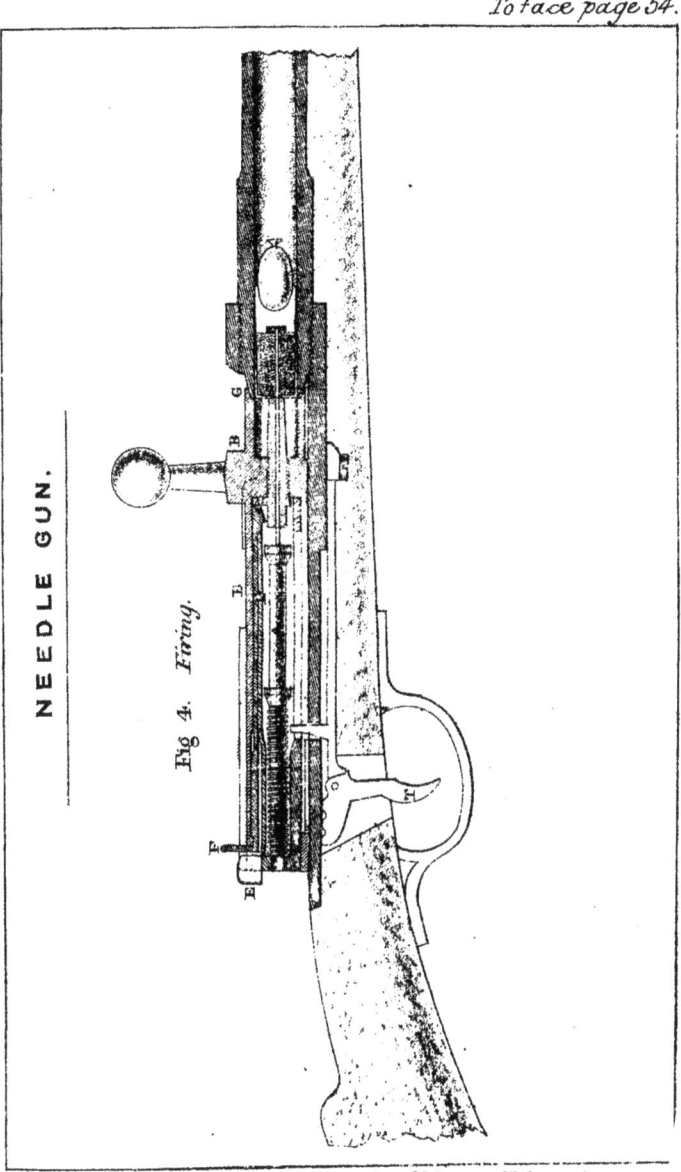

To face page 54.

NEEDLE GUN.

Fig 4. *Firing.*

DANGERFIELD, LITH 22 BEDFORD ST COVENT GARDEN.

To face page 55.

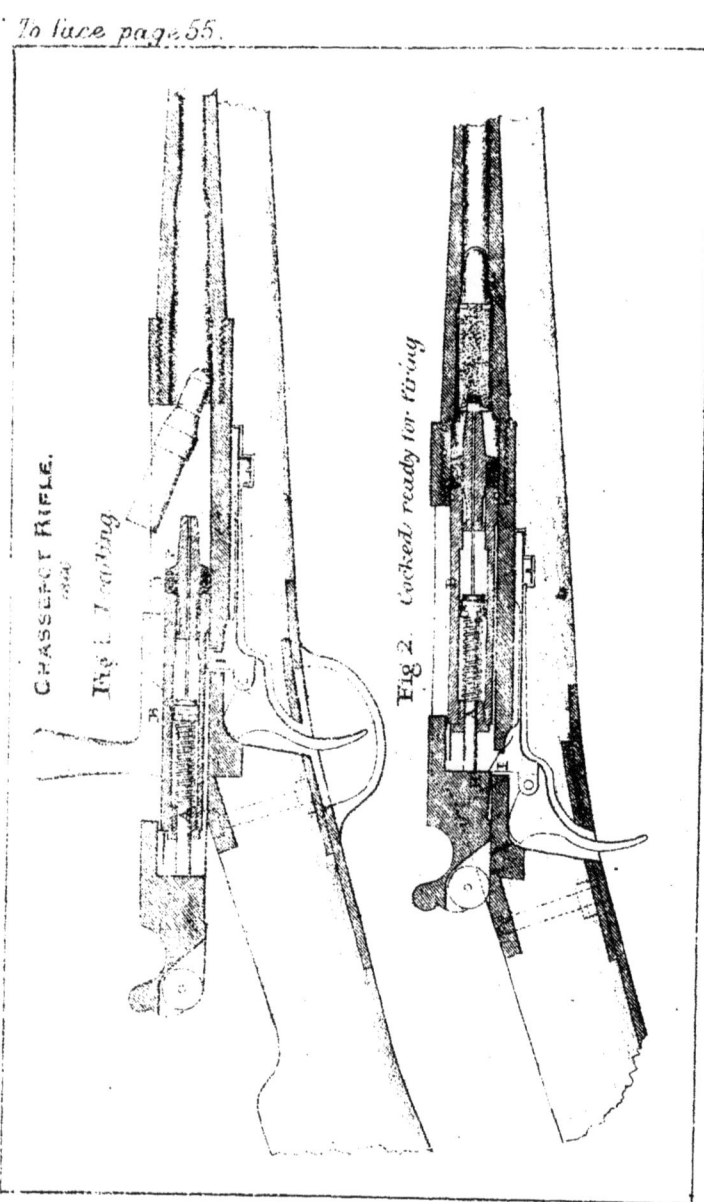

CHASSEPOT RIFLE.

Fig. 1. Loading

Fig. 2. Cocked ready for firing

DANGERFIELD, LITH. 22. BEDFORD S⟵ COVENT GARDEN.

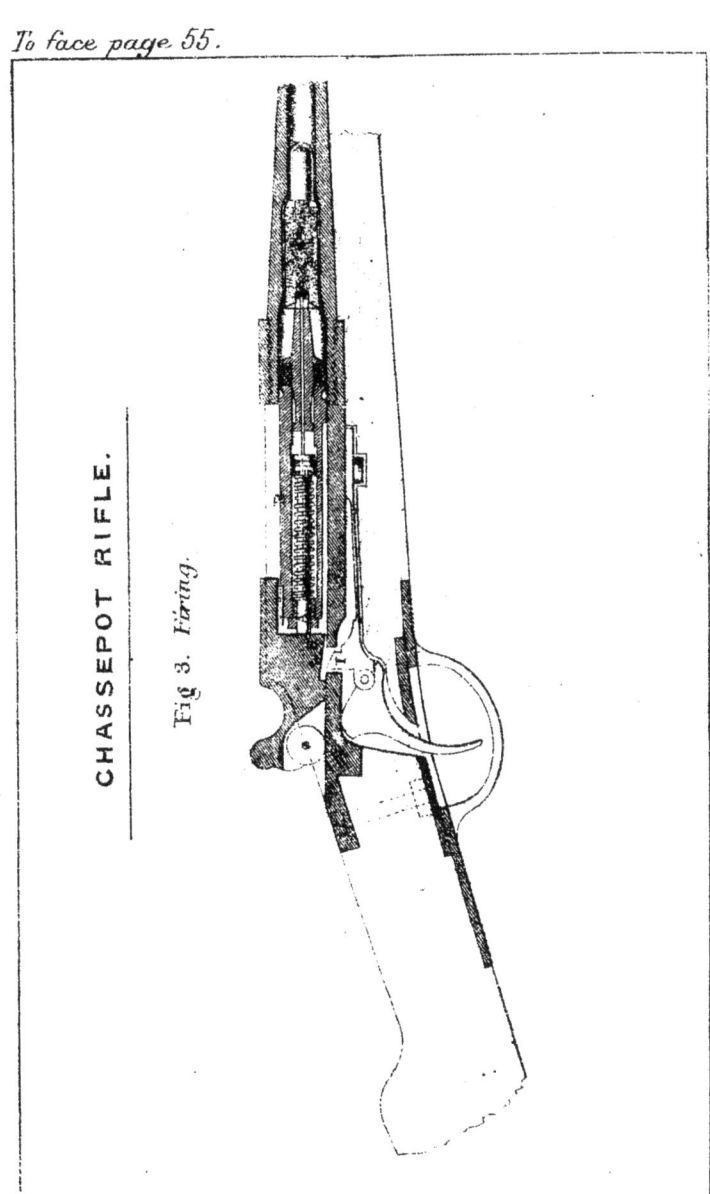

To face page 55.

CHASSEPOT RIFLE.

Fig 3. *Firing.*

French Chassepot.

This arm is an improved needle gun; the action is simpler and the bore smaller viz., ·433 with grooves of left hand twist. It is of interest as being the rifle used by the French in their late war with the Germans; the present French rifle the Gras, is a modification of it.

The motions of loading are the same as with the needle gun, but the spiral mainspring is partly compressed by the 1st motion of pulling back the hammer, and the final one of pushing in the thumb piece becomes unnecessary.

It will be seen that the internal sliding tube in the bolt of the needle gun is dispensed with.

The closing of the breech is effected by a cylindrical plug P Fig. 1, with a packing ring of india-rubber J which is pushed into the barrel (Figs. 2 and 3), and is compressed and bulged out laterally by the back pressure of the explosion, so as to make a tight fit to the bore of the barrel; the front metallic face of the plug is made with a stem sliding within the hinder portion in order to allow of the packing ring J being compressed.

It is found, however, that this elastic packing is liable to injury by use and by exposure to the heat of long-continued firing, and that it fails to keep the breech gas-tight; this escape causes great inconvenience to the firer.

This arm has a paper cartridge which is supposed to be consumed, but it is found that a residue is often left which fouls the breech chamber and renders loading difficult. The weight of bullet is 385 grains; charge of powder 87 grains.

The Mauser, Beaumont, and Gras actions are modifications of the Chassepot; they act on the same principle, and only differ from each other in minor details. The bolt in each is made up of three pieces externally, viz., the rear piece or hammer; the centre piece with lever or handle; and the front piece carrying the extractor, which is a spring capable of hooking and drawing out the empty cartridge case.

The hammer and front piece can only move longitudinally; the centre piece can both rotate a quarter circle and move longitudinally.

GERMANY.

Mauser Rifle.

This is a bolt gun with steel barrel. Four circular grooves; diameter of bore 0·433 inch; twist, one turn in 22 inches. Right-handed twist.

To the barrel is screwed the body or shoe, Fig. 1, in which the bolt moves, cut down in front on the right side for the purpose of facilitating the loading and extraction, and to receive the handle or lever when turned down to the right in the final motion of closing the breech.

The bolt Fig. 2 consists of three principal pieces, viz., A the hammer or rear piece; B the centre piece with handle N; and C the front piece carrying the extractor F; a nut D secures the rear end of the striker to A; the striker O Fig. 10 passes internally through the pieces A, B, and C. The centre piece B contains a coiled spiral mainspring encircling the striker. There is a helix or curved inclined portion cut out of the centre piece at L Fig. 2 into which a corresponding shaped projection M on the hammer fits, when these two pieces are in actual contact. To load, strike up the handle N from the right until it is vertical, as in Fig. 2, in this movement, the handle first slides up the inclined surface of the shoe at R Fig. 1, and slightly moves the entire bolt to the rear, at the same time the hammer A being incapable of rotation, its projection M is forced to slide up the inclined surface of L, and to come into the position shown in Fig. 2; this movement, besides separating the hammer and centre piece, compresses the main spring. The entire bolt can now be drawn to the rear until the washer at P Fig. 2, strikes against the upper part of the shoe at V Fig. 1, which stops it. By this motion the empty cartridge case is withdrawn, and can be removed by hand. A fresh cartridge is now inserted, and the bolt pushed forward by the handle which sends it into the chamber. When the above movement is almost completed, the projecting trigger nose X Fig. 10, catches the hammer A and retains it. The centre piece is now turned to the right by the handle into the recess of the shoe, and this has the effect of slightly moving forward the centre piece B as

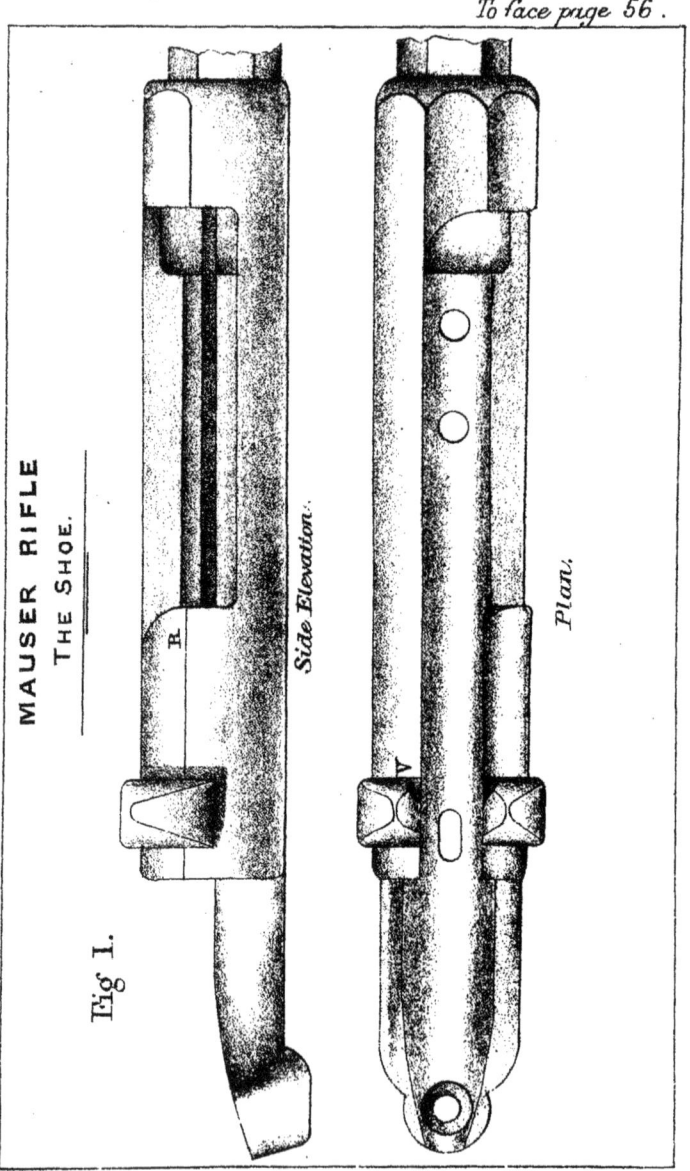

To face page 56.

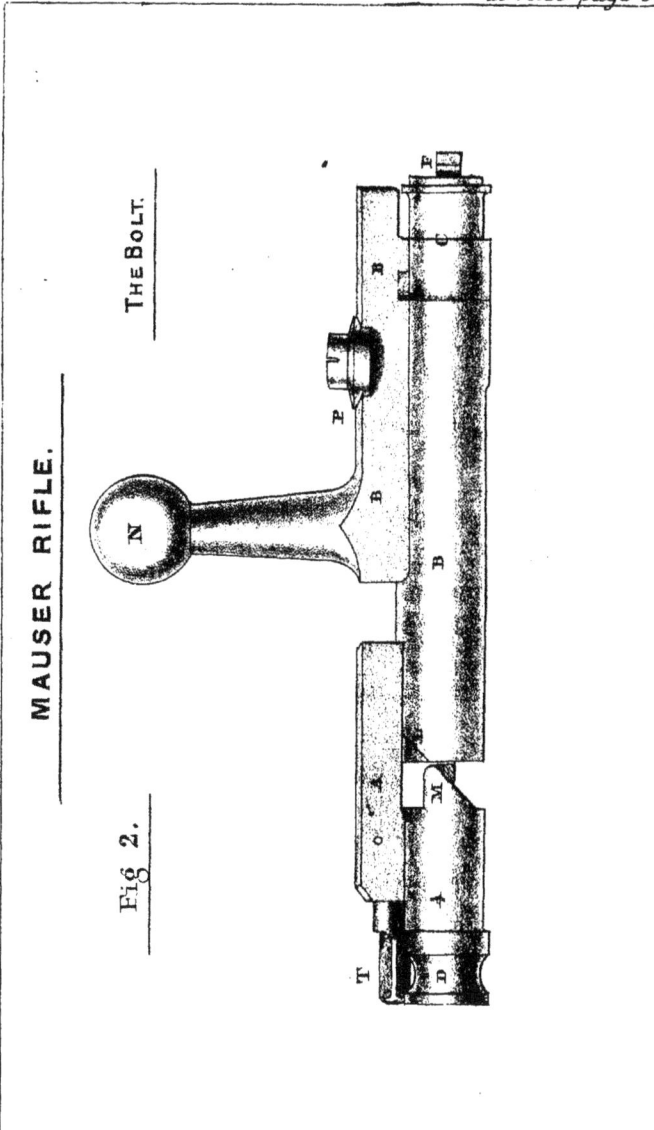

To face page 56.

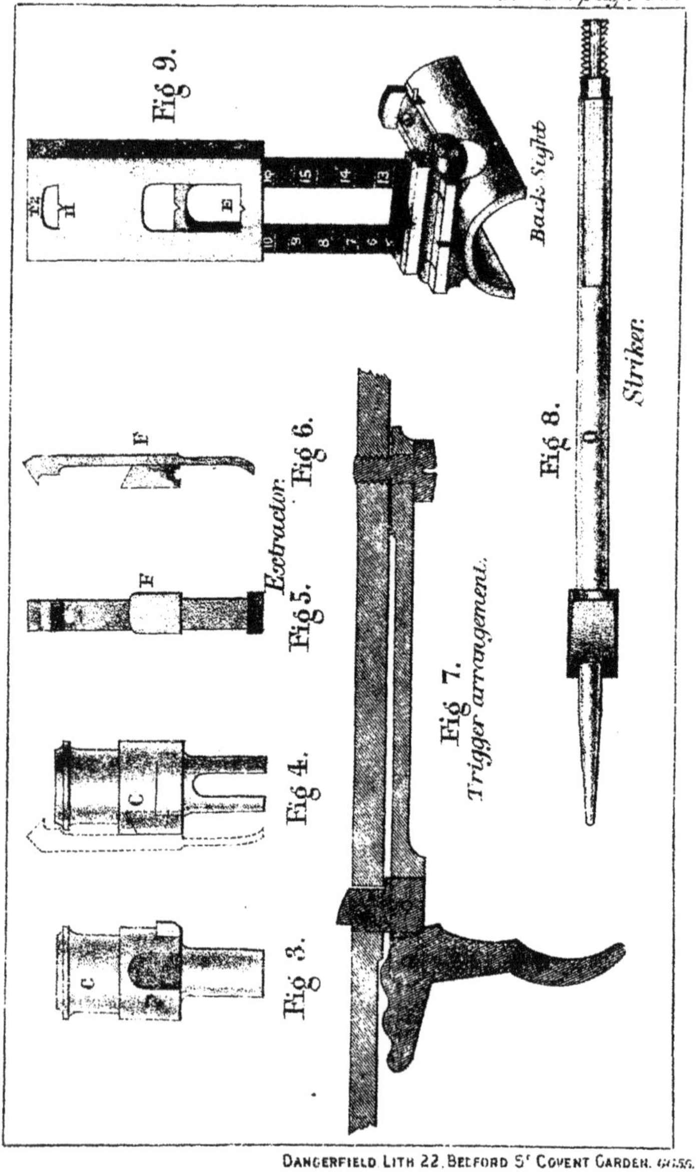
Fig 3.
Fig 4.
Fig 5.
Fig 6.
Extractor.
Fig 7.
Trigger arrangement.
Fig 8.
Striker.
Fig 9.
Back Sight

DANGERFIELD LITH 22, BEDFORD S^T COVENT GARDEN.

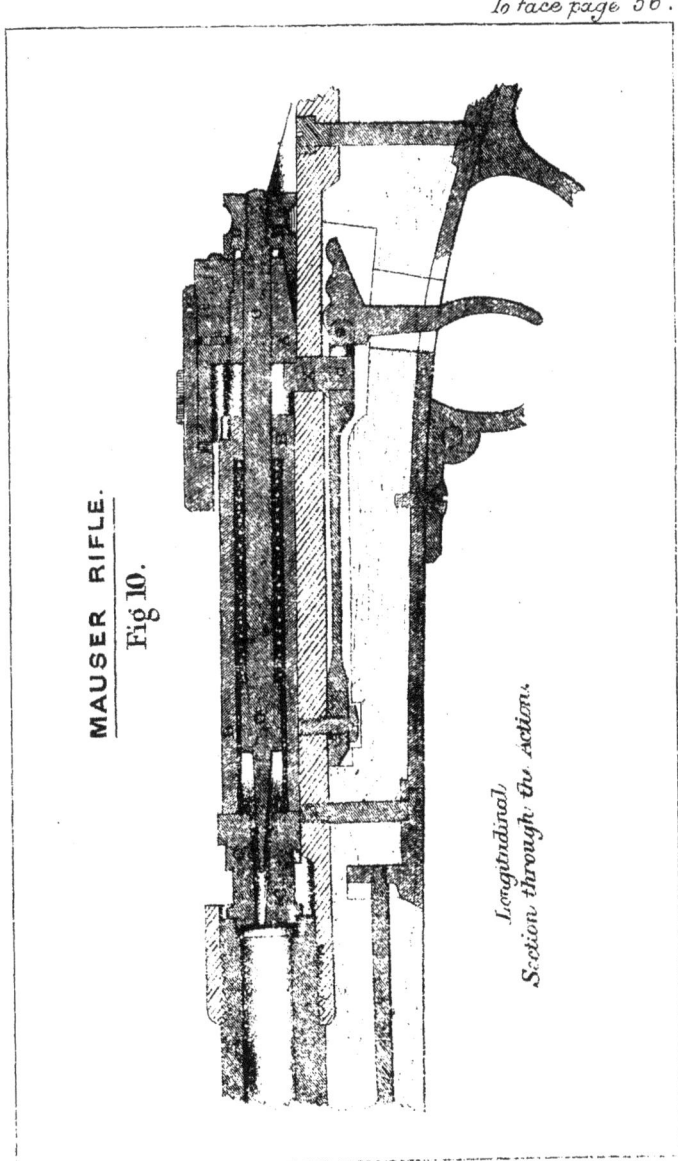

MAUSER RIFLE.
Fig 10.

Longitudinal Section through the action.

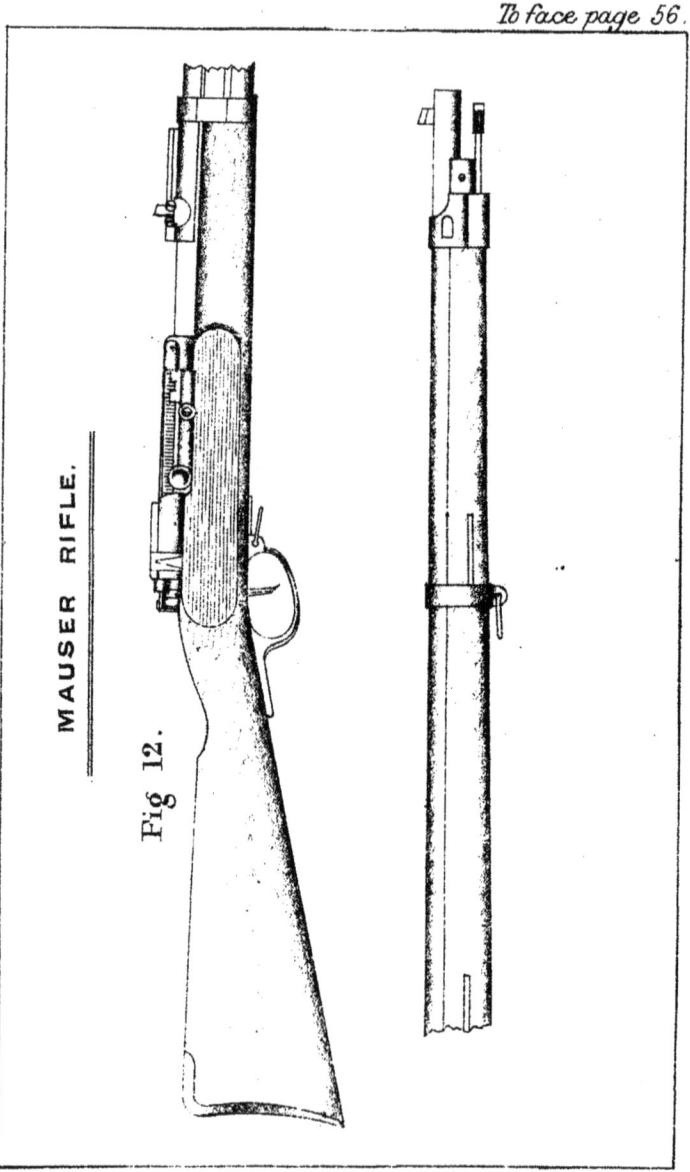

well as the front piece C, and gives a final slow motion to the cartridge into the chamber, and thus lessens the risk of a premature explosion. The pressing down of the handle to the right also further separates the hammer from the rest of the bolt, it also increases the tension of the mainspring, and brings the cavity L, Fig. 2, exactly opposite the projection M. On pulling the trigger, the trigger nose X is depressed, and the hammer set free, the latter then moves forward under the action of the compressed spiral mainspring carrying the striker with it until the projection M falls into the cavity L and the point of the striker, passing through a small hole in the face of the front piece, strikes the percussion cap and explodes the cartridge.

There is a half-round safety bolt attached to the rear piece of the bolt rotated by a thumb piece T Fig. 11. When the flat side of this safety bolt is under, it does not act, but, when the thumb piece is turned to the right, it brings the round side down into a cavity in the centre piece B and keeps this piece and the hammer or rear piece firmly apart, and in this position of the safety bolt the arm cannot be fired.

The extractor F shown in Fig. 2 moves in a groove S cut in the interior surface of the shoe, Fig. 1. Figs. 3, 4, 5, and 6 show the position of the extractor and how it is attached to the front piece of the bolt:—

The trigger arrangement, Fig. 7, resembles that of the needle gun.

The back-sight Fig. 9 gives elevation to 1600 metres. It is of a complicated character, having no less than five notches suitable for different ranges.

1st notch on base up to 300 metres.

2nd notch in small hinged flap turning down to the rear for 400 metres.

For higher elevations there is a flap and slide, on the latter of which there are three notches. The left side of the flap is graduated to 1000 metres; and with these graduations the lowest notch on the slide at E is used.

For 1100 and 1200 metres the slide is pushed down to the base of the flap, and the notches marked 11 and 12 give the correct elevation for those distances.

For further distances, up to 1600 metres, raise the slide and take the figures on the right of the flap, using the highest notch marked 12 in taking aim.

The motions in loading are—

1. Open the breech by striking up the handle and drawing back the bolt.
2. Insert the cartridge.
3. Close the breech by pushing forward the bolt and turning the handle a quarter circle to the right.

HOLLAND.

The Beaumont Rifle.

Steel barrel, 4 grooves; bore ·433 inch; right-handed twist.

The bolt for closing the breech slides in a shoe H, with a recess cut on the right side, into which the handle is turned on the breech being securely closed. The shoe is screwed to the barrel.

The bolt consists of three pieces, A, B C, which are similar, and perform the same functions as in the Mauser.

The centre piece is capable of rotating a quarter circle and moving longitudinally; the front and rear piece can only move longitudinally.

The same interlocking action takes place between a projection on the rear piece and the recess on the centre piece as shown at M and L. L is on the opposite side of the bolt, but its position is shown by the dotted lines. It will be observed that the projection and recess are in slightly different positions on this bolt from those in the Mauser.

The mainspring is a flat one, and is enclosed in the handle, instead of being a spiral coiled round the striker.

The extractor D slides in a groove in the interior of the shoe Y and limits the backward motion of the bolt when it comes to the end of the groove. The extractor is connected to the front piece C by a screw.

The striker O is attached to the rear piece A by a screw S Fig. 5.

There is a locking bolt with spring shown at N (Fig. 6), it is a clumsy device.

To face page 59.

GRAS RIFLE.

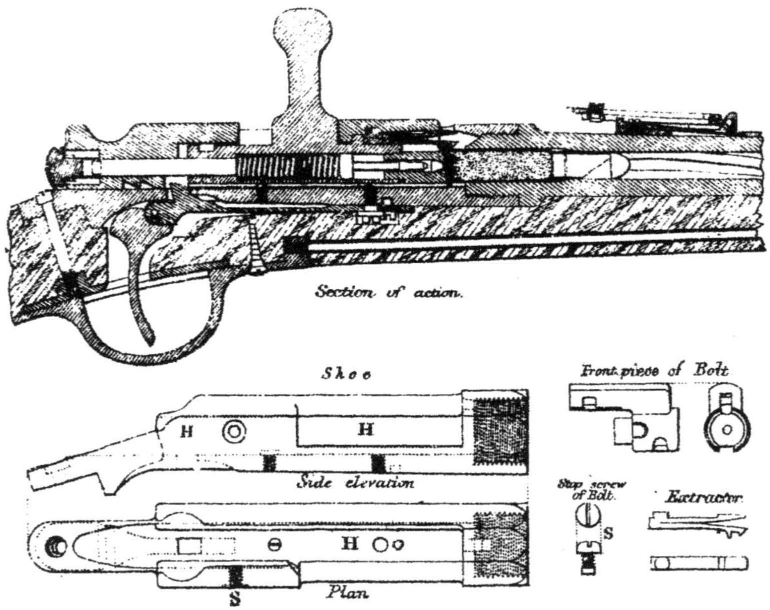

Section of action.

Front piece of Bolt

Extractor

Stop screw of Bolt.

Shoe

Side elevation

Plan

DANGERFIELD, LITH. 22 BEDFORD ST COVENT GARDEN   6648

To face page 59.

GRAS RIFLE.

It will be seen that the principle of this action is exactly the same as in the Mauser, and the trigger arrangement is almost identical. The motions in the loading are also the same.

The back-sight is of the quadrant form, the graduations for distance being marked radially on the quadrant.

FRANCE.

Gras Rifle.

Bolt action; barrel cast steel, 4 grooves, of equal width with the lands; left-handed twist, making one turn in 22 inches.

The bolt for closing the action slides in a shoe H with recess cut out on right side, into which the handle is turned to secure the breech.

The bolt consists externally of three principal pieces, the functions of which are precisely the same as in the Mauser and Beaumont.

The backward movement of the bolt is limited by a screw S, which passes through the right side of the shoe, and its extremity works in a groove cut in the centre piece of the bolt; this groove is seen in the centre piece of the bolt at N.

The extractor is a spring composed of two arms, with a stud on the upper, which connects it with the front piece of the bolt. The lower arm is provided with a claw to grip the base of the cartridge. It will be noticed that on closing the breech the upper arm is constrained to slide up an inclined plane, thus bringing the spring to tension, and ensuring the lower arm taking a firm grip of the rim of the cartridge. The lower arm has also sufficient play to pass easily over the cartridge rim in closing the breech.

The back-sight is hinged to a bed, which is soldered to the barrel. It consists of a flap and a sliding bar. These can be turned down to the front or the rear, or can be maintained in a vertical position by means of a flat spring in the bed. With the bar and slide, elevation can be given for a range of 1800 metres (1969 yards).

Motions in loading and firing the same as in Mauser and Beaumont.

1. To open the breech, turn the handle from right till vertical, then draw back the bolt; these motions put the mainspring at tension, and extract the empty cartridge case.

2. Insert the fresh cartridge, pressing it home.

3. Push forward the bolt and turn the handle down to the right until in its place; the rifle is then ready for firing.

4. Pull the trigger; this frees the rear piece of the bolt, which with the striker is carried forward by the spiral mainspring, and strikes the cap in the base of the cartridge.

ITALY.

The Vetterli Rifle.

This is the military rifle now used in Italy. It is a bolt gun of peculiar design.

The shoe or body A Fig. 5, is screwed to the barrel; within this slides a bolt B Fig. 1, with projections J which fit corresponding grooves cut on the inside of the shoe.

To load.—1. Raise the handle N vertical; this causes the striker E within the bolt to run up the inclined plane K at the same time drawing the striker back and compressing the mainspring G. The bolt can now be drawn back until the forward end of the extractor D strikes a small quoin or bolt at O Fig. 5, which stops it.

On the bolt being drawn back, the rear end of the extractor, so soon as it is free of the shoe, being a spring, catches and locks the handle by entering a recess in that part, the position of which is shown by the dotted lines at Z Fig. 3 and ensures the mainspring being kept at tension. The cartridge is now inserted through the slot or opening in the upper part of the shoe and the bolt pushed forward, sending it into the chamber; during this movement the rear end of the extractor comes against the quoin at O which unlocks the handle N and allows it to be turned down to the right, thus

To face page 61.

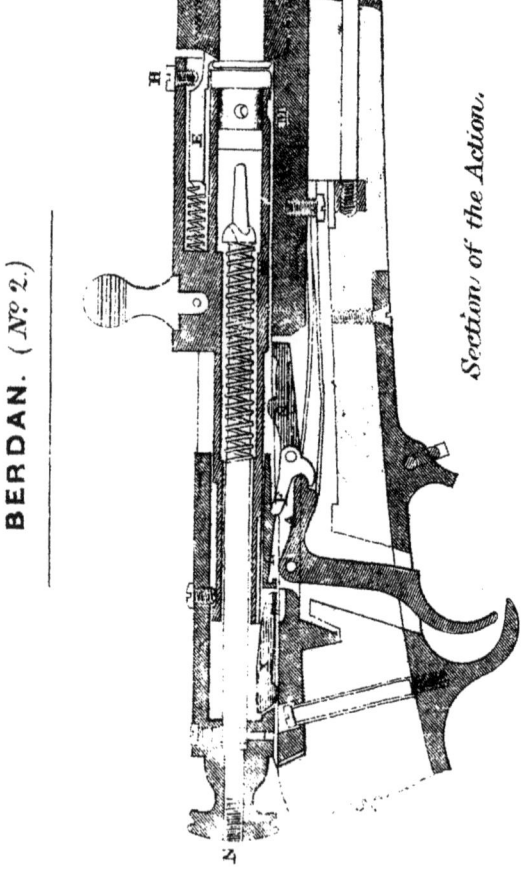

BERDAN. (N° 2.)

Section of the Action.

securing the bolt firmly. The projection on the striker E Fig. 5, is at the same time caught by the trigger nose, which retains it and keeps the mainspring at tension, the arm is now ready for firing. On pulling the trigger, the trigger nose is depressed, allowing the mainspring to drive the striker forward, and explode the cap in the base of the cartridge.

The trigger arrangement is shown Fig 4; the pulling of the trigger depresses the trigger nose as in other bolt guns.

There is a locking bolt at Y Fig. 5, in connection with the trigger, so that the arm can with safety be carried loaded.

The back-sight is of the quadrant form, marked radially and does not appear adapted for fine shooting.

RUSSIA.

Berdan No. 2.

This is the military rifle now used in the Russian Army.

No. of grooves, 6; twist one turn in 21 inches.

The bolt consists of three pieces; it slides in a shoe.

The extractor E is attached to the centre piece; its action is novel, being actuated by a small spiral spring, which pushes it out and by a screw H which keeps it up to its work, but at the same time allows it a certain play.

The extractor, being attached to the centre piece of the bolt, which rotates a quarter circle, must rotate the same amount round the rim of the base of the cartridge.

To load, raise the handle vertical. This motion slightly draws back the entire bolt. Draw the bolt to the rear until the catch N enters the recess M in the bolt and stops it; this movement withdraws the empty cartridge case. Insert a fresh cartridge and push forward the bolt; the sear nose F falls into the first catch, shown at A, and retains the rear piece, the mainspring not being at any tension, as was the case with the Mauser, Gras, &c. Continue the movement of pushing forward the bolt; this compresses the mainspring. Turn the handle down to the right, which secures the bolt. The arm is now ready to fire.

On pulling the trigger the sear nose is released from the catch, and the rear piece with striker connected moves forward under the action of the mainspring and explodes the cartridge.

There is a half-cock catch at L, so that the arm can be carried loaded with safety; to cock the arm from this position, pull the button at N until the sear falls into the foremost notch at A. There is also a small bolt or latch at X attached to the rear piece of the bolt, which falls into a recess underneath in the shoe when the rear piece moves forward on firing; this is for the purpose of strengthening and giving rigidity to the bolt. The action is a very weak one, and does not appear suitable for firing heavy charges.

BLOCK SYSTEMS.

The Peabody.

In July, 1862, Mr. Peabody of Boston, America, invented a breech-loading action. His principle was to close the breech by a longitudinal falling block B which is hinged on a transverse pin at the rear end, and falls at the front end sufficiently to clear the opening of the barrel, the upper surface of the block being hollowed out to allow a free entrance for the cartridge into the barrel in loading the rifle. The breech block is lowered and raised by a curved lever L which forms the trigger guard when closed ready for firing, and lifts the block by an arm entering a notch on its under side. The hammer H is an external cock at one side, actuated by an ordinary gun lock; the blow of the hammer is conveyed to the base of the cartridge, which is a rim-fire one by a striking bar J sliding in a curved groove in the side of the breech block. The extractor E is a bent lever, which is struck by the breech block B when lowered, and is made to jerk the empty cartridge case out. The cocking of the gun has to be effected by a separate movement of drawing the hammer back.

There is another component actuated by a spring in

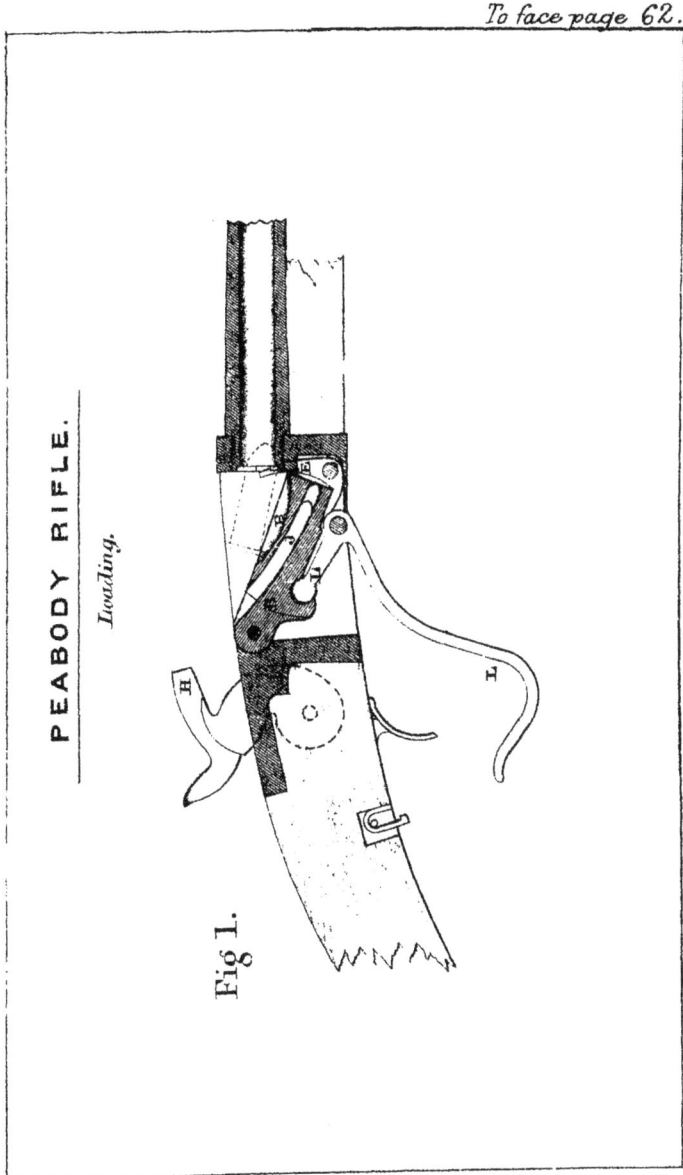

PEABODY RIFLE.

Firing.

Fig 2.

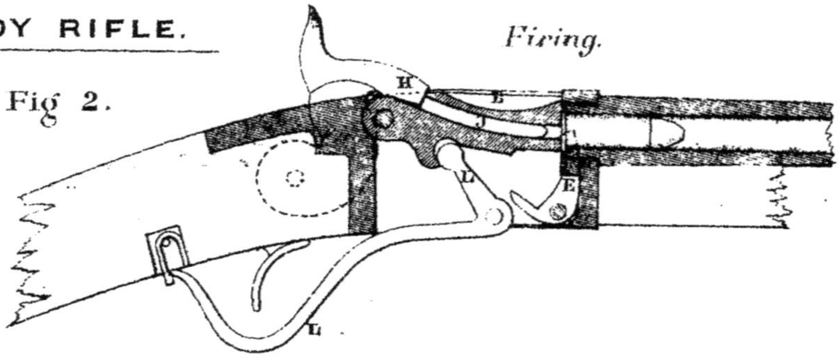

Plan. when cocked.

Fig 3.

To face page 62.

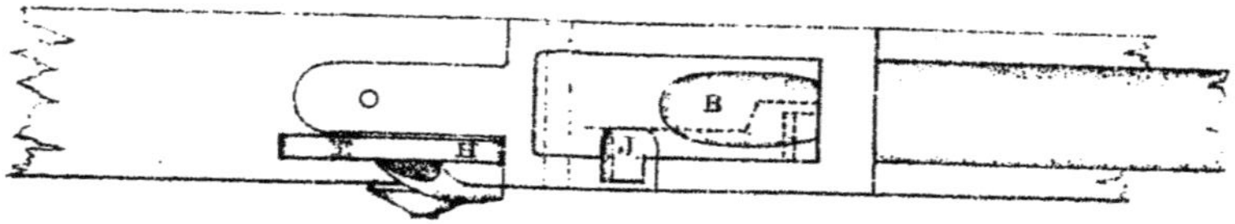

Dangerfield Lith 22, Bedford St Covent Garden

To face page 63.

MARTINI BREECH ACTION.
(Closed and Fired.)

Fig. 1.

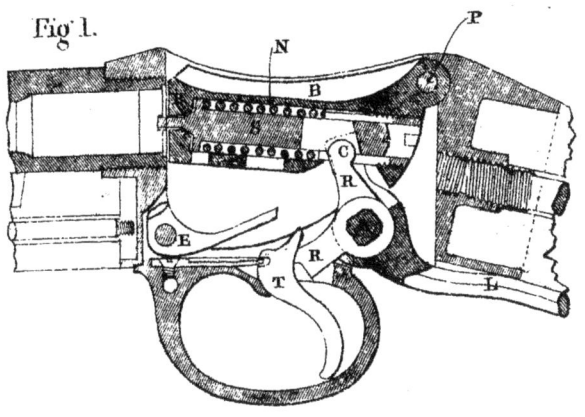

MARTINI BREECH ACTION.
(Open.)

Fig. 2.

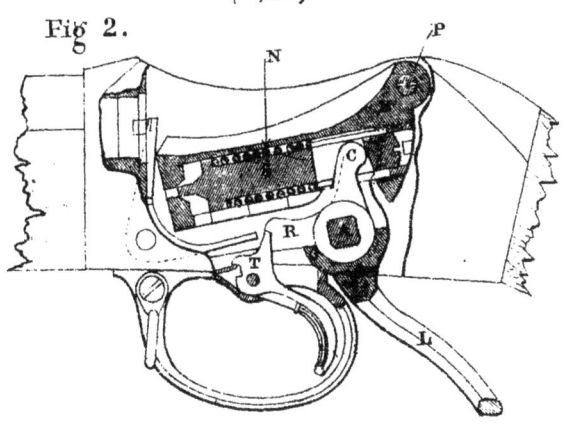

DANGERFIELD, LITH. 22, BEDFORD ST COVENT GARDEN.

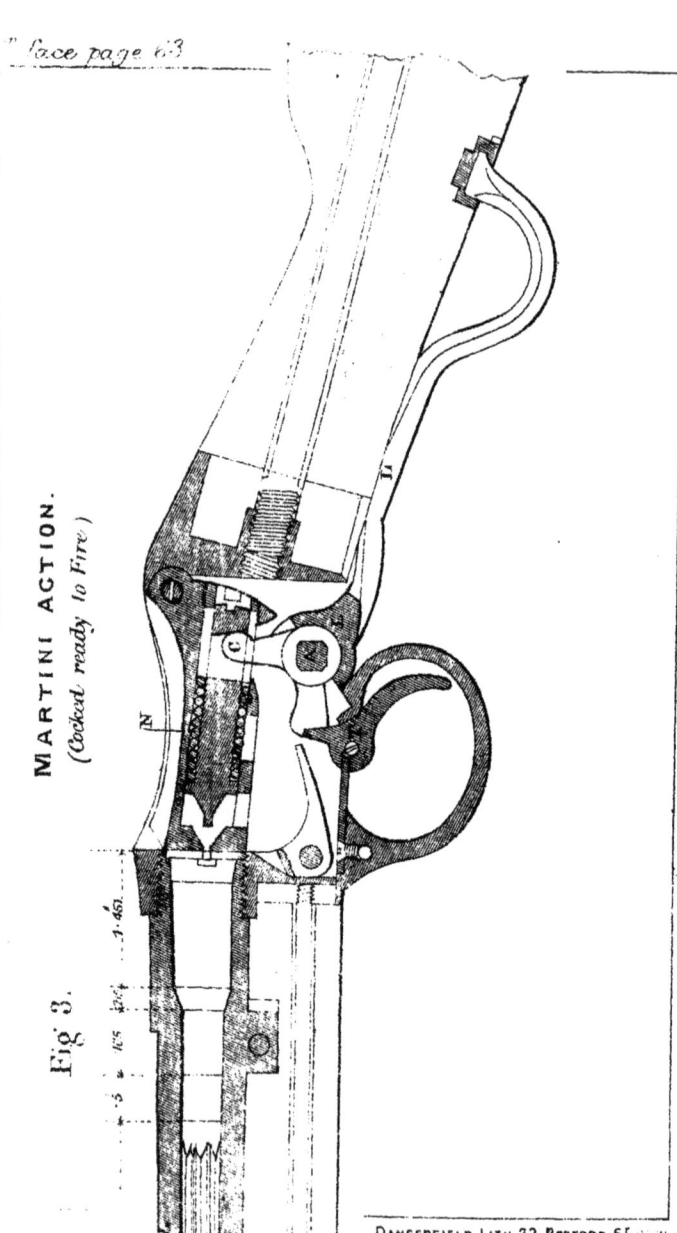

"face page 63"

Fig 3.

MARTINI ACTION.
(Cocked ready to Fire)

DANGERFIELD LITH 22, BEDFORD ST

the block for the purpose of accelerating the movement of the latter, which is omitted in the figure.

Martini-Henry Rifle.

The action of this rifle resembles the Peabody, but considerable ingenuity was displayed by M. Martini in doing away with the side lock and replacing it by one in the breech block, which is cocked by the same movement as that which opens the breech.

The rifle consists of a barrel screwed into a shoe or body V (see Fig., page 98), a butt, and a fore end. The body contains the breech action, which is the mechanism for closing the breech, firing the cartridge, and extracting the empty cartridge case.

The breech is closed* by a block B which swings on a pin P passing through the upper rear end of the shoe or body, the recoil being taken by the back and sides of the body, and not by the pin. The cartridge is exploded by the striker S which is driven by the action of a strong spiral spring N within the breech block. A lever L in rear of the trigger guard acts by means of two horns on the breech block, so that the action of lowering the lever causes the block to fall and to strike the extremity of the lower arm of the extractor E, thus ejecting the cartridge case. With the same motion and at the same time the lever carries the tumbler R round until the trigger nose falls into the bent of the tumbler, and retains that component in the cocked position (Figs. 2 and 3). The action of the lever in the above movement also draws back the striker and compresses the mainspring N by means of the crane C of the tumbler, which engages in a slot cut through the striker S.

On returning the lever to its former position the block is raised by the horns so as to close the breech, and the mainspring is still further compressed, but the tumbler does not move; it is retained and held firmly by the trigger nose. The arm is now cocked and ready for firing.

To make the above clearer it is as well to point out that the lever and tumbler are upon the same axis pin or spindle

* See Figs. 1 and 2.

A which is square at the central part, the seat of the tumbler, and this component is incapable of rotating upon it, while the outside parts of the same pin on which the lever works are round, and so the lever is free to rotate upon them. On lowering the lever a projection on it at O Fig. 2, pushes the tumbler R round until the latter engages the trigger nose which holds it. The lever is then free to rotate on the axis pin back to its former position.

There is an indicator on the right side of the action at I (see Fig., page 98) forming part of this axis pin, which at all times shows the position of the tumbler, and whether the arm is cocked or otherwise.

On pulling the trigger to fire the arm, the trigger nose is freed from the bent of the tumbler; the striker moves forward under the action of the compressed mainspring, rotating both the tumbler and axis pin, as shown by the indicator outside, and striking the cap in the base of the cartridge.

The barrel is of steel, which, owing to its greater strength, elasticity, and hardness, is far superior to wrought iron. It is rifled with seven grooves, ·03 inch of the original bore being left between the grooves as lands; the centres of the grooves and the surface of the lands are both contained in the circumference of a circle with the axis of the bore as centre; this may be understood by considering that the cutting tool which forms the groove is not rounded like a gouge, but is right-lined like a chisel, consequently the centre of the tool is the last point which touches the circular bore, and when this takes place the groove is of the proper depth.

The depth of the grooves is progressive for the first 11 inches from the breech, then they are of uniform depth to the muzzle.

A groove is ·009 inch deep at the breech, progressing to ·007 inch at 11 inches from it, and continuing at that depth to the muzzle.

The bore is slightly enlarged towards the breech for 8 inches.

The chamber is coned 018 inch to facilitate extraction.

The stock is made from Italian walnut, and is in two

parts, the butt and the fore-end. The butt is secured in the socket of the shoe or body by means of a screw bolt; and a loop and pin and two bands connect the fore-end to the barrel. In the latest pattern rifle the loop and pin have been replaced by a fore-end hook, which engages into a recess in the front of the body.

Length of rifle with bayonet fixed, 5 feet $11\frac{1}{2}$ inches.
Do. without bayonet, 4 feet $1\frac{1}{2}$ inches.
Weight of rifle without bayonet, 9 lbs. It is sighted to 1450 yards.

MARTINI-HENRY CARBINES.

The carbines of the cavalry and artillery patterns have the same calibre as the Martini-Henry rifle (0·45 inch), and have also the same twist and form of rifling, but the barrels are only 19 inches in length. The processes of manufacturing the various parts are precisely the same as those for the rifle, with which most of the components are interchangeable.

Weight, 7 lb. 8 oz., cavalry carbine.
" 7 lb. $10\frac{1}{2}$ oz., artillery carbine.
Length, 3 feet $1\frac{11}{16}$ inches.

The artillery carbine is made to take a sword bayonet, and is fitted with swivels for a sling; in these respects it differs from the cavalry carbine.

These carbines are sighted to 1000 yards.

MANUFACTURE.

The following description of the manufacture of the Martini-Henry rifle is from notes by Major W. McClintock, R.A., Assistant Superintendent R.S.A. Factory, Enfield Lock, who has kindly placed them at my disposal:—

THE STOCK.

The stock, which consists of two parts, the butt and fore-end, is made of Italian walnut; this wood, owing to its lightness, hardness, and closeness of grain, being found well suited for the purpose. The rough

(S.A.) E

butts and fore-ends are obtained by contract, and on arrival in the factory are examined, when, should any of the following defects be observed, they are rejected:—

1. Under size.
2. Crooked (fore-end only).
3. Galls (the results of wound in tree)
4. Shakes (cracks).
5. Rind galls (the result of injury to bark of tree when young).
6. Discoloured wood.
7. Bines or knots.
8. Cross grain.
9. Bad quality (perished wood).
10. Fly holes and worm.
11. Impregnated with salt water.

The first ten defects are readily detected by the examining viewers, and should the appearance of the wood lead them to suppose that it has been damaged by salt water, a shaving is taken off with a spokeshave, and is dipped in a solution of nitrate of silver (1 grain to 1 oz. distilled water), when, should any salt be present in the wood, a white precipitate is formed (chloride of silver). Should wood which has been damaged by salt water be used for a stock, it will rust any steel or iron with which it comes in contact, and no method is known by which to remove the salt from wood which has once been damaged.

The butts and fore-ends are usually in a half-seasoned condition when received from the contractor, and are stacked to season in the stock stores.

Green wood requires about three years to season. If it is necessary to hasten the seasoning of the wood, the rough butts and fore-ends are placed in the desiccating room, and subjected to a heat of 60°, gradually increasing to 90° or 100° Fahrenheit. If half dry when placed in the desiccating room, they will be ready for use in about six or seven weeks.

BUTT.

Principal Processes in Manufacture.

The principal machine operations are as follows:—

1. Boring for stock bolt
2. Rough turning.
3. Sawing to length.
4. Bedding butt plate.
5. Finished turning.
6. Bedding for shoe, and lever catch-block.
7. Counter-sinking and facing for body.
8. Hand-finishing.

Fore-end.

1. Rough turning.
2. Grooving for barrel.
3. Sawing to length.
4. Fitting nose-cap.
5. Finished turning.
6. Bedding for body, rod-holder, and fore-end hook.
7. Boring for rod.
8. Hand-finishing.

THE BARREL.

Material.

The barrel is made of soft or mild steel, prepared by the "Siemens-Martin" process, this metal having been found to be of a very uniform nature. The barrel bars or moulds are obtained by contract in lengths of 15 inches, the diameter for rifle bars being $1\frac{1}{2}$ inch.

The Smithery.

Forging.—The barrel bar is heated to a white heat and passed through the barrel rolling-mill, which consists of ten pairs of rolls arranged alternately horizontally and vertically, when it is drawn out in one heat to the full length required (about 36 inches), taper in form, and solid. It is next passed to the Ryder forging machine, where the "Knox form" is forged on the breech end and the barrel cut to length, then passed through a straightening machine, examined for straightness, and viewed as finished forged.

Barrel Machine Room.

Machine Operations.—The ends of the barrel are clamp-milled for size and length, and then drilled up about $1\frac{1}{2}$ inch at each end, the diameter of the holes drilled being 0·430 inch. This operation is called "entering the bore," and is very carefully tested to see that the starting of the bore is true and correct. The barrels are now ready for drilling.

Drilling.—The barrels, while being drilled, are placed vertically in a machine, where they revolve with a speed of about 300 revolutions per minute, the holes already made at each end acting as guides for the set of three drills used in this operation. The method of using these drills ensures a long hole of small diameter being drilled perfectly true, and until this method was adopted this was found to be a most difficult task. The drills consist of, first, the "core drill," for roughly cutting away the metal. This is run in half an inch, when the barrel is taken out and emptied of swarf or cuttings by placing it over a jet pipe, when a strong stream of washing liquor thoroughly clears out the bore. Another half inch is drilled in the same manner, and the bore again washed out. The second drill, or half-round bit, is now used. This drill is 0·430 inch in diameter, and having only a cut of 0·05 inch to make in clearing the hole, is run down the one inch the core drill has cleared without any risk of deviating from the truth.

The barrel is now again washed out, and No. 3 drill made use of. This has a stock fitting the hole already bored, and ending in a small $\frac{3}{16}$-inch drill, which, being supported by the stock, drills away the centre perfectly true with the axis of rotation, ready for the "core" or "roughing drill" to start again. If this system is rigidly carried out inch by inch, it is possible to drill a hole three or four feet deep with an error of less than 0·005 inch. A set of drills consists of these three just described, and three sets of different lengths are used. When one half of the barrel has been drilled, it is turned end for end, and the operation repeated until the holes meet in the centre.

This system of drilling originated at the Royal Small Arms Factory, and is not in use elsewhere.

After drilling, the hole is broached out with long square bits, on one side of which a strip of oak is placed. Long strips of writing paper are evenly placed between the strip and bit, one upon another, and the bit is run through the barrel until the hole is broached out to the required diameter. This operation is more of a burnishing character than a cutting one, producing a fine clear polished surface, down which a shade is readily thrown by holding the barrel at the proper angle to the light. As shadows thrown off straight surfaces are projected in straight lines on any true surface on which they are thrown, the eye can be taught by practice to detect any inaccuracy in the bore of a barrel by the appearance of the edges of the shadow thrown down it. In order to ensure absolute certainty that no barrel should be passed on for the exterior to be turned, which had not the bore perfectly true, the following mechanical test has been devised, viz.:—A steel rod is stretched taut between two horizontally fixed head-stocks, having a collar in the centre and at one end, which fit the bore loosely, so that the barrel can freely revolve on the rod. If the bore is straight, the end of the barrel where there is no collar on the rod will run perfectly true; but if not straight it will revolve eccentrically, and its motion is easily detected by any unskilled person. Every barrel is passed through this test before the exterior is commenced upon. The bore is also tested for size by the collars on the rod.

The next operation is to support and hold the bore true, while the outside is turned perfectly concentric with it. After a number of experiments to find out a means of fixing a *true turned bush* or collar on a rough exterior, the present method of running sulphur in a liquid state between the barrel and bush was adopted. By this means the exterior of barrel can be turned perfectly true with the bore, without injury to the inside. The barrel is placed vertically, when two plugs, whose centres coincide with the axis of the barrel, are placed in the breech and muzzle; the bush is then held over it, and melted sulphur is poured in between barrel and bush. This gives a bearing for the outside perfectly true with the bore.

Turning.—The barrel is now rough-turned, finished-turned, draw-polished. gauged, chambered for proof, and screw-thread cut in breech end to take the "hutts" used to close the breech during first proof.

This system of turning a barrel enables its exterior to be brought to a definite size, and is greatly superior to the old method of grinding barrels on a large stone, and afterwards striking them up.

First Proof.—The barrels now undergo the first proof test, which is necessary in order to detect inferior quality of metal, and flaws which do not appear on either the exterior or interior surfaces. The first proof charge is 7½ drams of powder, a lead plug of 715 grains, and over the latter a cork wad half an inch in thickness. Twenty barrels are proved at the same time in a cast-iron proof battery.

Finished Milled.—The seat for the front sight is now cross-milled and dovetailed, and the steel for the front sight is sawn to length and brazed on. The barrel is now finished, bored, and set, and is then ready for rifling.

Rifling—The rifling is done with a cutter having a head of suitable form for the rifling required. This is fitted into a groove cut in a box about eight inches in length, and fitting the bore. It is drawn through the barrel by a rod fastened to one end of the cutter box, the other end of the rod being coupled into the spindle of the head-stock or traversing saddle. On the spindle is a pinion geared into a sliding rack carried by the same saddle. The end of the rack is fitted to slide backwards and forwards along a fixed bar, which can be set at any angle necessary to rotate the spindle and cutter box to the amount of spiral required. From four to five cuts are needed for each groove, and the cutter is fed up by a screw tapped into the end of the cutter box, to which a rod is attached, which works through the centre boss of a hand wheel. A spiral groove is cut along this rod, in which a feather fixed in the boss of the hand wheel slides, enabling the feedscrew to be screwed in or out by the hand wheel as required. An index is connected with the hand wheel, enabling the operator to read off the depth of cut. The barrel is fixed in a rotating chuck, which is divided so that any number of grooves required can be cut inside the bore. The rifling is of a uniform twist of 1 in 22 inches, or one and a half turns in the length of bore (33 inches). The form of rifling is that known as the "Henry rifling;" the grooves are seven in number, and are 0·007 inch in depth.

Screwing and Chambering.—The barrel is suspended inside a hollow rotating spindle by a plug inside the muzzle end, running on a plug fixed in headstock at the breech end. A guide-screw is securely fixed on the rotating spindle, and carries a nut fixed to traversing tool-holder, which holds a peculiar form of chasing tool. The teeth for cutting the screw-thread on the breech end are on the under side, so that, being set over the top of the rotating barrel, it can be lifted in and out of the thread which is being cut, in the shortest possible time and distance, without chopping the thread.

The screw being finished, the barrel is driven from it, while the breech end is chambered up for the cartridge. This is an ordinary operation of boring and reamering in a lathe.

Second Proof.—The barrel is now breeched up to body, the action assembled for proof, and the rifle undergoes the second proof test. The second proof charge consists of 5 drams of powder, a bullet weighing 715 grains, and a ½-inch cork wad. The barrels are proved in a proof battery something similar to that used for the first proof.

Sighting.—The back-sight bed is soldered on to the barrel, and also secured in its place by two screws. Both the back-sight and front-sight are adjusted and regulated from the axis of the bore, and when viewing the barrels for sighting, the greatest care is taken to see that both sights are exactly in position.

Browning.—The body and barrel are browned separately, the following being the browning mixture at present in use:—

Spirits of wine				5 ounces.
Spirits of nitre				8 ,,
Tincture of steel				8 ,,
Nitric acid				4 ,,
Sulphuric acid				3 ,,
Blue vitriol				4 ,,
Water				1 gallon.

The process is as follows :—The barrels and bodies are first scalded in a solution of soda for twenty minutes, and are then washed in clean water. The browning mixture is applied, and they are placed in a damp heat for about one and a half hour, when they are scalded again, and, when cool, the rust is scratched off.

This process is repeated four times, and then the barrels are cleaned off and oiled. The whole operation of browning takes about eight hours.

THE BODY.

Material.—The body is made from a specially tough class of mild steel. Bars of this metal, 4 or 5 feet in length, and 2 inches by $1\frac{1}{2}$ inch in section, are obtained by contract.

Forging.—The body is blocked direct off the end of the bar by five blows under a 15-cwt. steam-hammer.

The first blow gives a rough figure, and measures off the quantity of metal required.

The second blow fullers in the sides of the body, to displace the metal when working the hole through it.

The third blow, by means of a chisel in the upper die, splits the metal in the centre, driving out the sides of the body to fill the die, and leaving the impression of the hole, to be made through the body, full size at top.

The fourth blow drives a full-sized drift, placed in the hole just made by the chisel, clean through; shearing down the sides, and driving through the small piece left at the bottom of the hole. The hole made through the body is now 3 inches by $\frac{7}{8}$ inch by $2\frac{3}{4}$ inches, and the metal wasted is only $3\frac{1}{2}$ oz. in weight.

The fifth blow cuts the body off the bar. A mandril is now driven in the hole, and a blow is struck upon the ends to square them up, when the body is ready for stamping.

Stamping.—The body is reheated and a cold steel mandril driven into it, when it is at once placed under a powerful steam-hammer. On the anvil of this hammer is the lower die of a pair, the impression cut in the pair of dies being that of the finished size of forged body. One heavy and sudden blow is given, with force sufficient to make the metal flow into every corner of the impression. If this is not done at the first blow, it cannot with safety be attempted by a second blow without reheating, as the surplus metal flows over between the faces of the dies in the form of a thin fin, chilled and black, and this would swallow up itself the force of a second blow, and perhaps split one of the dies.

The body is next annealed, scale pickled off, fin trimmed, and passed as "finished forged."

Machine Operations.—The hole in the body is first drifted out by means of long, slightly tapered drifts, which are drawn through it, and the hole thus produced is used as a starting-point for all the subsequent operations. After drifting, four bodies are placed on a revolving cross-shaped fixing, the arms of which exactly fit the holes in the bodies, while a transverse slide carrying two tool-holders, one on each side, turns up both sides of the four bodies at one eperation. This operation leaves the sides of the body equal in thickness, and true with the centre hole.

Twelve bodies are next fixed on a revolving head, and the barrel ends are all cut square and true, the stock ends being treated in the same manner.

The hole for the barrel is then drilled, tapped, and the burr thrown up by tapping is smoothed down. The face is eased, so that when a gauge is screwed in, it stands exactly true. The body is now placed in a drilling jeg, and the adjusted face is screwed tight up against a rib in the jeg, while the six axis holes of various sizes are drilled, three in each side. The drills run through hardened steel bushes fixed in the sides of the drilling jeg.

These axis holes, after being tested for accuracy, become, in conjunction with the large hole in the body, the base points for the remaining operations.

A number of drilling machines now operate to cut away the metal, so as to form the socket to receive the stock butt. The hole is drilled and tapped to receive the screw end of the stock bolt, which secures the butt in the socket. Pins in the axis holes in the left side of the body hold it while the knuckle seat for breech block is roughly cut out, and the seat milled out square and true. A number of minor milling, drilling, and tapping operations bring the body into the shape and figure required, and it is then screwed on, or "breeched up," to the barrel. The barrel is now placed vertically with the end of the chamber resting on the collar of a plug, which enters and exactly fits the chamber, and the face of the barrel is drawn tight down on this collar by means of plugs pushed through axis holes in the body. Small mills are now run on a spindle through the block axis-hole, and finish cutting out the knuckle seat of the block to a positive length from the face of the barrel. This length between the knuckle seat of the block and the face of the barrel is rigidly maintained, so as to ensure that any block will interchange or fit in any body. In order to ensure that this may the case, each breeched-up barrel and body is accurately gauged with hardened steel gauge blocks. Care is also taken to see that the striker hole, in the face of gauge block, coincides with the axis of the bore of barrel, to ensure the cap of the cartridge being struck in the centre.

The barrel and body are now passed on for assembling the action for second proof.

Emery Wheels.

A particular form of emery wheel, called a "rim wheel," has been introduced for finishing up some of the components. Its use has enabled unskilled labour to take the place of a high class of skilled workmen, and the work is better finished. For instance, the slot of the back-sight leaf is first drifted to its true size. By this it is held in a fixing attached to a vertical axis, and both edges with cap attached can be passed across the face of the rim wheels, maintaining it perfectly true, and grinding the edges of the leaf and cap parallel to each other. The sides are done in the same manner.

Having given a short description of the processes of manufacture for the rifle, barrel, and body, it will be unnecessary to describe the manufacture of the other components. The method pursued in the manufacture of all is precisely that followed in the case of the body. All the parts are first of all forged in dies, the fin is trimmed off, they are pickled to remove scale, and then undergo numerous milling, drilling, and other machine operations, until they are brought to the correct figure, when they are viewed, gauged, and either case-hardened, browned, blued, hardened, and tempered, &c., as the case may be.

The barrels of carbines and pistols are treated in the same manner as the rifle barrel. In order to ensure an absolute interchangeability of the various parts, the most exact system of gauging is a necessity, and the strict view which is enforced, prevents the possibility of any defective parts being assembled in an arm.

The following list gives the nomenclature of the remaining parts of the rifle, and the materials of which they are made:—

Name.	Material.	Name.	Material.
Band, lower	wrought iron.	Swivel, guard	wrought iron
Band, upper	,,	Washer, stock bolt	,,
Block	,,	Cleaning rod	steel.
Butt plate	,,	Extractor	,,
Fore-end hook	,,	Front sight	,,
Guard	,,	Indicator	,,
Lever	,,	Rod-holder	,,
Lever catch block	,,	Sight leaf	,,
Nose-cap	,,	Sight slide	,,
Nut, upper band	,,	Stop-nut	,,
Sight bed	,,	Striker	,,
Sight cap	,,	Trigger	,,
Stock bolt	,,	Tumbler	,,
Swivel, band	,,		

Screws.

Butt screws (2)	wrought iron.	Indicator keeper screw	steel.
Guard swivel screw	,,	Sight bed screw	,,
Lower band screw	,,	Sight cap screw	,,
Nose-cap screw	,,	Sight spring screw	,,
Rod-holder screws (2)	,,	Stop-nut keeper screw	,,
Upper band screw	,,	Trigger screw	,,
Extractor axis screw	steel.	Trigger spring screw	,,
Fore-end hook screws (2)	,,		

Springs.

Lever catch block spring	steel.		Sight spring	..	.. steel.
Main spring	..	.. ,,	Trigger spring	..	.. ,,

Pins.

Block axis pin	..	.. steel.	Sight axis pin	..	.. steel.
Lever catch block pin	..	,,	Upper band pin..	..	,,
Lower band pin..	..	,,			

HARDENING AND TEMPERING COMPONENTS.

Case-Hardening.

The breech-block, lever, butt plate, and iron screws, are case-hardened. This is done by carefully packing them in iron boxes, in which they are surrounded with bone cuttings or animal charcoal. An iron plate is laid on the top of the box, and it is placed in a furnace and raised to a red heat. The length of time that the various articles are left in the furnace, depends on the amount of case-hardening required; and when removed from the furnace they are chilled in a tank of cold water. They are then cleaned, oiled, and examined by gauges to ascertain whether the case-hardening has altered their form.

Tempering.

The following components are hardened by being raised to a certain temperature, and then cooled in oil. They are afterwards tempered by "blazing," that is, by heating them again until the oil or suet with which they have been covered, bursts into a flame:—

Striker, main-spring, indicator, extractor, sight spring, catch block spring, trigger spring, block axis pin, extractor axis, sight slide, and steel screws, &c.

The following components are blued:—

Upper and lower bands, upper and lower band pins, guard and band swivels, fore-end hook screws, sight leaf, lever catch block and pin, guard, nose-cap, rod-holder, &c.

They are polished, cleaned with lime to remove grease,

To face page 77.

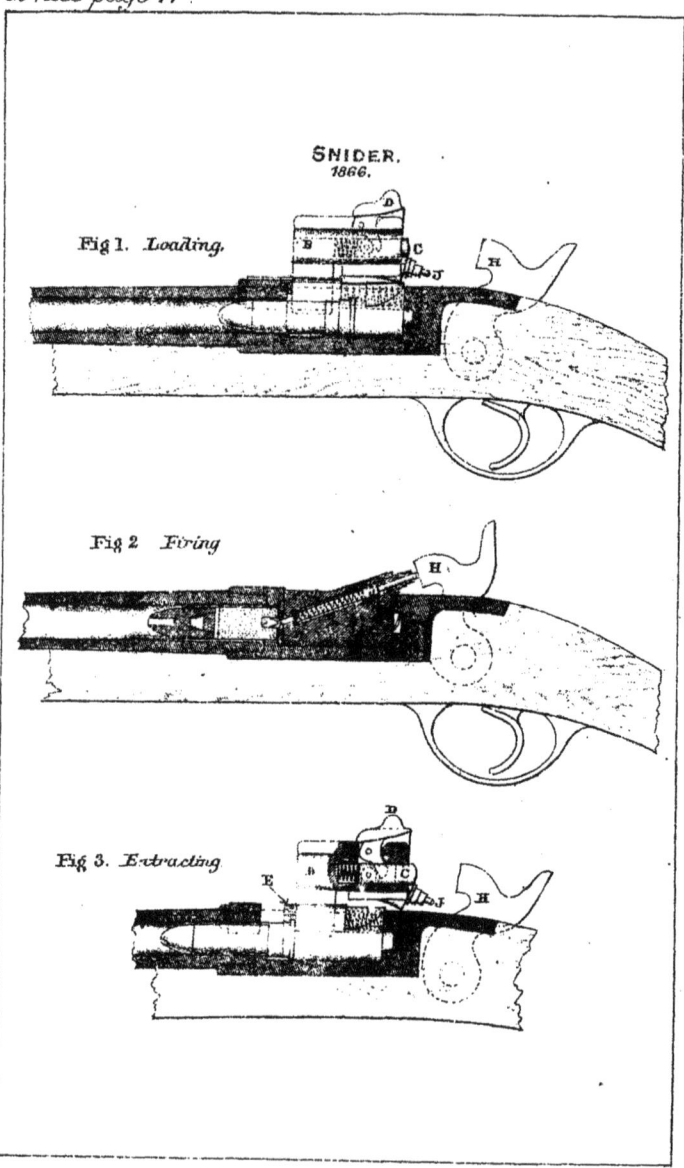

and are then covered with powdered charcoal and raised to a temperature of about 550° Fahrenheit.

TURKEY.

Peabody-Martini Rifle.

This rifle was manufactured in America on the model of the English Martini-Henry; it differs from it in being heavier, and having a smaller chamber to suit the solid drawn cartridge case used with this arm.

SNIDER RIFLE.

The Snider action was adopted in 1865 as the mode of altering the existing muzzle loaders.

The shoe L is screwed to the barrel, the breech is closed by a block B which lifts and turns over laterally for opening the breech, being hinged on a longitudinal pin on one side of the action; the breech is then open for inserting the cartridge in loading. When closed again (Fig. 2) the block is securely locked in its place by a spring catch C which is withdrawn by a lever D pressed by the thumb in the act of lifting the breech block. The firing of the cartridge is effected by an ordinary hammer and percussion lock propelled by a flat main spring in the usual manner, and acting upon a striker J which passes obliquely through the breech block, and terminates at the centre of the cartridge base; this pin has a light spiral spring to draw it back after striking the cap. For extracting the empty cartridge case an arm E is provided, which slides upon the hinge-pin of the breech block. When the breech is open, the breech block being drawn back, brings with it the extractor which seizes a portion of the rim of the cartridge and draws it out of the chamber, so that it can be dropped out or picked out by hand.

The breech block is then forced forward again by a spiral spring on the hinge pin which is covered by two hollow cylinders sliding the one into the other. The Snider rifle is of the large bore class, ·577 inch calibre, bullet 480 grains, fired with a charge of 70 grains of powder.

There are five motions in loading :—1. Cock the hammer. 2. Open the action. 3. Remove the empty cartridge. 4. Introduce fresh cartridge. 5. Close the action.

Snider rifles are sighted as below :—
Snider long Pn. 53 to 950 yards.
Snider short Pn. 60 to 1000 yards.
Snider Artillery carbine Pn. 61 and Snider Cavalry carbine to 600 yards.

For further particulars see Table II at end of this chapter.

AUSTRIA.

Werndl Rifle.

This arm has a rotating breech block consisting of a solid longitudinal cylinder B which turns one-quarter round upon a centre pin P at each end, situated just below the axis of the barrel (Figs. 1 and 2). A cylindrical groove is cut out along one side of the block, and when this groove is turned opposite the barrel, the breech is left entirely open (Fig. 1) ready for inserting a fresh cartridge ; by reversing this operation the breech is closed. The breech block is held at either extreme of its rotation by a spring S bearing against the projecting end of its centre pin P (Fig. 1), which is formed with two inclined flat sides for this purpose as shown in the end elevation (Fig. 4). A striker J is carried obliquely through the breech block for conveying the blow to the centre of the cartridge base from the hammer H which is on one side, similar to the ordinary percussion-lock hammers.

The cartridge extractor is carried on a transverse pin, I just below the barrel, and on the other end of the pin is a horizontal arm shown dotted in Fig. 1, having at its extremity a lateral projecting stud which enters a groove G cut round the cylindrical surface of the breech block, Fig. 3 ; by the rotation of the block in opening the breech, the end of the groove is brought down upon this stud, and depresses the arm of the extractor sufficiently to withdraw the cartridge partially from the chamber as in Fig. 1. The breech block is made with a

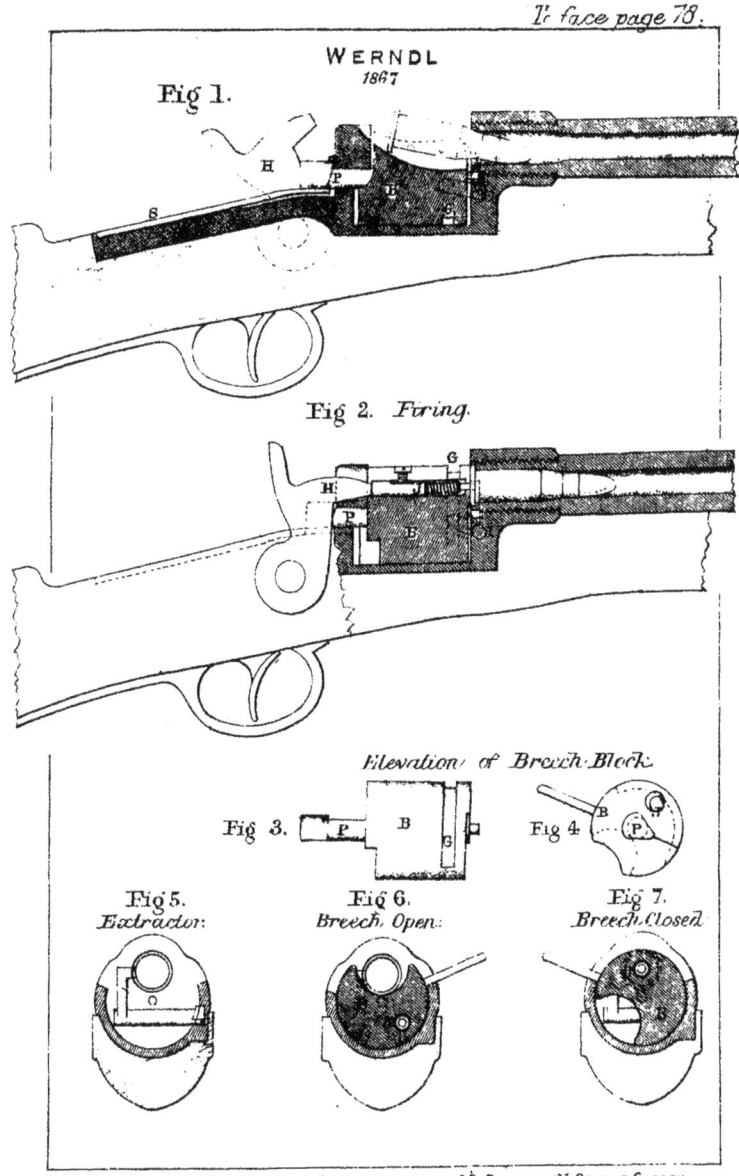

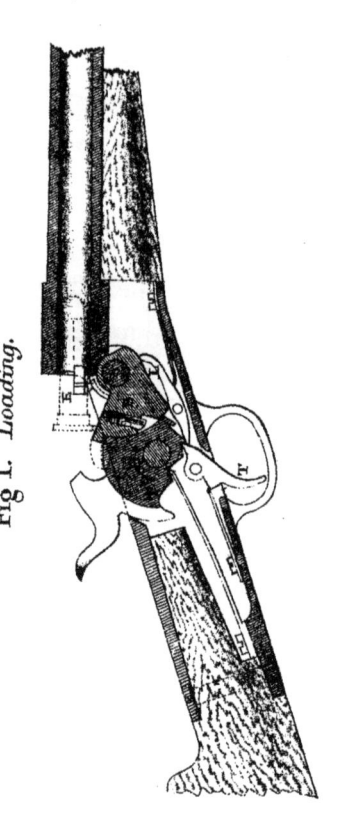

REMINGTON.
1867.

Fig 1. Loading.

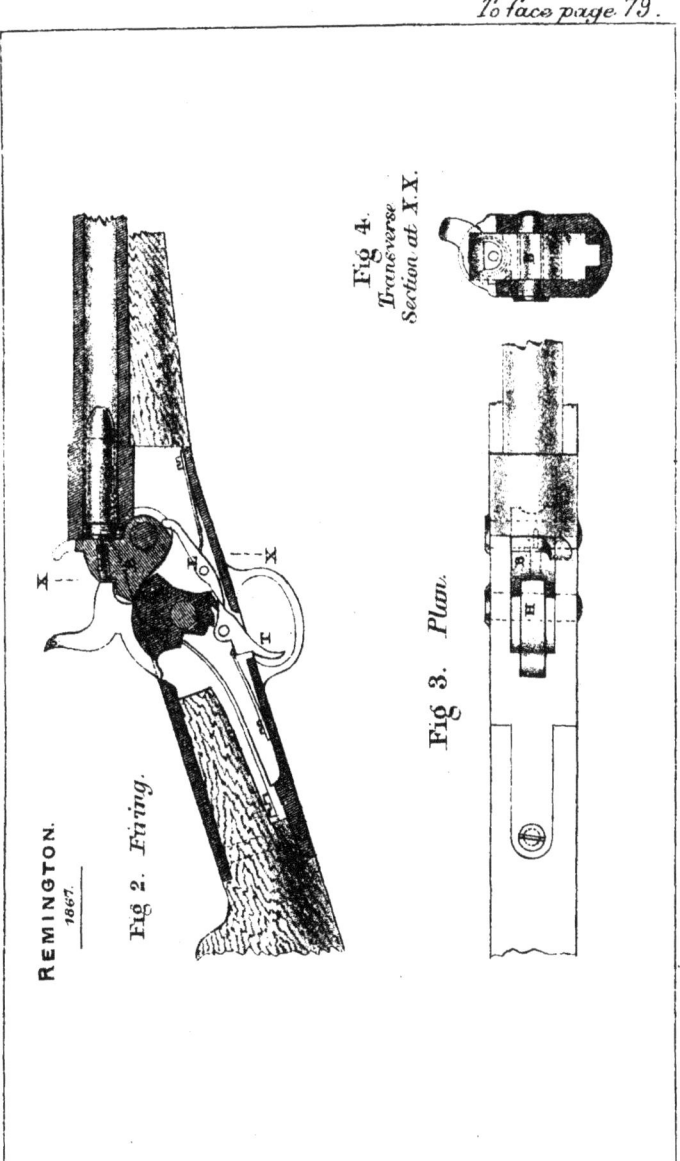

To face page 79.

REMINGTON.
1867.

Fig 2. Firing.

Fig 3. Plan.

Fig 4. Transverse Section at X.X.

slightly spiral face at the rear end, as shown in the side elevation, Fig. 3, by which it is driven home against the end of the barrel in closing the end of the breech as in Fig. 2; and in opening the breech the stud on the horizontal arm of the extractor bearing against the rear side of the groove G in the block which is cut slightly spiral for the purpose, gives the block a slight longitudinal movement backwards from the end of the barrel, as in Fig. 1. The extraction is evidently a weak point in this arm.

SPAIN, NORWAY, SWEDEN, DENMARK, EGYPT.

The Remington Rifle.

The breech is closed by a block B shaped like the sector of a circle, which turns down backwards to open the barrel, revolving upon a transverse pin, and when closing the barrel it is held up against the breech by a second sector-shaped block H turning on another transverse pin behind the breech block, the two sectors mutually detaining and slipping past each other alternately, as shown in Figs. 1 and 2. The front sector B forming the breech block has a square notch in it fitting close to the end of the barrel Fig. 1; the back sector, H, carries the hammer which strikes a firing pin in the breech block. The front side of the hammer sector is hollowed out to fit the top cylindrical surface of the breech block, as shown in Fig. 1, and the rear of the breech block is similarly hollowed out to fit the top of the hammer block as shown in Fig. 2. When the breech block is open as in Fig. 1, it holds the hammer back and prevents it from moving, and when the breech is closed and the hammer in the act of firing as in Fig. 2, the breech block is prevented from moving by the hammer block bearing against the hollow surface of the rear of the breech block. The two blocks combine in resisting the backward force of the explosion when the gun is fired. The extractor is a horizontal slide E Fig. 1, at the left side of the barrel laying hold of the base flange of the cartridge; a projecting nose on the underside of the extractor is caught and drawn backwards a

short distance by the breech block in the act of opening
the breech and the empty cartridge case is thus drawn
slightly backwards and can be picked out by hand. A
lever L pressed by a spring into a recess at the bottom
of the breech block holds it steady in its position when
closed, and the tail end of the same lever is made to act
as a stop to the trigger T Fig. 2, preventing it from
being pulled off until released by the front end of the
lever entering the recess in the breech block, when the
breech is fully closed, as in Fig. 1.

BELGIUM.

Albini-Braendlin.

The breech is closed by a hinged block B that opens
upwards and forwards turning upon a transverse pin at
the end of the barrel; when closed the block is held
down by a spring catch C shown dotted in the plan,
Fig. 3, which is withdrawn by the lifting handle D of
the block in the act of opening the breech. The breech
block contains a striker J as in the Snider, which is
struck by an ordinary external hammer H but the blow
is conveyed through a sliding pin P which is hinged
upon the hammer, and passing through a guide enters a
short distance into a recess in the breech block before
reaching the striker as shown in Fig. 2. This plan prevents any risk of the arm being fired without the breech
block being fully home in its place, and the sliding pin
P serves as a steady pin to hold the block firm at the
instant of firing.

The breech block in the act of closing has the effect
of forcing the cartridge home into its place in the
chamber. The extraction of the empty cartridge case is
effected by an arm E Fig. 1 hanging freely on the
hinge pin of the breech block, and laying hold of the
base of the cartridge; a projection on the front of the
arm is struck by the breech block in the last portion of
its movement in opening, causing the extractor to jerk
the cartridge case clear out of the barrel. The extractor
is made double with an arm on each side of the cartridge.

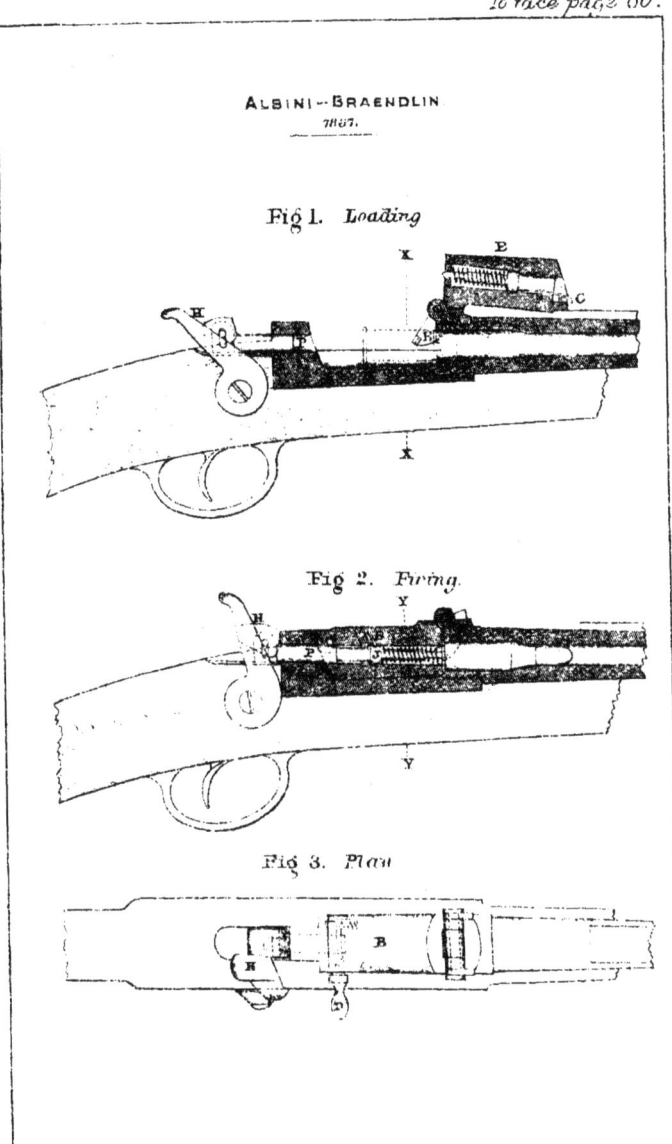

To face page 80.

ALBINI—BRAENDLIN
1867.

Fig 1. *Loading*

Fig 2. *Firing.*

Fig 3. *Plan*

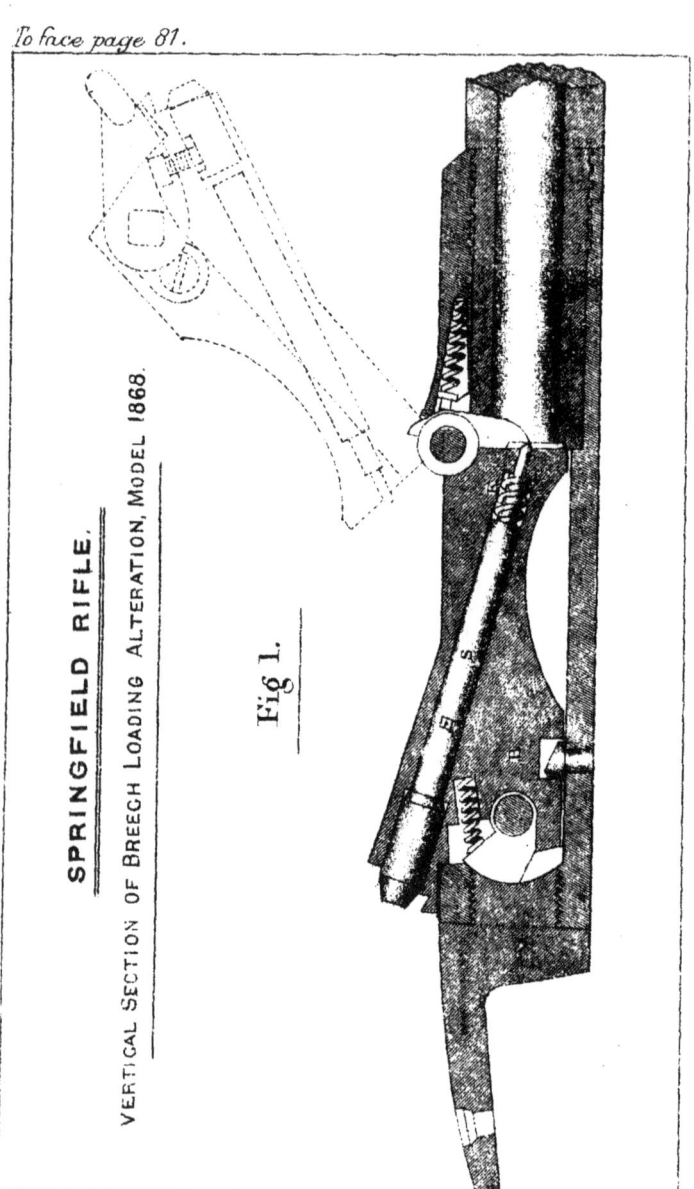

UNITED STATES.

Springfield Rifle.

This rifle has a block action; it resembles the Albini Braendlin; the block pivots on the rear end of the barrel, and is fastened down when closed by a bolt N and spring actuated by means of a projection on the right side of the action E.

The striker S and spring K for its withdrawal are contained in the block.

The striker is struck by the ordinary hammer of a front action lock.

Deeley-Edge Military and Match Breech Loading Rifles.

The Deeley-Edge rifle was introduced in 1873; it is on the sliding block system. In 1877 the Metford system of rifling was adopted with the barrel. In 1878 improvements were made in the action. In 1881 further improvements were made, and a fresh patent taken out; these consisted in a reduction of the weight of the action by nearly half a pound, and an increase in the extracting power, besides the substitution of a side lever for the lever underneath, which in the original pattern formed the guard and trigger plate.

Messrs. Deeley and Edge claim that the latest pattern action thoroughly embody the main desiderata in a rifle action, viz., strength, simplicity, rapidity, lightness, and symmetry. Messrs. Westley Richards are the sole manufacturers of these rifles in two patterns. In the one used for military purposes, there is a small main lever on the right side of the body; this lever depresses the block, raises the hammer to full cock, and extracts the empty cartridge case at a single movement; the other pattern is used for match and sporting rifles, for which it is desirable to have a half-cocking arrangement; with this pattern the main lever on the right side of the action merely brings the hammer to half-cock when depressed, so as to admit of cleaning and loading. There is a small secondary lever in addition on the left hand side of the body; when the main lever is depressed the action is at half-cock, and in

(S.A.)

that position is loaded and closed, and then by the movement of the secondary lever the arm can be full-cocked ready for firing. Both levers can be securely belted if desirable. The Metford system of rifling is used with these rifles, and has obtained great success in various competitions.

The peculiarities of this rifling seem to be the shape of the shallow grooves and the increasing twist, which is not regular, but varies in different portions of the barrel, with the object, it is stated, of giving the bullet equal increments of rotation in equal times, and thus lessening friction.

The shallow grooves adopted are of sufficient depth to allow the bullet, which has a cavity in the base, to expand into the rifling so as to form an effectual gas check, and to ensure the paper on the bullet being removed at the muzzle without cutting into and altering the shape of the bullet to any extent.

The grooving adopted until last year was of two kinds: for the military arm an easy segmental cut, so that there might be no angle which might be likely to hold dirt or fouling, and might be effectually swept out at each discharge by the wad employed. The military rifling has seven grooves. The match rifling has five grooves the edges of these grooves having an upright cut similar to that of the Snider. The recent regulation of the N.R.A. with respect to cleaning out, has caused the manufacturers to adopt a rifling similar to the military arm for all rifles.

The Deeley-Edge Metford military rifle is constructed in accordance with the conditions laid down by the National Rifle Association for military breech-loaders: its weight is $9\frac{1}{4}$ lbs. A new wind gauge sight has been fitted to the back-sight.

The match rifle weighs 10 lbs., and is fitted with orthoptic sights, level, &c. Two beds are fitted so that the back-sight may be used upon the grip or upon the heel as preferred. Both the back and front sights of these rifles are fitted with a shifting zero, for which the manufacturers claim advantages.

To face page 82.

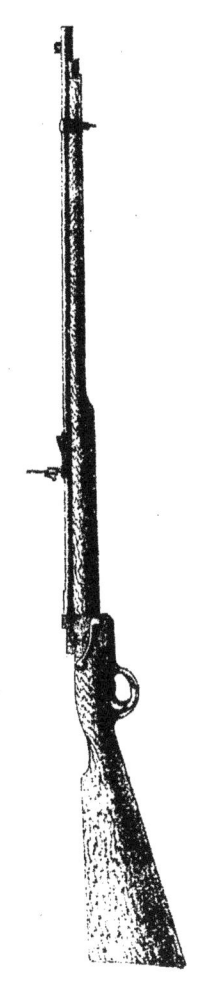

DEELEY EDGE MILITARY RIFLE.

DANGERFIELD, LITH 22 BEDFORD ST COVENT GARDEN

To face page 83.

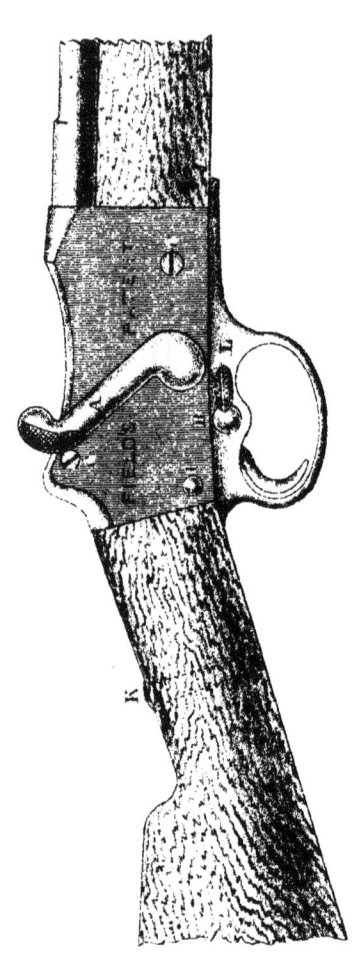

FIELD RIFLE.

Dancerfield, Lith 22, Bedford S.' Covent Garden

The Field Rifle.

The "Field" rifle, so called from the name of the inventor of this action, is now in much favour; several eminent gunmakers have adopted it with their barrels.

The action is made in two forms:—

1. With hinged falling block suitable for a military arm.
2. With a block which slides vertically into a recess, leaving a clear view through the barrel, suitable for match rifles.

The hinged falling block and the shoe or body in the first are very similar to the Martini-Henry.

The lever of the Martini-Henry is replaced by a side lever for actuating the block, which is pushed forward, and by this arrangement certain advantages are claimed in loading in the lying-down position, and when mounted.

The firing apparatus consists of a mainspring of moderate strength and V form, acting upon a heavy hammer H. In the lower part of this hammer is a bent for full cock of the ordinary kind, and with this the trigger nose engages when the lever is actuated. A shoulder upon the lever spindle also acts upon a similar shoulder upon the hammer, and effects the compression of the mainspring. The disengagement of the trigger nose on pulling the trigger allows the mainspring to act on the hammer which strikes the head of the firing pin or striker and propels it against the cap in the base of the cartridge. The striker is governed by a simple spiral spring, so that as soon as it becomes relieved from the pressure of the hammer it flies back, and is ready for the next blow of the hammer. The extractor differs from the Martini in being made in two pieces. The attachment of the butt to the shoe is also different.

The Farquharson-Metford B.L. Rifle.

This rifle is manufactured by Mr. George Gibbs, Bristol. It consists of the Farquharson action patented in 1871, attached to the Metford barrel, patented in 1865. It is made both as a military and match rifle.

The action is on the sliding block system, actuated by a lever beneath the trigger guard. When the block is depressed and action opened a full view is obtained through the barrel.

A description of the Metford rifling has been given under the head of the Deeley-Edge rifle.

Very good results have been obtained with these rifles in various competitions.

The Fraser Rifle.

The Messrs. Fraser, Edinburgh, make use of a side lever action patented by them about three years ago The breech is closed by a block which slides vertically, and is actuated by a lever on the right side; this lever is pressed down backwards to open the action instead of being pushed forward as in the case of the Field action. The mainspring is in the front part of the action underneath the barrel.

Since the new order prohibiting wiping out between rounds, the Messrs. Fraser have modified their previous rifling; the number of grooves is now seven of a form which may be termed a hollow ratchet; the bearing edge of the groove is sharp and well defined, while the other edge is hollowed up into the bore.

The twist in the new barrel begins straight at the breech, finishing at the muzzle at 1 in 17 inches; width of groove ·150″, depth ·007″.

Charge of powder used is 85 grains Curtis and Harvey's No. 6 powder; two felt wads fitting the barrel rather tightly. Bullet 530 grains, hardened with antimony.

Ingram Rifle.

Mr. Charles Ingram of Glasgow fits his barrels to different actions. He has for a long time used the ratchet form of rifling, and claims being the inventor of this principle which he adopted 35 years ago. He gives the ratchet grooves an increasing twist from 1 turn in 8 feet at the breech to 1 turn in 18 inches at 4 inches from the muzzle, and this twist is continued uniform for the remaining 4 inches. He also makes

To face page 84.

THE FARQUHARSON METFORD MATCH RIFLE

Dancerfield Lith. 22 Bedford S.t Covent Garden.

To face page 84.

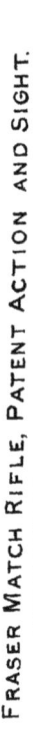

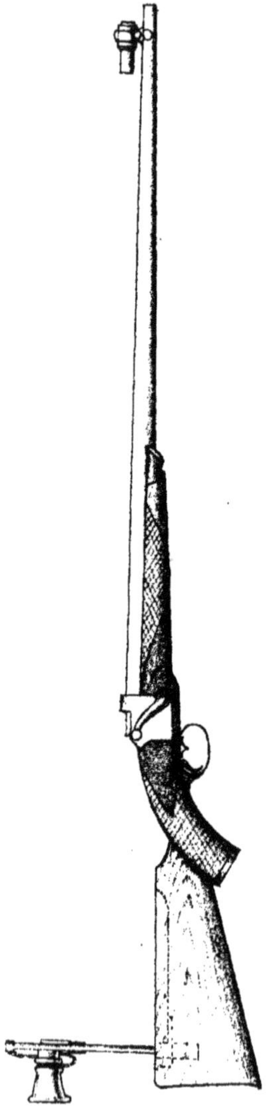

FRASER MATCH RIFLE, PATENT ACTION AND SIGHT.

DANGERFIELD. LITH 22 BEDFORD ST COVENT GARDEN

To face page 85.

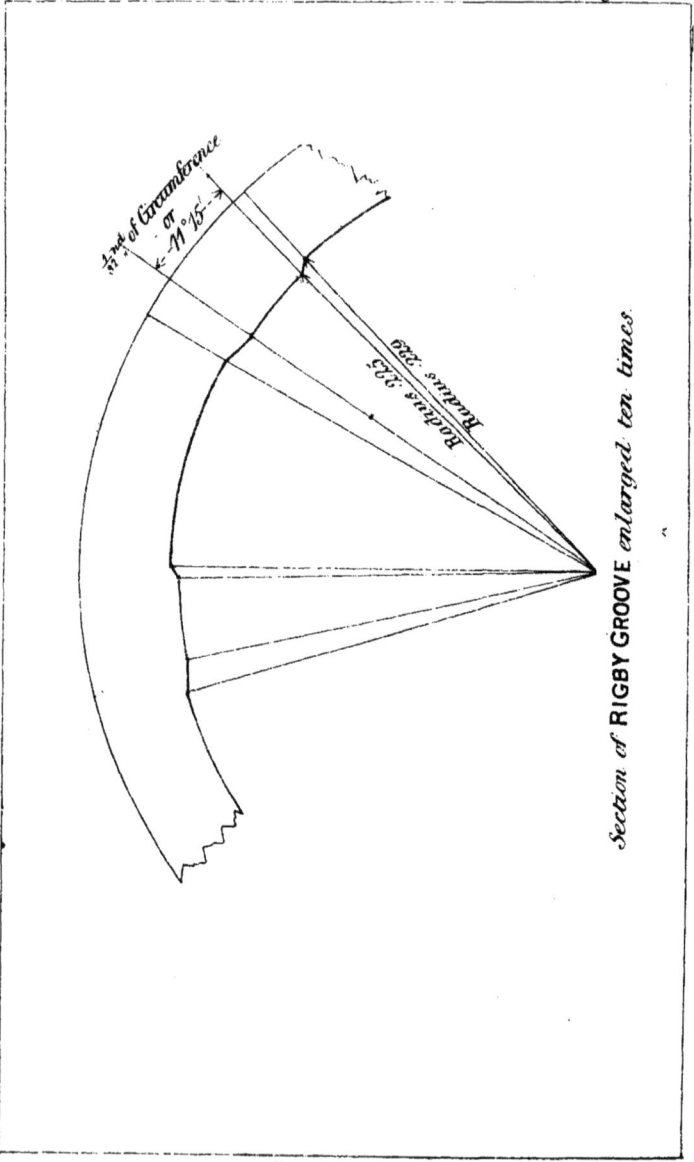

the grooves shallower towards the muzzle, and the lands broader than the grooves at the muzzle, but narrower at the breech.

Rigby Military B.L. Rifle.

The grooves of this rifle are eight in number, ·004 inch in depth, and are concentric with the axis of the bore.

The twist of rifling is uniform, 1 turn in 18 inches. The diameter of the bore is ·450 inch.

The design of this grooving will be understood by reference to the section, but in practice the angle made by the curved line forming the bottom of the groove and the side of the "land" is filled up by rounding off the angle of the cutter.

The cartridges used with these rifles are solid drawn, cylindrical in form; 2·6 inch long, charge 85 grains powder; bullet, 530 grains in weight; point ogival, rather acute, and hardened by a certain process which gives them a specific gravity greater than the alloys of lead and tin in general use.

This rifle was first used at Wimbledon in 1883. The Dudley prize, 10 shots at 1000 yards, open to any match rifle, was won with one of them, fitted with match sight. the score made being 49 out of a possible 50.

Rigby B.L. Match Rifle.

This rifle was first used by the Irish Eight in 1880, when they were successful in winning the Elcho Shield. It had then a somewhat different cartridge from that described above, the rules at that time permitting the rifle to be cleaned out after every shot. In 1883 the Council of the N.R. Association debarred cleaning, and under the new rule the match rifle is loaded with the same cartridge as that for the military rifle. It has also the same rifling as the military arm. The Irish Eight, several of whom used these rifles, were again successful in the Elcho Shield match in 1883. The "Field" action with sliding block has been generally employed with both these rifles. In 1882 Messrs. J. Rigby and Co.

brought out a new action called the Rigby-Banks, for which certain advantages are claimed in compactness, and having a strong attachment to the stock. The following is a description :—

NEW ACTION FOR MILITARY AND OTHER RIFLES.

Rigby-Banks Patent, 1882, *and Rigby's Patent,* 1884.

This is a sliding block action with hammerless lock, and possesses the following distinctive features. In place of the stock bolt used with the Martini-Henry, there is a steel tube screwed into the frame or body, having at its rear end a screwed nut, which serves to hold the butt firmly in its place. Inside this tube is a coiled mainspring 5 inches in length, within which slides a steel rod R; this rod after delivering the blow upon the striker S is made to rebound by the spring shown at L, and so to leave the breech block B free to move up or down. This arrangement also places the hammer and mainspring in a closed tube out of the way of wet or fouling. The rebound action removes the risk of accidental discharge in loading. The lever for working the action is on the right side in a convenient position, the action is opened by pressing with the thumb downwards on the lever, and closed by raising it again with the forefinger.

A spring J bears on the axis of the lever in such a way that when a part of the upward or downward movement is effected by the hand the pressure of the spring completes the remainder.

The striker plays freely in the breech block without a spring; it is provided with a parallel pin also sliding in a hole in the block, and so placed that should the striker from any cause fail to return into the block after discharge, the arm which lowers the latter comes first against the end of this pin, and compels it to retire into its place before it commences to lower the block. It is claimed for this invention that it remedies the defect to which sliding block rifles which depend upon a spring to retire the striker are liable, viz., that should the striker become stiff or stick in the cap, and the

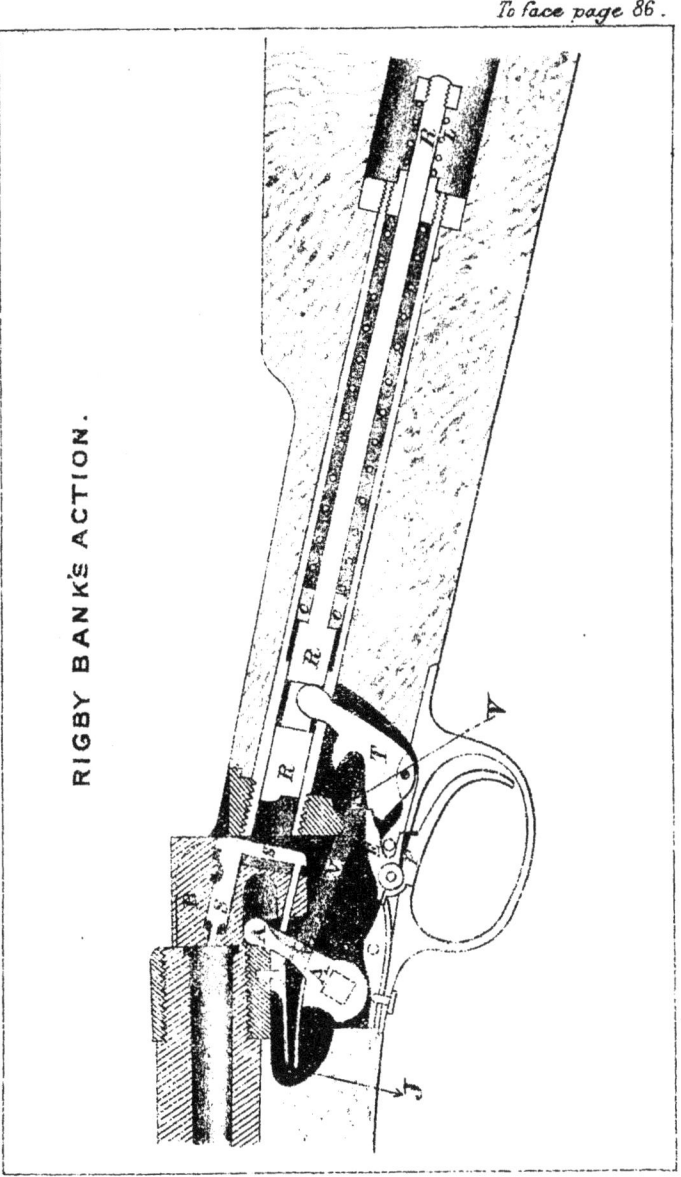

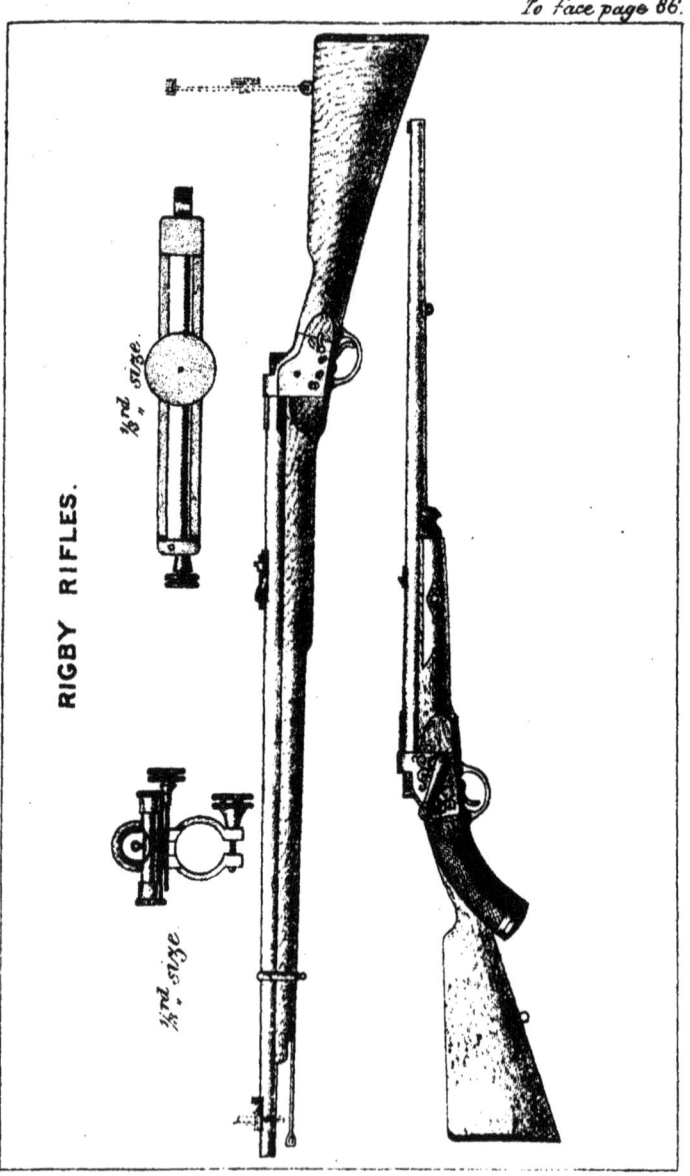

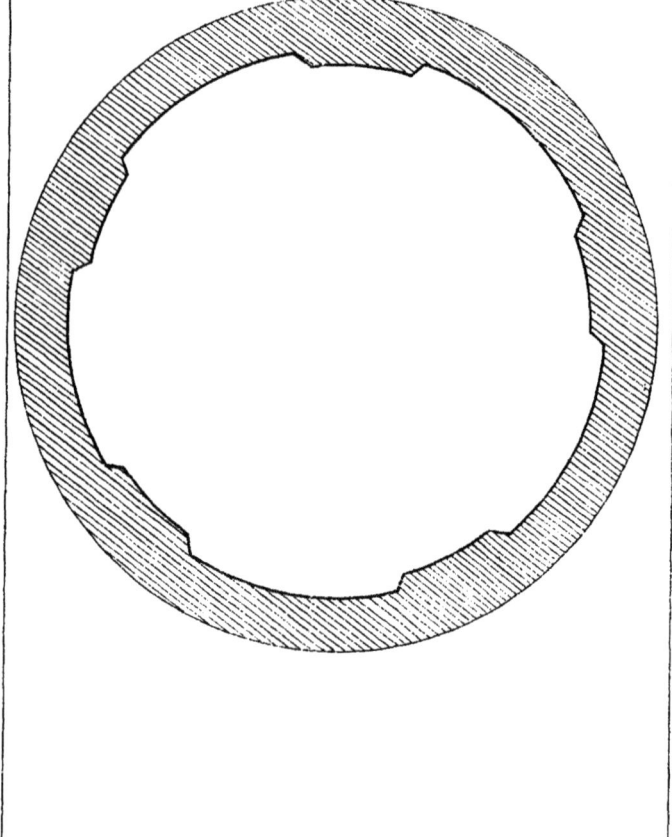

striker spring unable to withdraw it, the breech of the rifle cannot be opened.

The action of this rifle is fitted with a novel arrangement of the sear and trigger, which is the subject of a separate patent; the object is to secure a safe full cock combined with an easy finger pull for the trigger.

The extractor, a single one acting on the right side, has an accelerated motion which throws the fired cartridge clear of the arm when loading rapidly.

A is the arm actuated by the external lever on the same spindle which lowers and raises the block B, and works the tumbler by the connecting bar N, which is pivotted to A, but presses back the tumbler by means of a stud V.

B the sliding breech block, into which fits the striker S with parallel pin.

R the rod or hammer, a slot in which receives the crane of the tumbler T.

C the collar sliding in the tube and also on the rod R, which is thereby made free to strike and rebound.

E the sear shown in the tumbler bent, and holding that component at full cock.

F the trigger.

The Turner Military B.L. and Match Rifles.

These rifles are manufactured by Mr. T. Turner, Fisher Street, Birmingham. He uses the "Field" action. The bore is ·461, and the grooves either 5 or 7 in number, generally 7, ·005 inch in depth, of the form shown in the Figure, on an enlarged scale; the spiral is an increasing one, finishing at the muzzle at 1 turn in 20 inches.

The military rifle is made in conformity with N.R.A. rules.

The match rifle is made on the same principles.

Some excellent scores have been made with these rifles at long ranges.

The cartridge is solid drawn brass, charge 80 grains No. 6 powder and hardened bullet of 530 grains; bullet inserted according to the N.R.A. rules.

The Webley-Wyley Military Breech-Loading Rifle.

This rifle was designed and manufactured by the firm of Messrs. P. Webley and Son, Weaman Street, Birmingham, in 1879, and is one of those used in the various competitions at Wimbledon and other parts of the country. It complies with the regulations laid down by the N.R. Association for rifles of the military class.

The manufacturers claim for it a high degree of accuracy at long ranges, combining strength, simplicity, and moderate cost of production.

The action is made as light as possible, and the additional weight is thrown into the barrel, which weighs about $4\frac{1}{2}$ lbs.; considerable advantages are said to be gained by this distribution so long as the gross weight of the arm is not unduly increased or its balance impaired.

The action is opened, hammer cocked, and empty cartridge case extracted by turning the vertical lever on the right side of the action to the right; the action is closed by a reverse of this movement. There is a clear view through the barrel when the action is opened.

The cartridge is exploded by the blow of a hammer working in a slot in the centre of the action, and striking a pin or striker passing through the breech-block which closes the breech.

This hammer is capable of being also operated externally, and can be full and half-cocked with the thumb.

The diameter of the bore is ·458 inch, it is rifled with 7 grooves of the ratchet form, and having a uniform twist of 1 turn in 20 inches; the grooves are of the same depth from breech to muzzle.

The cartridge has a solid drawn slightly bottle-shaped case, charge of powder 82 grains with lubricated wads, and a hardened paper patched bullet with cavity in the base.

REPEATING AND MAGAZINE RIFLES.

Considerable attention has of late been directed to this class of arms, and numerous experiments have been

BREECH VIEW OF THE WEBLEY-WYLEY M.B.L. *rifling enlarged about 6 times. The depth of groove is exaggerated for the purpose of clearly showing the system.*

To face page 89.

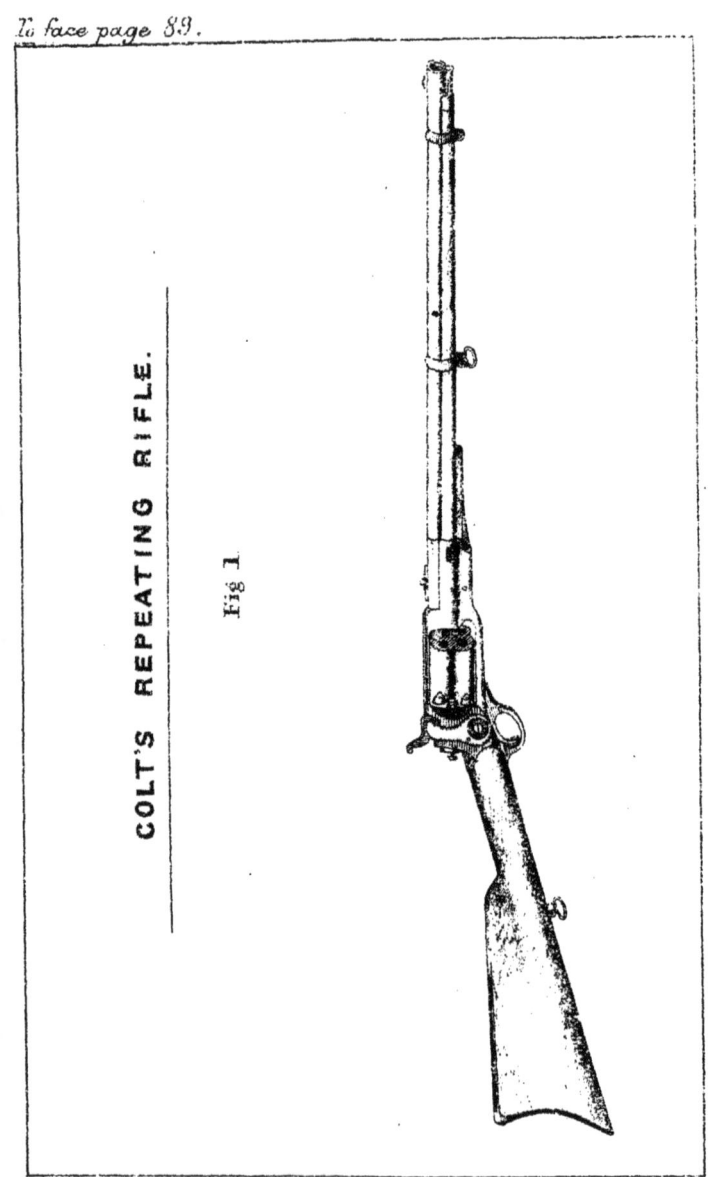

COLT'S REPEATING RIFLE.

Fig 1

Dangerfield Lith 22 Bedford St Covent Garden 1857

carried on both in this country and abroad with a view to testing the relative merits of different systems. It is now pretty well accepted that if a magazine arm could be obtained simple in construction, of moderate weight, not liable to get out of order, and capable of being used at will, as either a single-loader or a magazine arm, certain advantages would be gained. Up to the present time, the increased complexity of construction (except perhaps with the Lee) and the greater liability to derangement, have prevented their universal adoption.

In addition, their opponents say that they would lead to such a waste and outlay of ammunition as to require large reserves to meet the expenditure, and that the soldier would undervalue each particular round. It will be remembered that on the introduction of breech-loaders similar objections were raised which were not found to hold on service.

At close quarters in the attack and defence of positions, in repelling the sudden attacks of cavalry, in the hands of disciplined men either in the *mêlée* or contending against superior numbers, the capacity of being able to fire a series of rounds in rapid succession, say in the proportion of three to two, as compared with single-loaders, combined with the power of being able to keep the eye steadily fixed upon the object during the act of loading, all point to advantages to be obtained from this nature of arm.

Repeating and magazine rifles* may be classed as follows:—

1st. Repeating rifles identical with the ordinary revolver pistol in their construction and action, the cartridges being placed in revolving cylinder Fig. 1. It has been found that this nature of arm is unable to stand the strain of the heavy charges of powder now employed, the escape of gas at the joint between the revolving cylinder and the fixed barrel being always excessive.

2nd. Magazine arms in which the cartridges are placed in a tube or magazine under the barrel: to this class belong the Winchester, Vetterli, and Kropatschek.

---

* These terms are sometimes used indifferently; it seems better to make a distinction.

The base of each cartridge rests on the point of the bullet of the next, and owing to the jar of rapid firing, or an over sensitive or projecting cap, cartridges have occasionally been found to explode accidentally in the magazine. It will be also noticed that owing to the position of the magazine, the balance of the rifle constantly alters as the magazine is being emptied.

3rd. Magazine arms in which the tube or magazine is placed in the butt as in the Spencer, Hotchkiss, &c. As the butts of rifles are shorter than the barrels, the magazines of this class hold fewer cartridges than Class 2, but the arm is not subjected to the same variations of balance. The objections to the base of the cartridges resting on the points of the bullets exist here as in Class 2.

4th. Magazine arms with detachable magazines as the Lee. The cartridges are placed lying one upon another in a rectangular shaped wrought-iron box, which can be inserted underneath just in front of the trigger-guard into a corresponding slot or mortice in the action. As soon as one magazine is emptied it can be instantly removed, and replaced by another filled one. From the position of the magazine, the balance of the arm is maintained under all circumstances.

5th. In addition may be mentioned appliances and devices to hold cartridges for the purpose of expediting the loading of single-loaders, as the Mayhew and Krinka cartridge holders.

Spencer Magazine Rifle.

This rifle was patented in Boston, America 1860 and was the first of this class of arms used in actual warfare.

The magazine containing seven cartridges is placed in the stock; the cartridges are fed up to the action by means of a spiral spring in the magazine tube.

The arrangement for closing the breech, Fig. 2, consists of three principal parts—B the Block; C the Central Piece; and L the Lever.

The striker S fits in a groove on right side of the block, and strikes against the rim of the cartridge, which is a rim-fire one.

To face page 91.

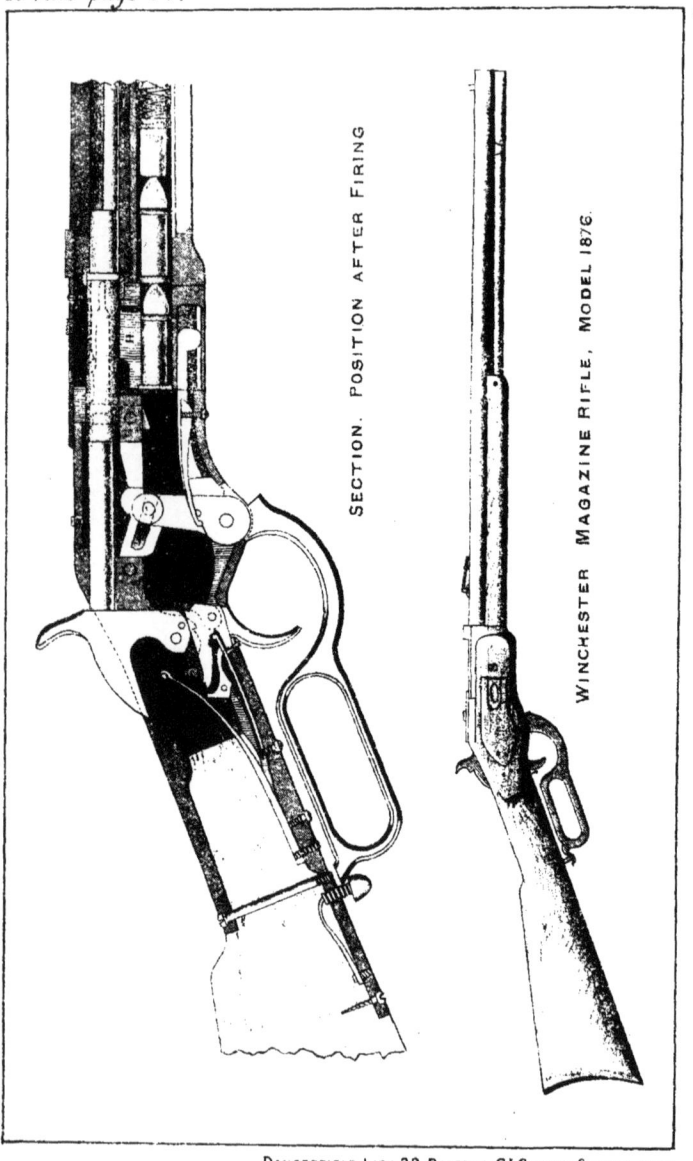

The block can slide vertically into a recess in the central piece Fig. 2, which carries on its left face a moveable extractor E shaped like the blade of a knife. A spiral spring keeps the block and central piece separated when the breech is closed.

The lever is attached to the central piece by a hinge, while a cylindrical bolt M connects it with the block B.

A screw pin traversing the central piece and the shoe serves as an axis of rotation.

A flat piece K is acted upon by a spring; it presses continuously upon the block; it is for the purpose of guiding the cartridge into the chamber—it also acts to eject the empty cartridge case.

To open the action.

On pressing down the trigger guard or lever, the block closes into the recess in the central piece, Fig. 1, and then both pieces together are rotated by the lever, and the action opened. This movement also withdraws the empty cartridge case which is placed upon the conductor K at the same time a fresh cartridge is fed up from the magazine and passes between the conductor and the block.

On closing the action by means of the lever, the block catches and guides the cartridge into the chamber. At the same time, the block acted on by the spiral spring rises and completely closes the cartridge chamber.

The upward movement of the block also causes the conductor K to throw the empty case sharply out of the action.

Henry Magazine Rifle (America).

The magazine is placed beneath the barrel in the fore-end, the cartridges are pushed towards the breech by a spiral spring.

The magazine is capable of holding 15 rim-fire cartridges.

This rifle was used with effect in the American war.

The Henry has been lately improved by the Winchester Company, and in the new form is called the Winchester magazine rifle.

In this rifle the magazine or brass tube under the barrel is filled from the breech end through a spring cover S which closes automatically after the insertion of each cartridge.

From the magazine the cartridges are transferred to the barrel by a carrier or hopper H which is actuated by the lever forming the trigger guard. The motion of lowering the lever cocks the gun, ejects the empty case, brings a fresh cartridge from the magazine to the barrel, and on raising the lever to its original position, the hopper is lowered, and the gun ready to be fired.

The Vetterli Magazine Rifle.

This arm, on the bolt principle, resembles the single-loader already described.

The cartridges are contained in a magazine underneath the barrel, which contains a spiral spring, and are inserted through an aperture at the side, as in the Winchester.

On opening the breech by pulling back the bolt a stud on the latter strikes against the upper extremity N of a bell crank lever L, and causes the other extremity to raise a cage or carrier H containing the cartridge, and to bring it on a level with the cartridge chamber of the barrel.

When the bolt is pushed forward the cartridge is sent into the chamber, and a projection on the bolt striking the bell crank lever lowers the carrier to its original position ready to receive another cartridge from the magazine.

Hotchkiss Magazine Rifle.

The breech action of this rifle is on the bolt system.

The magazine is a brass tube contained in the butt. A hole is drilled in the shoe at its rear end and below the breech bolt, and through this hole the cartridges from the magazine are fed into the chamber, being pressed up by a spiral spring in the magazine.

There is a cartridge stop C at the end of the magazine next the shoe, and when the magazine is filled, which is done by pressing the cartridges into it through the hole in the shoe, they bear against this stop, which retains them in the magazine. On pulling the trigger

To face page 32.

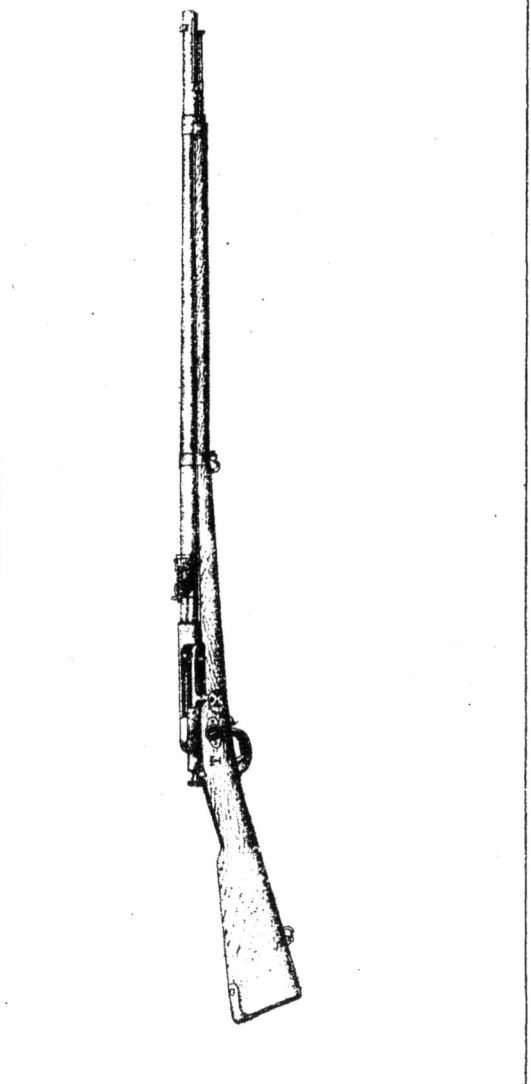

HOTCHKISS MAGAZINE RIFLE.

DANGERFIELD LITH 22 BEDFORD S.T COVENT GARDEN 6657

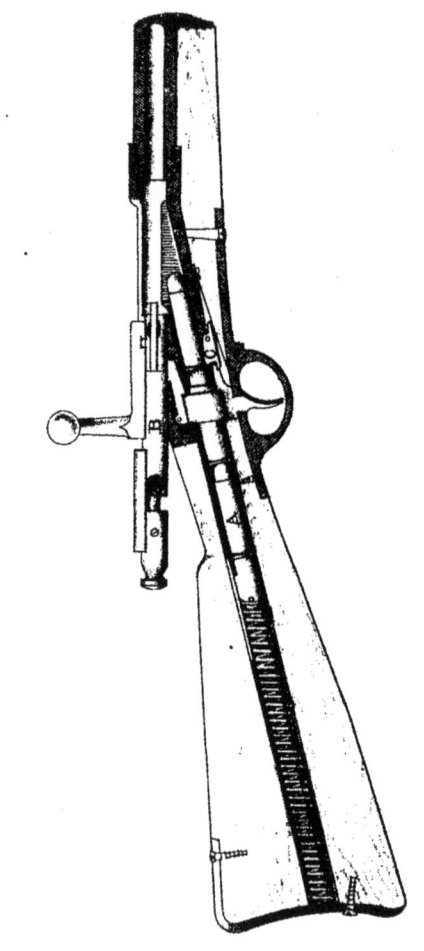

To face page 92.

THE HOTCHKISS MAGAZINE RIFLE.

DANGERFIELD, LITH 22, BEDFORD ST COVENT GARDEN.

To face page 93.

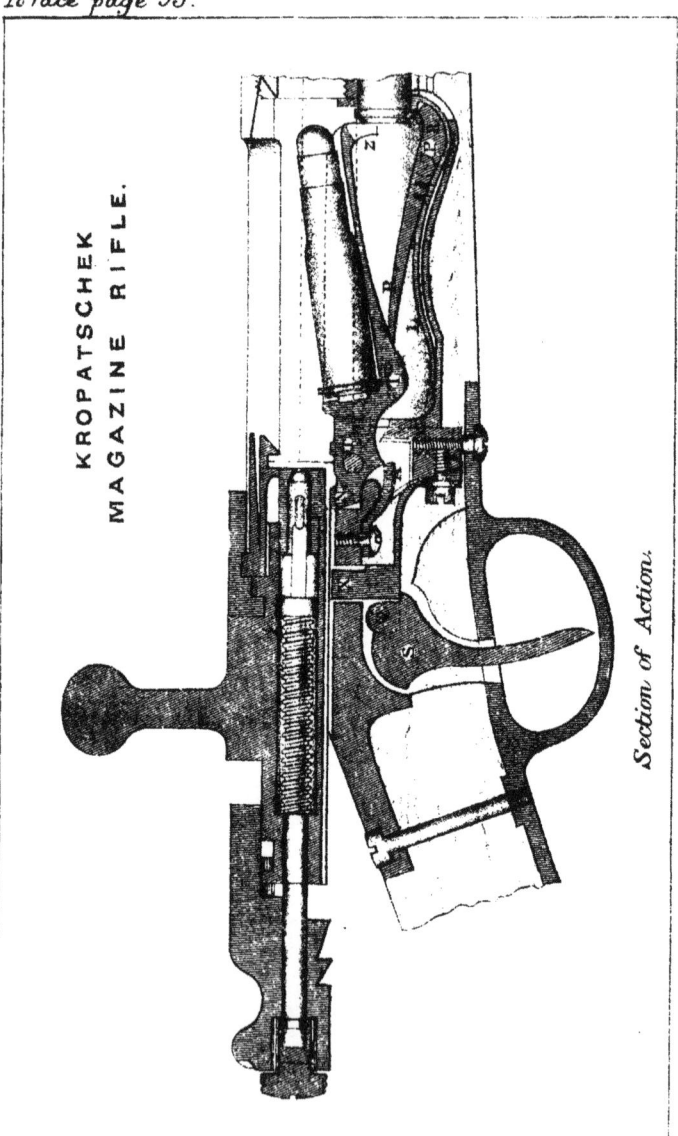

KROPATSCHEK MAGAZINE RIFLE.

Section of Action.

DANGERFIELD LITH. 22. BEDFORD S.* COVENT GARDEN

the cartridge stop is depressed, and the cartridge nearest the chamber is pushed by the magazine spring past the stop, against the under side of the bolt. When the bolt is drawn back the cartridge slips quickly into the shoe, while the one following it is caught and detained by the cartridge stop C which has been only depressed while the trigger is being pulled. It will be seen therefore that the pressing of the trigger to fire one cartridge permits the next one to partly enter the shoe, the operation being completed when the bolt is withdrawn with the empty cartridge case.

There is a thumb-bolt on the right side of the stock at T, by turning which the magazine can be cut off, and the arm used as a single-loader. A reverse operation brings the magazine into play.

The arm carries five cartridges in the magazine.

As a magazine-gun two motions are necessary to load, viz., opened, closed.

As a single-loader three motions are necessary, viz., opened, insert cartridge, closed.

Kropatschek Magazine Rifle.

This is a rifle now used in the French Navy; it is on the bolt system, and in that respect resembles the Gras. The magazine is a brass tube under the barrel, as in the Winchester and Vetterli, and contains six cartridges; another cartridge can be placed in the trough or carrier T.

When the action is opened by pulling back the bolt a projection on the latter strikes the trough at N, and causes the other extremity Z to rise and occupy the position shown in the Figure. This movement is accelerated by the spring A acting against a knife-edge projection on the trough T. In the upper position of the trough the spring acts upon one face of the angle, and in the lower position upon the other. On closing the action the bolt pushes the cartridge into the chamber, and on turning the handle down to the right a part of the bolt presses against a stud, and pushes down the trough ready to receive another cartridge from the magazine. The magazine can be cut off, and the arm used as a single-loader by pushing forward a stud on the right side of the action, the effect of so doing is that on turning down the handle to close the breech securely; the bolt does not act upon the stud and depress the trough.

T is the trough or carrier.

Z a projection of the trough, which prevents the cartridge in the magazine from coming out more than a certain distance while the trough is in the upper or loading position.

R a supplementary cartridge stop pivoted at its centre P, with a spring underneath it L, it retains the cartridges in the magazine; and its action in conjunction with Z prevents more than one cartridge at a time from passing out of the magazine; it also retains the cartridges in the magazine when the latter is being filled.

Lee Magazine Rifle.

This rifle has a bolt action, and the principle does not differ from those already described. The magazine M is detachable, and is inserted from underneath into a slot or mortise in front of the trigger guard.

The magazine M is of sheet iron, and when inserted is held in its place by a magazine catch C, which engages in a notch N in the rear of the magazine; the magazine can be released by an upward pressure on the magazine catch at its lower end, where it projects inside of the trigger guard. The cartridges are placed in the magazine one over the other in nearly a horizontal position, each slightly in advance of the one below it, rendering it impossible for anything to impinge on the caps of the cartridges. The cartridges are pressed up in front of the bolt by a magazine spring D situated in the lower part of the magazine box.

The magazine is simply a sheet-iron box of a sufficient size to hold five cartridges, but there seems to be no reason why it should not be made of larger dimensions.

The magazine must be detached before the arm can be used as a single-loader, but in a late pattern there are two notches in the magazine at N. When the magazine is only inserted as far as the first notch, the arm can

To face page 94.

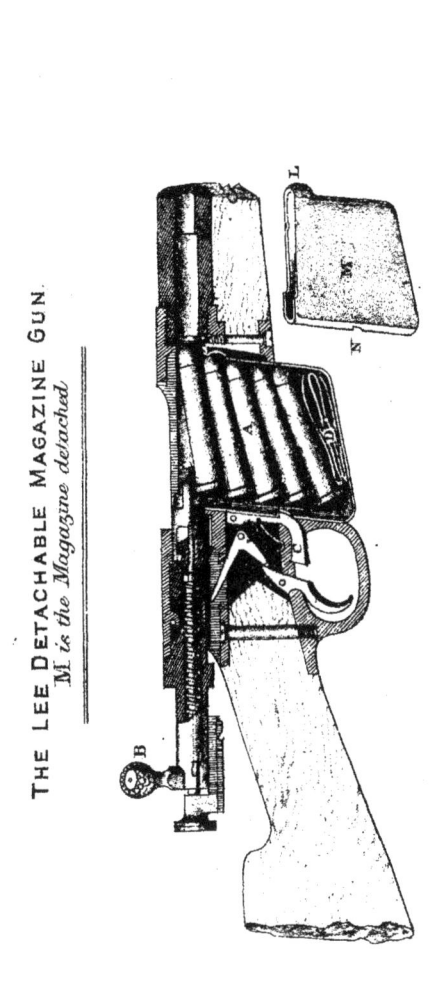

THE LEE DETACHABLE MAGAZINE GUN.
M is the Magazine detached.

Dangerfield Lith. 22 Bedford St. Covent Garden 6696.

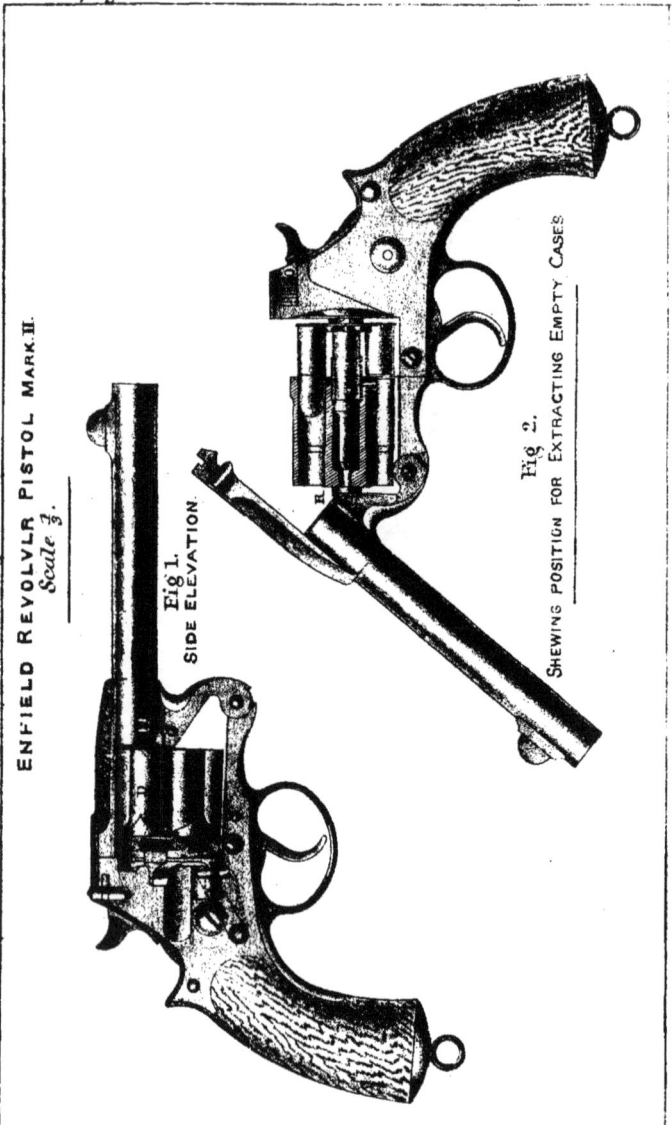

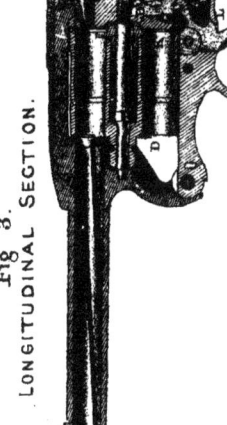

Enfield Revolver Pistol Mark II.
Scale 7/3

Fig 3.
Longitudinal Section.

only be used as a single-loader, but by pressing in the magazine to the second notch it immediately comes into play. There is a spring plate in the shoe, which is pushed aside by the insertion of the magazine, but immediately springs out on its removal. This plate nearly fills the upper aperture of the magazine slot, and prevents cartridges from falling through when the arm is used as a single-loader.

The action must in all cases be closed before a magazine is inserted.

When the magazine is filled the bullet of the top cartridge is pushed into the projection L and this keeps the other cartridges securely and firmly in their places. On withdrawing the bolt to open the action the top cartridge is slightly drawn back, and this frees the cartridges, and allows them to be fed up by the spring D.

REVOLVERS.

Enfield Revolver Pistol, Mark II.

This pistol has a rebounding lock, and it differs from other patterns usually met with in its method of extracting the empty cartridge cases.

The barrel is $5\frac{3}{4}$ inches in length, and the diameter of bore and form and twist of rifling are the same as in the M.H. rifle.

The cylinder contains six chambers, and the pistol is loaded in the ordinary way.

The act of pulling the trigger cocks the pistol and fires it, and upon the release of the trigger the trigger rebounds to half-cock.

The stock is of walnut, the remaining parts of steel.

Weight of pistol, 2 lbs. $8\frac{1}{2}$ ozs.

Description of Action.

The pistol may be fired on the single-acting principle by cocking in the usual manner, a bent being provided on the hammer to engage and rest on the trigger.

For firing the pistol by automatic pull-off of trigger only, the action may be described as follows:—

The trigger A and the pawl B being connected by an axis at C, they are both carried upwards by pulling the trigger, and the pawl rotates the cylinder D by means of ratchet-teeth cut on the cylinder face near the axis pin; on the lower end of pawl B a projection or horn C is formed; this engages and begins to cock the hammer F directly the trigger is pulled, and releases it at the end of the pull.

The main-spring G, is of the common V form, the ends being shaped to act on the hammer F and lever H, the upper arm gives the hammer its striking power; the lower presses on the lever and hammer to give the rebound or half-cock position. On the lever a small swivel K is fitted to engage the cylinder and prevent a return movement when the pawl is coming down and rubbing against the face of the cylinder teeth; a small spiral spring L is attached to the trigger to act on end of pawl and assist the trigger in returning to its position for the next shot. A knuckle is formed on the top of trigger to engage and fall into the indents on the outside of cylinder, whilst the upper end of pawl prevents it turning in the opposite direction at the moment of discharge. The shield N (Fig. 1) also exerts a pressure on the cylinder by means of its spring shown in dotted lines, and engages notches cut on the circumference of the cylinder to prevent it moving when the action is returning after firing.

To extract empty cases, the barrel catch O (Fig. 2) is drawn backwards by the thumb, and a sharp downward motion given to the pistol causes the barrel to revolve on its joint-pin, and draw the cylinder off its axis sufficiently to release the empty cases.

The ears R R, near the barrel front of cylinder, are for the purpose of opening the holster to allow the cylinder to pass.

Tranter's Self-extracting Revolver.

This pistol has been patented by Mr. W. Tranter, Lichfield Road, Birmingham, who has devoted considerable attention to this branch of manufacture.

The following are some advantages claimed for this pistol:—

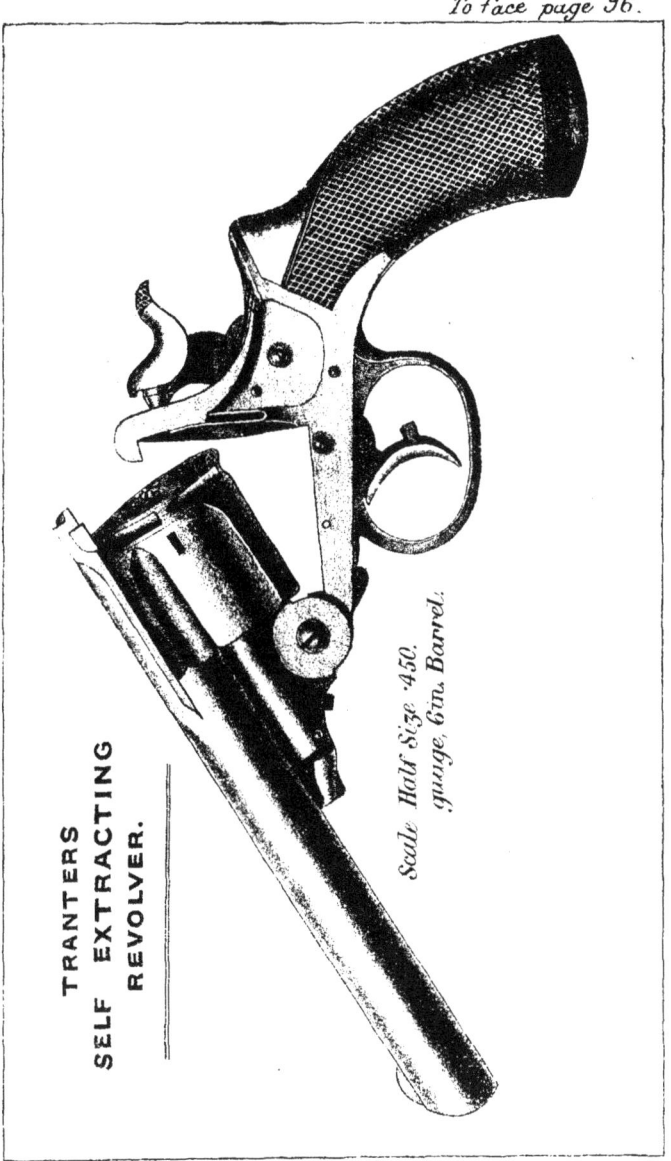

To face page 96.

TRANTER'S SELF EXTRACTING REVOLVER.

Scale Half Size ·450. guage, 6in Barrel.

To face page 97.

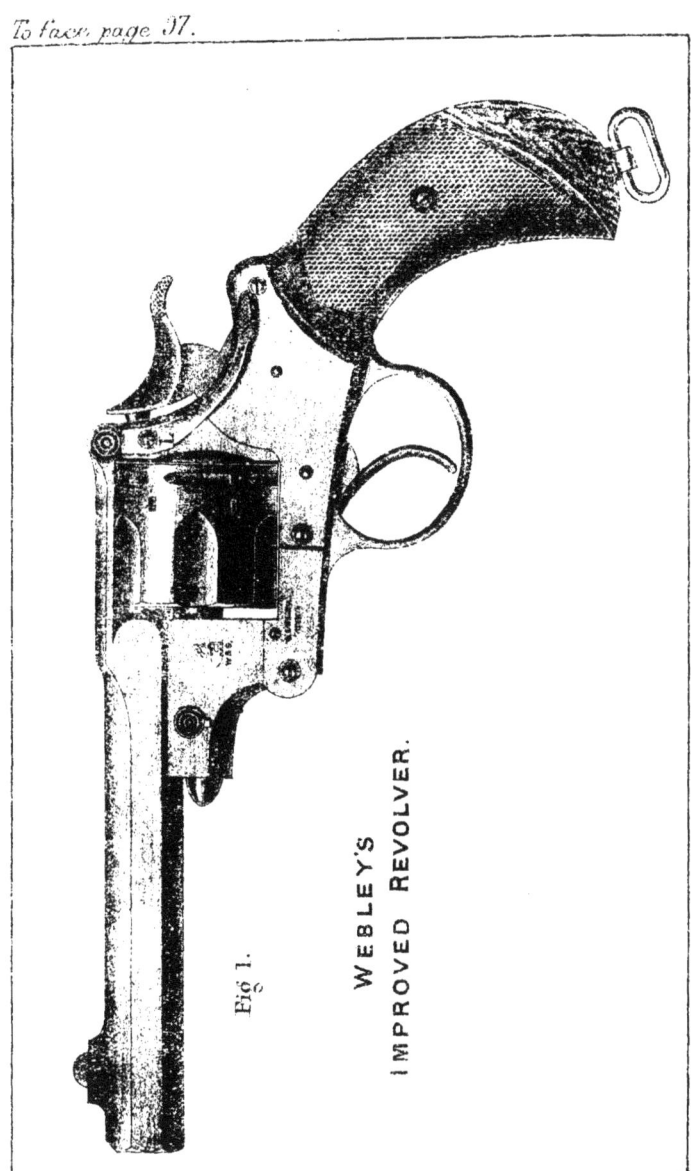

Fig 1.

WEBLEY'S IMPROVED REVOLVER.

Dangerfield Lith 22, Bedford S.' Covent Garden 6667

To face page 97.

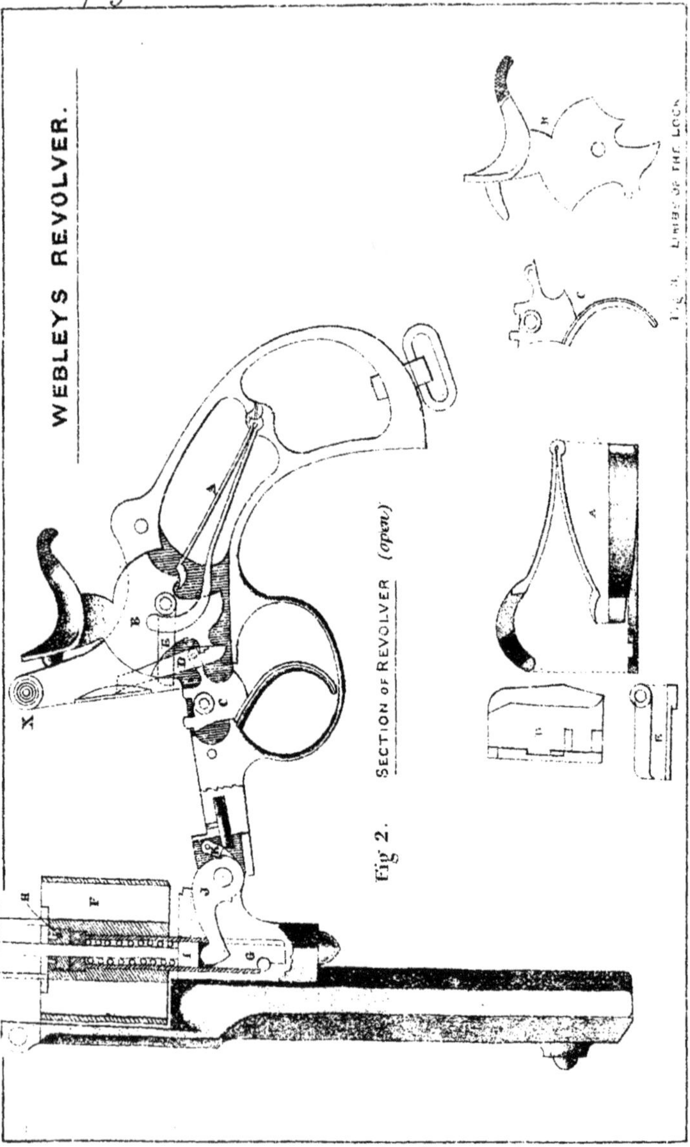
WEBLEYS REVOLVER.
SECTION OF REVOLVER (open)
Fig 2.
LIMBS OF THE LOCK
X
B
C
D
E
F
G
H
J
A

DANGERFIELD, LITH 22. BEDFORD St COVENT GARDEN 6657

1. It can be used with facility with one hand, and is easy to load when mounted.
2. It extracts the empty cartridge cases without discharging the loaded ones.
3. It has a rebounding lock, and cannot fire a charge until it is required.
4. All the parts are strong and serviceable, and not liable to get out of order.

Webley's Government Pattern Revolver, ·455 Bore.

This pistol, manufactured by Messrs. P. Webley and Son, Birmingham, is self-extracting, the components are few in number, simple, and for the most part interchangeable.

The lock mechanism is constructed upon an improved plan, resembling that of the Enfield pistol; it consists of five components, viz., the hammer B, trigger C, central lever E, and the mainspring A, all of which are interchangeable.

The hammer strikes the cartridge with considerable force, but when the pistol is used as a self-cocker it can be fired by a very moderate and even draw of the trigger.

When the empty cases require ejection, the fastening bolts securing the extension of the barrel to the body frame at X are withdrawn by means of the external thumb lever L, Fig. 1; the barrel can thus rotate into the position shown in Fig. 2, the extractor being thrust out by the lever J; this latter forming part of the joint on which the barrel moves, and this again is acted on and held in its position by the small catch K which only acts on it while the extractor moves out a certain distance, when it is so arranged that it disengages, and then the spiral spring, hitherto compressed during the extraction process, brings the extractor smartly back to its seat together with the lever J. It will be observed that the extractor I slides in the hollow axis or tube G upon which the cylinder rotates.

The two small projections or stops upon the upper part of the trigger C, Fig. 2, engage into the notches shown on the cylinder Fig. 1; one acting when the

(S.A)   G

pistol is at full cock, and the other when the hammer fires the cartridge thus the cylinder is always under the control either of one stop or the other, or of the lifter when rotating from one position to the next.

With this pistol, on pressing the thumb-lever, the cylinder is canted up and follows the motion of the barrel. With the Enfield the cylinder is drawn out horizontally along its axis sufficiently far for the empty cartridge cases to fall out. With both pistols the empty cases only are ejected.

TABLE I.—MILITARY RIFLES.

Country.	Supposed latest patterns.
Austria	Werndl, pattern 1873.
Bavaria	Werder, Mauser.
Belgium	Albini Braendlin, pattern 1867.
Brazil	Comblain, No. 2; Westley Richards.
China	Remington, Spencer, Snider.
Denmark	Remington.
Egypt	Remington.
France	Gras, Chassepôt.
Germany	Mauser.
Great Britain	Martini-Henry, Snider.
Greece	Gras, pattern 1874.
Holland	Beaumont, Chassepôt (modified).
Italy	Vetterli (single loader and magazine).
Japan	Murata.
Madagascar	Remington, Snider.
Montenegro	Krihk, Dreyse.
Norway and Sweden	Jarman (magazine), Remington.
Persia	Chassepôt.
Peru	Beaumont (modified).
Portugal	Martini-Henry, Snider.
Roumania	Peabody-Martini.
Russia	Berdan, No. 2, pattern 1871.
Servia	Peabody, Grün.
Spain	Remington, pattern 1871.
Switzerland	Vetterli (magazine).
Turkey	Peabody-Martini.
United States	Springfield.

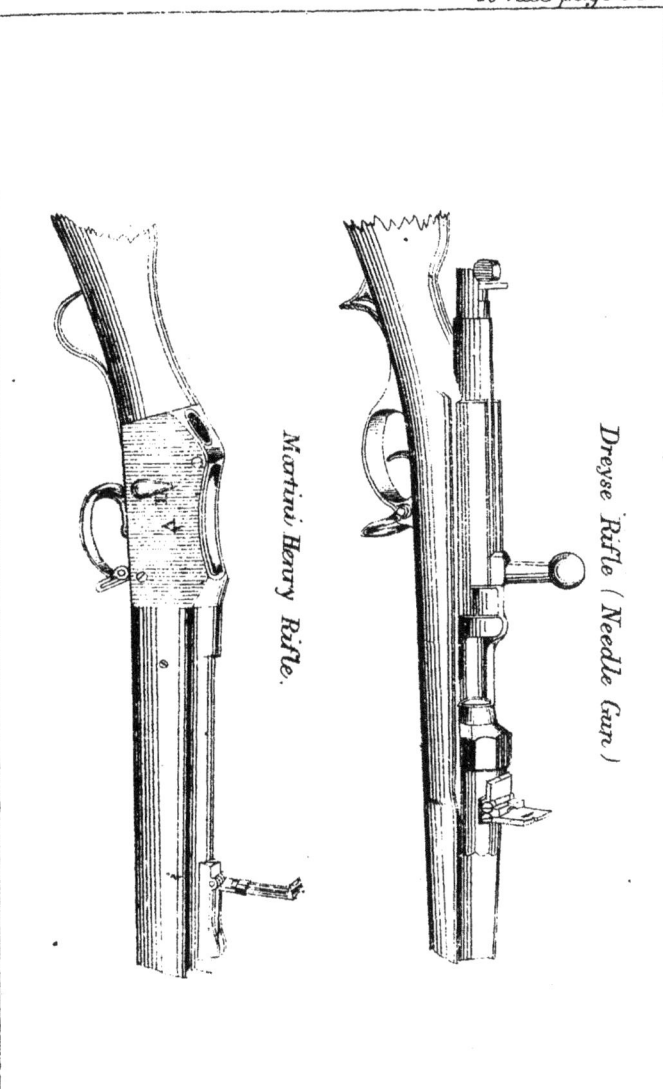

To face page 98.

Dreyse Rifle (Needle Gun)

Martini Henry Rifle.

MILITARY RIFLES.

Mauser Rifle.

Werder Rifle.

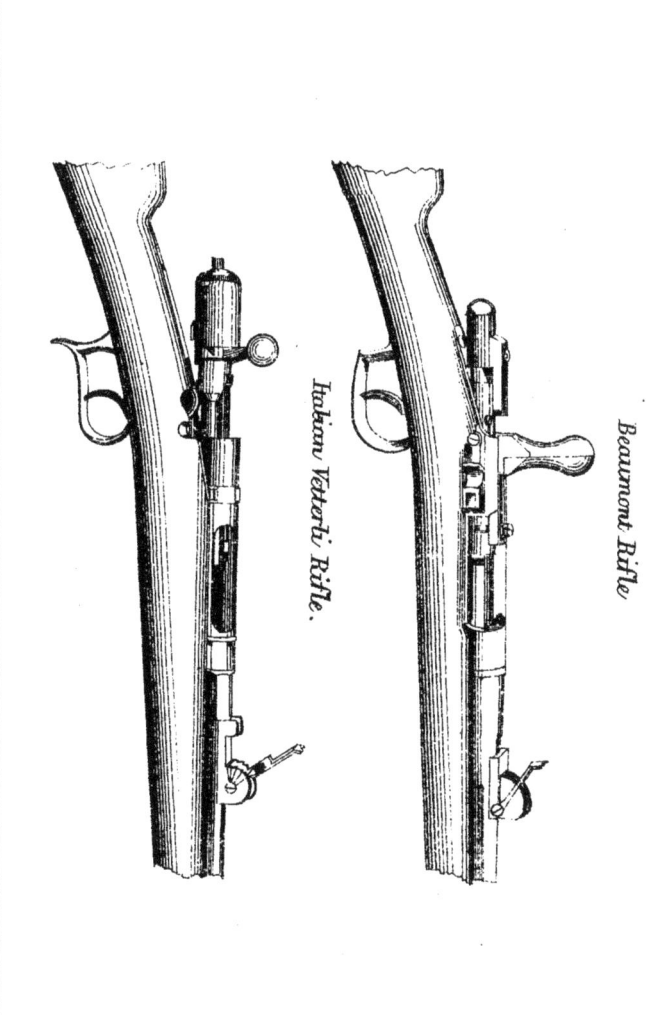

To face page 98.

Beaumont Rifle

Italian Vetterli Rifle.

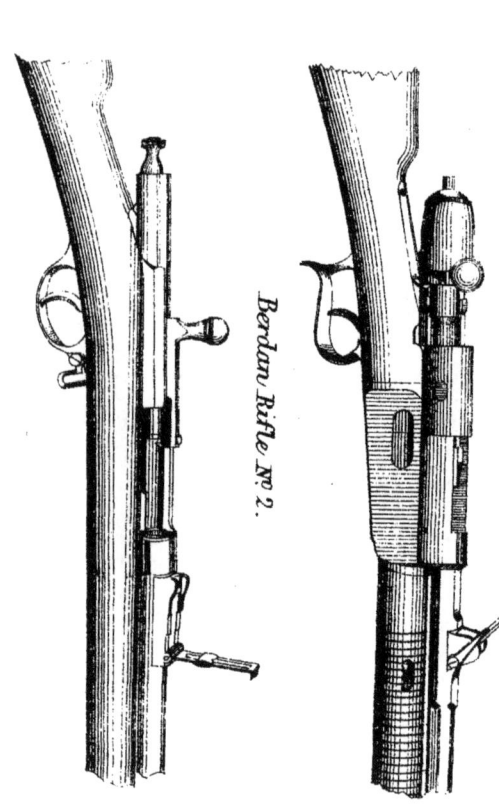

To face page 98.

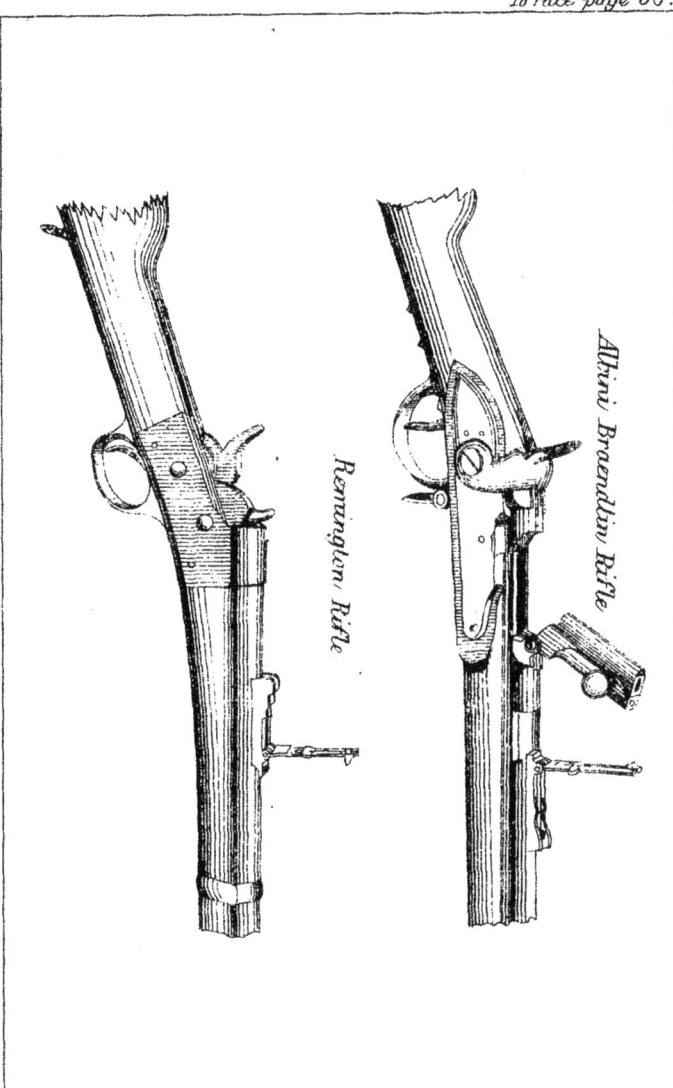

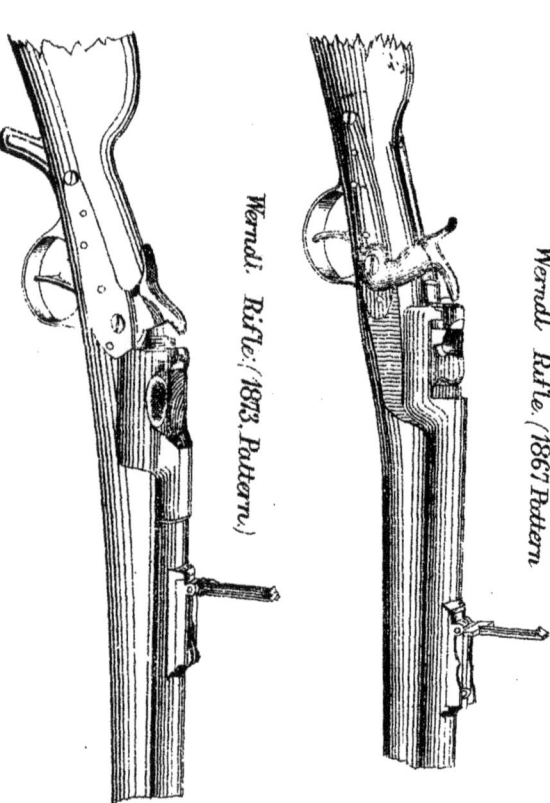

Werndl Rifle (1867 Pattern.)

Werndl Rifle (1873 Pattern.)

Table II.—Military Rifles: Lengths and Weights, &c.

System.	Calibre.	Weight.				Length.				Grooves.	
		Without bayonet.		With bayonet.		Without bayonet.		With bayonet fixed.		Number.	Width.
	ins.	lbs.	ozs.	lbs.	ozs.	ft.	ins.	ft.	ins.		ins.
Berdan	0·42	9	12½	10	12¾	4	5	6	1¼	6	0·16
Chassepôt	0·433	9	5½	10	12½	4	3½	6	2	4	0·17
Chassepôt modified	0·433	9	8½	10	6¼	4	3¾	6	0	4	0·18
Gras	0·433	9	11	10	$7\frac{9}{25}$	4	$3\frac{6}{25}$	6	$0\frac{21}{25}$	4	0·168
Jarman (Magazine)	0·397	10	1½	..		4	4½	..		4	0·16
Martini-Henry, long butts* (Mark III)	0·45	9	0	9	14	4	1½	5	11½	7	..
„ Cavalry carbine	0·45	7	8	..		3	$1\frac{11}{16}$	..		7	..
„ Artillery „	0·45	7	10½	†9	4¾	3	$1\frac{11}{16}$	†5	3⅜	7	..
Mauser	0·433	10	4	11	12	4	4¾	6	0½	4	0·18
Murata	0·432	9	10	11	3¾	4	3½	6	2	5	0·20
Peabody-Martini	0·45	9	10	10	8½	4	1	5	9	5	..
Remington	0·433	9	5½	10	13½	4	2¼	6	1	5	0·175
Snider, long rifle, Pn. 53 ..	0·577	9	0¾	9	14¼	4	7	6	0½	3	0·235
„ short, Pn. 60	„	8	12	†10	7½	4	0½	†5	11¼	5	„
„ Cavalry carbine ..	„	6	10¼	..		3	0⅞	..		5	„
„ Artillery „ ..	„	7	7	†9	3	3	4¼	†5	3	5	„
Springfield	0·45	9	5¼	10	1	4	3½	5	9½	3	0·24
Vetterli single-loader (Italy) ..	0·408	9	9	10	14½	4	5½	6	2	4	0·165
„ Magazine (Italy) ..	0·408	10	15	11	10½	4	4¼	5	11¼	4	0·18
„ „ (Swiss) ..	0·409	10	6	11	3½	4	4	5	11	4	0·18
Werder	0·433	9	13	11	6½	4	$3\frac{5}{7}$	5	10¼	4	0·16
Werndl	0·433	9	13½	11	8½	4	2	6	0	6	0·15

* M.H. rifle, Mark II, is the arm in use with the Infantry, and its weight is 8 lbs. 12 oz.

[To face page 98.

Depth.	Length of one turn.	Mechanism.		Proportion of weight of powder to weight of bullet.	Weight of one cartridge.
		Closing.	Striking.		
ins.	ins.				grains.
0·011	21	Bolt.	Spiral spring and striker.	1 : 4·743	610
0·010	22	,,	,, ,,	1 : 4·425	492
0·012	30	,,	,, ,,	1 : 4·911	609
0·010	22	,,	,, ,,	1 : 4·825	675
0·010	22	,,	,, ,,	1 : 4·37	620
0·007	22	Falling hinged block.	,, ,,	1 : 5·65	758
0·007	22	,,	,, ,,	1 : 5·857	684
0·007	22	,,	,, ,,	,,	684
0·012	22	Bolt.	,, ,,	1 : 5·066	650
0·006	20	,,	,, ,,	1 : 5·06	697
0·007	22	Falling hinged block.	,, ,,	1 : 5·65	802
0·010	20	Sectorial block.	Flat spring and striker.	1 : 5·33	665
{0·005 / 0·012}	78	Turn over block.	Side lock and striker.	1 : 6·857	715
,,	48	,,	,, ,,	··	··
,,	,,	,,	,, ,,	··	··
,,	,,	,,	,, ,,	··	··
0·005	22	,,	,, ,,	1 : 7·143	752
0·009	26	Bolt.	Spiral spring and striker.	1 : 5·16	568
0·012	26	,,	,, ,,	1 : 5·63	468
0·009	26	,,	,, ,,	1 : 5·63	465
0·012	36	Falling hinged block.	Flat spring and striker.	1 : 5·14	543
0·018	28	Revolving block.	Side lock and striker.	1 : 4·805	655

† Sword bayonet.

TABLE III.—MILITARY RIFLES, VELOCITIES, &c.

System.	Calibre.	Length of barrel.	Charge. Powder.	Charge. Bullet.	Value of $\dfrac{d^2}{w}$.	Muzzle.	At 500 yds.	At 1000 yds.	At 1500 yds.	At 2000 yds.
	inch.	inches.	grains.	grains.		f.s.	f.s.	f.s.	f.s.	f.s.
Berdan	0·42	32¼	77	370	3·336	1444	873	645	476	353
Chassepôt	0·433	32·6	87	385	3·409	1373	848	623	457	338
Chassepôt, modified	0·433	32¼	68	384	3·930	1369	806	566	396	281
Gras	0·433	32·3/10	81	386	3·416	1493	878	643	471	348
Jarmann magazine	0·397	32	77	337	3·322	1536	908	675	504	377
Martini-Henry	0·45	33·1/16	85	480	2·958	1315	869	664	508	389
Mauser	0·433	33·5/16	75	380	3·453	1430	859	629	459	338
Murata	0·432	33·1/16	83	420	3·110	1487	905	679	512	387
Peabody-Martini	0·45	33·1/16	85	480	2·953	1380	888	678	519	397
Remington	0·433	35·8/16	75	400	3·281	1340	849	631	468	350
Snider	0·577	39	70	480	4·855	1240	711	458	299	196
Springfield	0·45	32¼	70	500	2·034	1301	875	676	523	404
Vetterli single loader (Italy)	0·408	33·7/8	62	310	3·759	1430	835	595	422	304
Vetterli magazine (Italy)	0·408	33·1/16	55	310	3·750	1389	824	588	417	300
Vetterli magazine (Switzerland)	0·409	33	55	310	3·777	1314	804	572	406	292
Werder	0·433	35	64	329	3·989	1424	815	570	396	280
Werndl	0·433	33	75	370	3·547	1439	854	620	449	328

Table IV.—Military Rifles: Heights of Trajectory.

Systems.	Greatest heights of trajectory.			
	500 yds.	1000 yds.	1500 yds.	2000 yds.
	feet.	feet.	feet.	feet.
Berdan	7·995	47·01	151·7	388·7
Chassepôt	8·594	50·44	162·8	417·3
Chassepôt, modified	9·243	56·62	193·8	528·9
Gras	7·769	46·60	151·8	389·9
Jarmann, magazine	7·235	42·97	137·6	348·5
Martini-Henry	8·594	47·90	147·1	357·85
Mauser	8·249	48·68	159·2	411·1
Murata	7·433	43·53	137·7	341·8
Peabody-Martini	8·097	45·395	139·77	341·67
Remington	8·539	50·42	160·3	403·1
Snider	11·85	75·58	284·5	866·2
Springfield	8·574	46·88	142·3	343·0
Vetterli, single loader (Italy)	8·527	52·17	176·3	469·9
Vetterli, magazine (Italy)	8·892	53·63	181·1	484·4
Vetterli, magazine (Swiss)	9·475	57·07	191·0	510·2
Werder	8·880	54·80	190·9	523·1
Werndl	8·252	49·41	162·6	426·0

TABLE V.—MILITARY RIFLES: TIMES OF FLIGHT.

Systems.	Times of flight over different ranges.			
	500 yds.	1000 yds.	1500 yds.	2000 yds.
	seconds.	seconds.	seconds.	seconds.
Berdan	1·409	3·418	6·139	9·826
Chassepôt	1·461	3·540	6·357	10.18
Chassepôt, modified	1·516	3·751	6·939	11·47
Gras	1·389	3·402	6·141	9·842
Jarmann, magazine	1·341	3·268	5·846	9·305
Martini-Henry	1·461	3·449	6·045	9·4287
Mauser	1·432	3·477	6·288	10·100
Murata	1·359	3·289	5·848	9·215
Peabody-Martini	1·4182	3·358	5·893	9·213
Remington	1·473	3·539	6·310	10·001
Snider	1·679	4·333	8·409	14·67
Springfield	1·460	3·417	5·946	9·23
Vetterli, single-loader (Italy)	1·455	3·599	6·618	10·80
Vetterli, magazine (Italy)	1·486	3·651	6·708	10·97
Vetterli, magazine (Swiss)	1·534	3·765	8·889	11·26
Werder	1·486	3·690	6·887	11·40
Werndl	1·432	3·503	6·354	10 29

TABLE VI.

The following table shows the "Accuracy Figure of Merit" of various military rifles at different ranges:—

	Ranges in yards.				
	100.	300.	500.	800.	1000.
Snider long rifle		0·62	0·89	2·80	5·09
Snider carbines			1·30		
Martini-Henry rifle	0·09	0·32	0·55	1·20	1·85
Martini-Henry carbines	0·11	0·45	0·75	2·01	2·21
Vetterli rifle (Italian)			1·045		4·435
Vetterli magazine rifle (Swiss)			0·71		2·19
Winchester magazine rifle			1·675		
Hotchkiss			0·59		2·415
Kropatchek			1·26		1·89
Murata rifle			0·74		2·975

Chapter IV.

SERVICE SWORDS, LANCES, SWORD BAYONETS, AND BAYONETS.

The swords used in the Service have of late years been supplied by contract, chiefly at Birmingham.

They are inspected, gauged, and tested at the Royal Small Arms Department, Birmingham, in two stages;

1st. The separate components of the sword unfinished.

2nd. The finished sword complete.

In the manufacture of swords the best cast steel should be used. It is obtained from Sheffield tilted in taper bars, each bar containing the material necessary for two blades; the bars vary in dimensions and form to suit the different natures of swords required. The forging is done almost entirely by hand. A tang of iron is welded to the upper end or shoulder of the blade for the purpose of attaching it to the hilt.

The tempering process is one requiring skill and experience. The blades are carefully heated to a red heat, and then plunged into a bath of water or oil. When drawn out they are nearly white, and so brittle as to be easily broken by the hand. They are then gradually heated until they pass from a white to a blue colour; after this they are "set" perfectly straight while still hot, and are ready for grinding.

The grinding is done on large circular stones revolving rapidly; each blade is ground to weight and to fit accurately standard troughs and gauges.

The blade when ground is ready for the 1st inspection by the Government Department. It is proved by being struck both back and edge a heavy blow on an oak block; it is also tested by the trough gauge and for weight, and it must spring regularly.

The other components of the sword are also separately

examined as to quality, soundness, &c., the whole are then returned to the contractor for mounting. When complete, the swords with the scabbards are again submitted for inspection. The soundness of the mounting of the hilt is tested by striking the blade on the oak block a smart blow. The sword is weighed, gauged, and sprung, and the distance at which the blade balances from the hilt is tested.

In springing, the blade is bent by placing the point on the ground and pressing down upon the hilt until the length of the blade is reduced a certain length—4 inches for the cavalry swords—this will detect anything wrong in the tempering.

Officers' swords obtained in this country are often either wholly or partially of foreign make, and in some cases are not reliable.

Cavalry Sword Patterns 1853 and 1864.

Fig. 1 represents the 1853 pattern cavalry sword and scabbard: the bar hilt is of iron, the scabbard of iron, lined with slips of wood. <small>Cavalry sword, pattern 1853.</small>

In 1864 a new sword with a sheet steel hilt was introduced; the blade was identical with the pattern '53, the scabbard of steel, and fitted with the solid wood lining; this necessitated its being of larger dimensions than the pattern '53. <small>Cavalry sword, pattern 1864.</small>

The sheet steel hilt was adopted, it having been found that the bars of the iron one were liable to break.

Both of these patterns are still in the Service, and are used by the Light and Heavy Cavalry, Horse Artillery, non-commissioned officers of Field Artillery,* and Commissariat and Transport Corps; but will be gradually superseded by the new patterns.

Some of the swords patterns 1853 and 1864 have been converted to pattern 1882, they will weigh from 1 to 2 ozs. more than new swords of this pattern.

---

* The bar hilt is used in the Field Artillery, the sheet steel hilt being found to injure the uniform when looped up.

Length of blade of '53 and '64 patterns....	2 ft.	11½ ins.
Weight of sword.....	2 lbs.	7¾ ozs.
,, scabbard...	2 ,,	1¼ ,,
Total......	4 ,,	9 ,,

Cavalry Swords, Pattern 1882—" *Long* " *and* " *Short.*"

Of these swords the "long" pattern is intended for Heavy Cavalry of the Line, and the "short," which is shown in Fig. 2, for all other mounted services except Household Cavalry.

The principal points in which they differ from the pattern 1864 are as follows:—

Sword.—The blade, which is slightly curved, is reduced in weight and length. The hilt, of sheet steel, is reduced in size, and its edges are turned up. The position of the slot for the sword knot has been changed from the back to the upper part of the guard as in the 1853 pattern.

Scabbard.—The scabbard is reduced in size and weight —it has fixed loops instead of loose rings; the object of this change is to prevent noise. It is fitted with a new mouth piece or sputcheon, carried by a band fitting outside the scabbard. This ensures the blade at once entering the solid wood lining, instead of having to pass through the iron sputcheon which was formerly fitted inside, and was found to blunt the sword blade.

The following table shows how these patterns differ as to length and weight from the patterns 1853 and 1864:—

It will be observed that the "long" or Heavy Cavalry sword is 2⅜ inches longer than the "short" pattern.

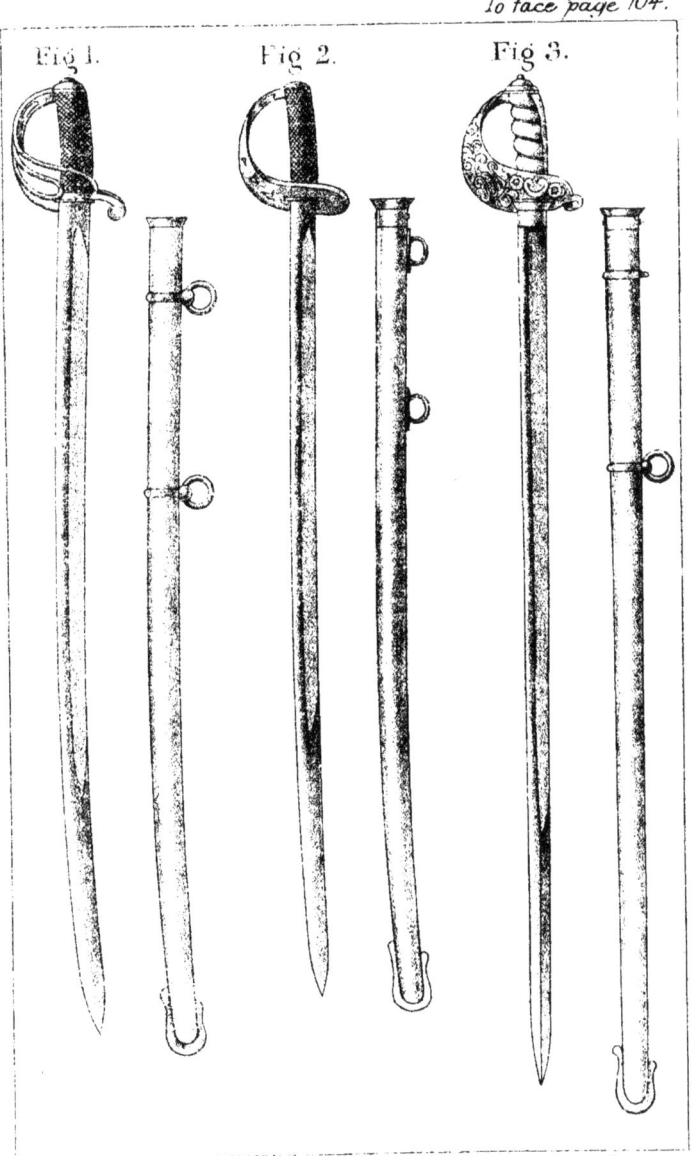

To face page 104.

Fig. 1.   Fig. 2.   Fig. 3.

DANGERFIELD. LITH. 22. BEDFORD S.T COVENT GARDEN.

	Patterns, 1882.		Patterns 1853 and 1864.
	Long.	Short.	
Length of blade	2 ft. 11⅜ in.	2 ft. 9 in.	2 ft. 11¼ in.
Total length	3 ft. 4⅜ in.	3 ft. 2 in.	3 ft. 4¼ in.
Weight of sword	2 lb. 2¼ oz.	2 lb. 0¼ oz.	2 lb. 7¾ oz.
Weight of scabbard	1 lb. 11½ oz.	1 lb. 9¾ oz.	2 lb. 1¼ oz.
Total weight	3 lb. 14 oz.	3 lb. 10 oz.	4 lb. 9 oz.

It is intended that the store of 1853 and 1864 pattern swords shall be gradually converted to the 1882 pattern.

Sword, Household Cavalry—" Long" and " Short."

The swords of the Household Cavalry are special to that branch of the service. In 1882, on the arrangements for the supply of their equipment being assimilated to those of the service generally, new patterns of swords common to the whole brigade were approved. In the "long" pattern, Fig. 3, which is for general use, the blade is 38⅞ inches long, and quite straight; the hilt of sheet steel is pierced to represent the letters H C, and scroll work, the scabbard is of steel, with solid wooden lining, and is fitted with the improved mouth piece, as with the new cavalry sword. The scabbard has the old pattern loose ring for its lower point of attachment to the sword belt; the upper attachment is to a staple or loop fixed to the side of the scabbard in line with the stud and eye shown in the figure, which is for the purpose of hooking up.

Sword, Household Cavalry, "long."

Length of blade ...... 38⅞ inches.
Weight of sword ...... 2 lbs. 4½ ozs.
  ,,   scabbard .. 1 ,, 14 ,,

Total .... 4 ,, 2½ ,,

The "short" pattern is for the bands of the brigade.

Household Cavalry, "short."

The sword and scabbard are lighter and 4 inches shorter than the long pattern. In every other respect they are identical.

Weight of sword......	2 lbs.	$1\frac{3}{4}$ ozs.
,, scabbard....	1 ,,	$11\frac{3}{4}$,,
Total.........	3 ,,	$13\frac{1}{2}$,,

The other swords and scabbards in use in the service are shown as under.

Sword, Staff Sergeants of the Line.

Fig. 4. Sword, Staff Sergeants of the Line: the hilt is gilt, with a device of a crown and VR in a monogram. The scabbard is of leather gilt mounted.

Length of blade	$32\frac{1}{2}$ inches.	
Weight of sword......	1 lb.	$14\frac{1}{2}$ ozs.
,, scabbard....	0 ,,	10 ,,
Total.........	2 ,,	$8\frac{1}{2}$,,

Sword, Staff Sergeants of Rifles.

Fig 5. Sword, Staff Sergeants of Rifles: steel hilt with a device of a crown and bugle, leather scabbard steel mounted.

Length and weights the same as for Staff Sergeants of the Line.

Sword, Staff Sergeants of Artillery.

Fig. 6. Sword, Staff Sergeants of Artillery and Conductors of Stores: steel hilt with three bars, and steel scabbard.

Length of blade	$32\frac{1}{2}$ inches.	
Weight of sword......	1 lb.	$14\frac{1}{2}$ ozs.
,, scabbard....	1 ,,	$1\frac{1}{2}$,,
Total.........	3 ,,	0 ,,

Sword, Staff Sergeants of Engineers.

Fig. 7. Sword, Staff Sergeants of Engineers: gun metal hilt and steel scabbard.

Length and weights the same as for Staff Sergeants of Artillery.

Claymore, Staff Sergeants of Highland Regiments.

Fig. 8. Claymore, Staff Sergeants of Highland Regiments: steel hilt, and leather scabbard, steel mounted.

To face page 106.

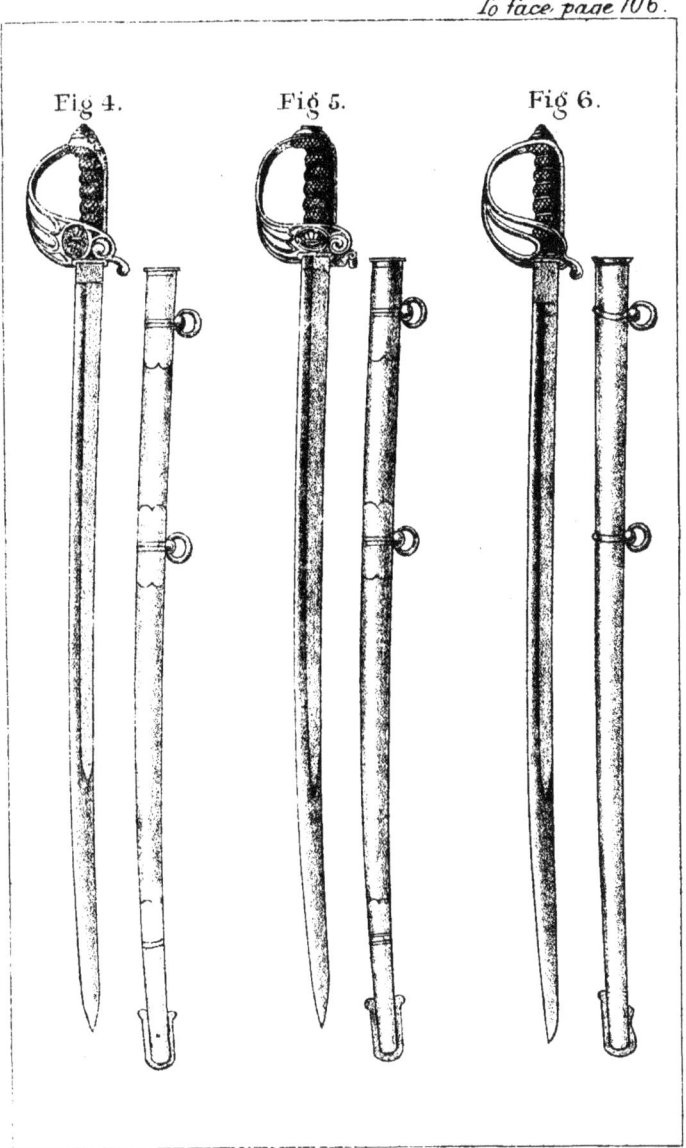

Fig 4.   Fig 5.   Fig 6.

DANGERFIELD, LITH 22, BEDFORD S⁺ COVENT GARDEN.

To face page 107.

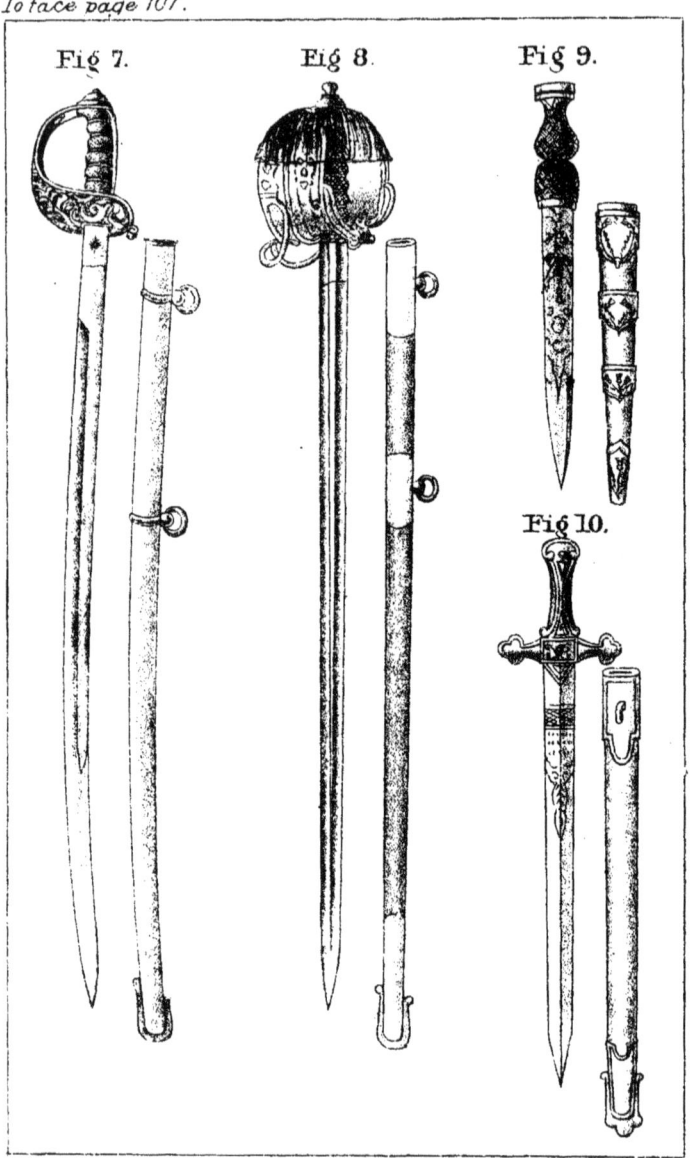

Length of blade ...... 32½ inches.
Weight of sword...... 2 lbs. 15½ ozs.
" scabbard.... 0 " 12⅓ "

Total........ 3 " 12 "

Fig. 9. Highland Dirk for Drummers and Band: this is substituted for the claymore that was formerly carried. *Highland Dirk for Drummers and Band.*

Length of blade ...... 12 inches.
Weight of dirk ...... 0 lbs. 13 ozs.
" scabbard.... 0 " 6½ "

Total........ 1 " 3½ "

Fig. 10. Sword for Drummers and Band of the Line: leather scabbard, brass mounted. *Sword, Drummers and Band of the Line.*

Length of blade ...... 19 inches.
Weight of sword...... 1 lb. 15 ozs.
" scabbard.... 0 " 9¼ "

Total........ 2 " 8¼ "

The Drummers and Band of Rifle regiments have a similar sword and scabbard, steel mounted. *Sword, Drummers and Band of Rifle Regiments.*

Length of blade ...... 19 inches.
Weight of sword.. ... 1 lb. 13 ozs.
" scabbard.... 0 " 8½ "

Total........ 2 " 5½ "

Fig. 11. Naval Cutlass: black japanned iron hilt, and brown leather scabbard, brass mounted. Spring inside locket to prevent cutlass falling out, cannot be attached to rifle. *Naval cutlass.*

Length of blade ...... 25½ inches.
Weight of cutlass .... 2 lbs. 5¼ ozs.
" scabbard .. 0 " 12 "

Total ...... 3 " 1½ "

Fig. 12. Pioneer saw-back sword with saw teeth for *Sword,*

Pioneer saw-back. cutting wood or branches of trees: brass hilt and leather scabbard, brass mounted.

> Length of blade ...... 22½ inches.
> Weight of sword........ 2 lbs. 4¼ ozs.
>   ,,   scabbard.... 0 ,, 13 ,,
> Total........ 3 ,, 1¼ ,,

Lead cutter. Fig. 13. Lead cutter; black japanned iron hilt, and leather scabbard with brass tip.

> Length of blade ...... 31 inches.

Sword, practice. Fig. 14. Practice sword; thick edged furrowed blade, with black japanned iron hilt; no scabbard.

> Length of blade ...... 32½ inches.

Foil, fencing. Fig. 15. Fencing Foil: white cord grip, wound on a wooden body covered with chamois leather, steel guard and brass pommel.

> Length of blade ...... 33¾ inches.

Lance, service. Fig. 16. Service Lance: mounted in bamboo; steel head in one piece, the socket as well as the iron shoe is bored out of the solid, and attached to the stave with shellac. The flag and sling are attached with leather thongs.

> Length of lance .... 108 inches.
> Total length of spear head .... 12⅝ ,,
> Total length of shoe ...... 6¾ ,,
> Total weight of lance.. 3 lbs. 13¾ oz.

Lance, practice. Fig. 17. Practice Lance; bamboo stave; pads on both ends.

Lance, old pattern. Fig. 18. The Old Pattern Lance, 1860, had an ash pole fitted with lanquettes.

Sword bayonets. Figs. 19—20. Sword Bayonet, Short Rifle, and Artillery Snider Carbine.

These are alike, except in the cross piece, the hole in which is larger in that for the short rifle. Scabbard for short rifle is of leather; for Artillery carbine of steel.

To face page 108.

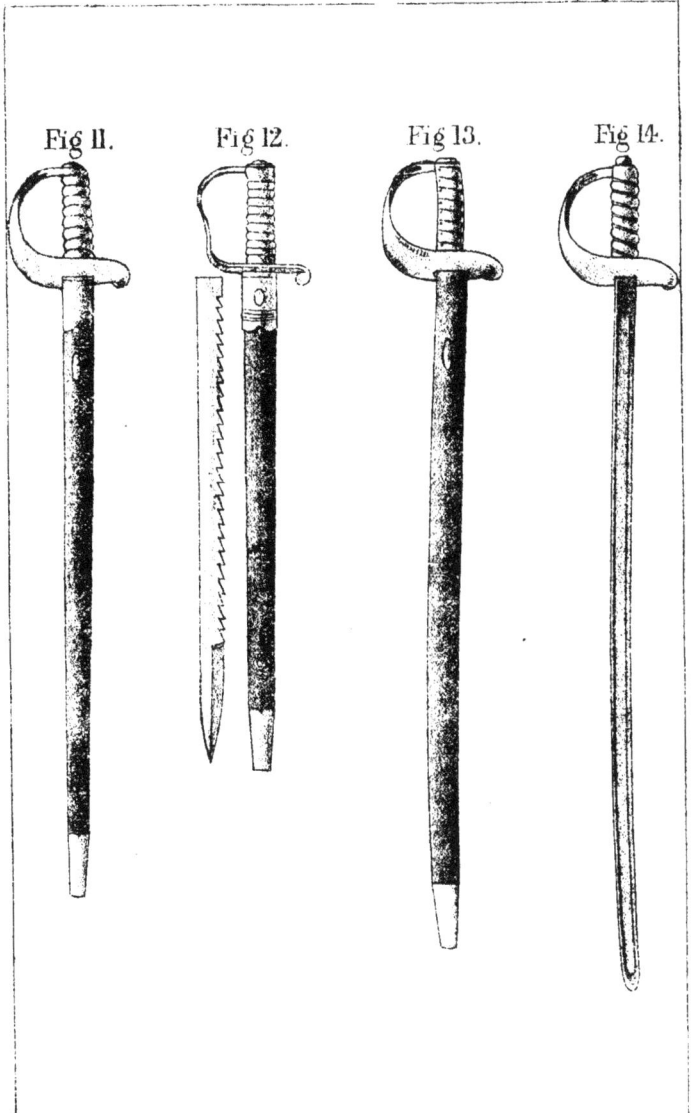

Fig 11.   Fig 12.   Fig 13.   Fig 14.

DANGERFIELD LITH 22 BEDFORD ST COVENT GARDEN

To face page 108.

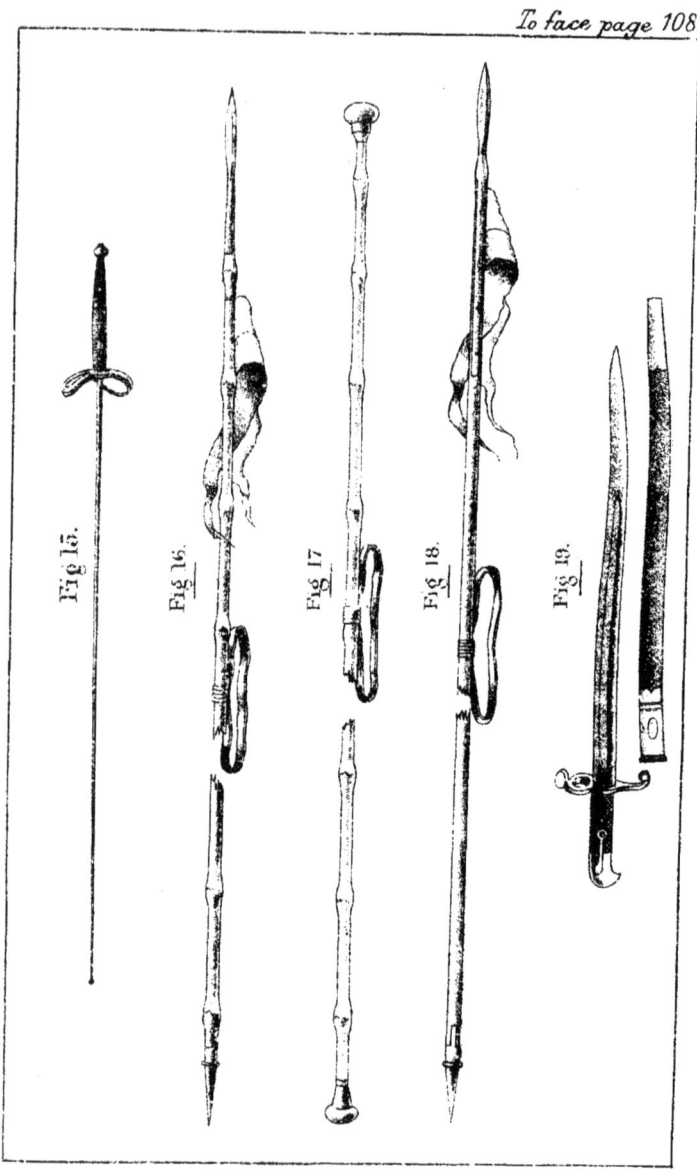

To face page 109.

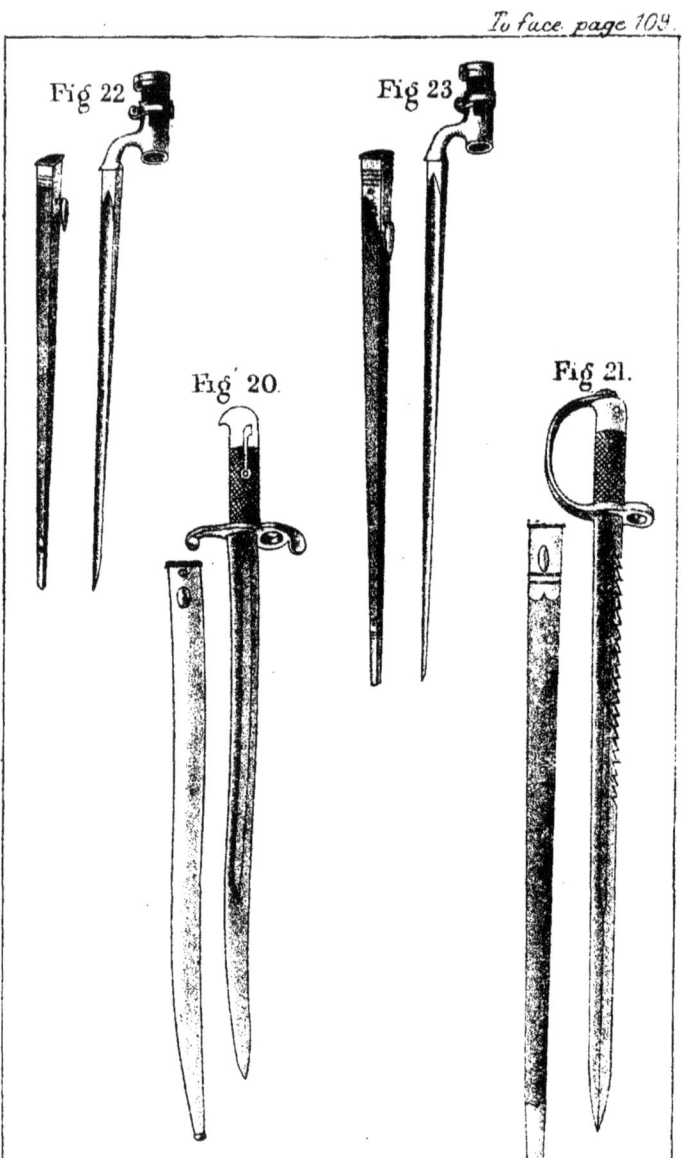

DANGERFIELD, LITH 22, BEDFORD S.T COVENT GARDEN

The sergeants of the Line and Rifle Battalions have a sword bayonet, the same as for the short rifle, except that it fits the Martini-Henry rifle; it is the old pattern sword bayonet, with the muzzle hole bushed to fit the latter rifle.

Total length of sword bayonet............ 2 ft. 4¼ inches.
Weight............... 1 lb. 12 ozs.
Scabbard, short rifle.. ⎫ Length, 23¼ inches.
„ M.-H. „.. ⎬ Weight, 7½ ozs.
Scabbard, Artillery ⎫ Length, 23¾ inches.
Snider carbine.... ⎬ Weight, 13 ozs.

Fig 21. Sword Bayonet for M.-H. Carbine. Artillery. Sword bayonet,
The blade of the sword bayonet is straight, and the M.-H.
back is cut as a saw of 41 teeth. carbine.

Length ⎧ of sword bayonet...... 31¼ inches.
⎨ of blade............. 25¾ „
⎩ of saw .... 9¼ „

Weight ⎧ of sword bayonet without scabbard........ 1 lb. 10¼ ozs.
⎨ of sword bayonet with scabbard .... 2 „ 2¾ „

The scabbard is of leather blackened, it has a steel locket and tip, and two springs in the locket to prevent the sword bayonet from falling out.

Length of scabbard ...... 26 13/16 inches.
Weight .... 8½ ozs.

Fig. 22. Bayonet pattern '53 for Snider rifle. Bayonet,
Total length .... 20¾ inches. pattern
Weight .... 13¼ ozs. 1853.

This bayonet has an outward cant when on the rifle.

Fig. 23. Bayonet, common, Martini-Henry, "long" Bayonet,
the blade of steel, the socket of wrought-iron. The blade M.-H.,
is hardened, tempered, ground, and polished; the socket "long."
browned, the locking ring blued; the blade is 21½ inches long, and is straight.

Total length......... 2 feet 1⅛ inch.
Weight............. 16 ozs.

Scabbard for ditto of leather is fitted with two springs long and short. The long spring is intended to strengthen the scabbard, and the short spring to prevent the bayonet from falling out. In Mark II the long spring is attached to the leather by two rivets.

Length .... $22\frac{1}{8}$ inches.
Weight .... $8\frac{1}{4}$ ozs.

CHAPTER V.

GUNPOWDER—COMPOSITION OF GUNPOWDER—
PROPORTION OF INGREDIENTS—FORCE OF
GUNPOWDER, HOW INFLUENCED—OUTLINE
OF MANUFACTURE—VENTILATION OF MAGA-
ZINES—LEAD AS A MATERIAL FOR BULLETS.

GUNPOWDER is an intimate mixture of the following ingredients:—
1. Charcoal (C) to supply the carbon or fuel.
2. Saltpetre or nitre (KNO_3) to furnish the oxygen required for the oxidation or burning of the charcoal.
3. Sulphur (S) to accelerate the combustion.

Composition.

Sulphur does not appear to be absolutely necessary, as good powder has been made without it.

The proportions of the ingredients vary in different countries; those used in the British Government factories are approximately saltpetre, 75 parts; charcoal, 15; sulphur, 10.

Proportion of ingredients.

The explosive action of gunpowder depends for its effect on the sudden evolution of a large volume of gas at a high temperature; this gas is chiefly derived from the combustion of the charcoal by the oxygen contained in the saltpetre.

Explosive action.

The gases formed would, if allowed to expand, freely occupy a space about 2000 times as great as that of the powder from which it was evolved.

The sulphur is said to lower the point of ignition of the powder and to increase the temperature and rapidity of combustion, thus increasing the volumes of the gases by expansion.

The explosive force of gunpowder is not determined alone by the amount of gas generated; it depends also upon the heat developed by which the expansion of the gases is influenced, and also upon the rate at which the gases are produced, and this again depends on the size and form of the grains, &c.

The great advantage possessed by gunpowder over other explosives hitherto tried, is our power of being able to regulate its rate of combustion and thus reduce the strain on the gun.

The chief disadvantages of gunpowder are the smoke and fouling attending its explosion.

The total theoretic work of gunpowder when indefinitely expanded is 486 foot-tons per lb. of powder. (The work stored up in 1 lb. of coal is about ten times as great.)

The following are the principal circumstances which influence the force exerted by gunpowder :—

1. Quality of the ingredients.
2. Proportion of the ingredients.
3. Density of the powder.
4. Hardness of the powder.
5. Proportion of moisture.
6. Size of grain.
7. Amount of space occupied by the charge in the bore.
8. Length of barrel.
9. Calibre.
10. Amount of charge.
11. Weight of bullet.
12 Windage.
13. Rifling.

Quality of the Ingredients.

One of the greatest difficulties of the powder maker in his endeavours to produce an uniform powder is the variability of the charcoal. The chemical constitution of the woods from which it is produced is affected by the climate in which the wood is grown, and even by the time of year in which it is cut. The wood for powder is always cut in spring. The nature of the charcoal itself can be modified to almost any extent in process of manufacture by varying the heat to which it is subjected and the length of time it is exposed to this heat. Underburnt charcoal is more easily inflammable, but is more hygroscopic than charcoal which has been burned the usual time. It therefore makes a stronger powder, but one which is liable to lose its strength by absorbing moisture from the air.

With regard to the other two constituents of powder (sulphur and saltpetre) there is no great difficulty in reducing them to a pure state and thus ensuring uniformity of quality.

Proportion of the Ingredients.

A slight increase in the proportion of sulphur is said to increase the rapidity and temperature of combustion. A slight diminution in the proportion of saltpetre diminishes both velocity and pressure.

Density of the Powder.

The denser the grains of a powder, *i.e.*, the higher their specific gravity, the more slowly they will burn, and the less the pressure they will exert in the bore of a gun, and the less the velocity they will impart to the projectile.

Hardness.

Hardness is independent of density; its effect is to retard the ignition of the powder. Glazing-like hardness retards ignition.

Proportion of Moisture.

The effect of moisture in powder appears to be to reduce the temperature of explosion by the steam developed, and thus to reduce both the pressure and the velocity.

Size of the Grains.

Suppose a powder similar in all respects, except in the size and shape of the grains; then conversion of the powder into gas depends on the rate of ignition of the grains and the time of combustion of each grain.

Rate of ignition.

Rate of combustion.

The rate of ignition of the grain depends on the facility with which the flame can penetrate to contiguous grains, *i.e.*, to the magnitude of the interstices between the grains, depending principally on the shape of the grain, while the time of combustion depends on the bulk or size of the grains themselves, *i.e.*, the smaller the *size* the quicker the combustion.

These conditions are, to a certain extent, opposed to one another, so that it will readily be understood that for a given charge of powder, there is some shape and size of grain which will give uniformity of ignition combined with the required rapidity of combustion.

Fine grain more rapid with small charges.

In small charges, such as are used in our rifles, the finer the grain the more rapid the ignition and combustion.

Amount of Space Occupied by the Charge in the Bore.

The greater the space unoccupied by the charge of powder in the chamber, the less the pressure and the less the muzzle velocity of the bullet. The Martini-Henry cartridge, owing to the nature of the case, has a greater air space than a solid drawn one, such as is used in the Peabody-Martini (America), and hence the muzzle-velocity is less.

Length of Barrel.

The object sought after in recent experiments is to distribute as far as possible the pressure over the whole length of the bore, and to obtain the maximum work from a given charge of powder without undue strain on either gun or projectile. A theoretically perfect result as to length of barrel would be obtained if the last atom of powder were converted into gas as the bullet was leaving the muzzle.

Calibre.

With the same charge and weight of projectiles an increase of calibre is said to give an increase of muzzle velocity; it is probable that this is only true to a limited extent.

Amount of Charge.

With small arms excessive recoil places a limit on the amount of charge.

Weight of Bullet.

By increasing the weight of the bullet the muzzle velocity is reduced.

Windage.

Windage has little influence with our present small arms.

Rifling.

The experiments of the Committee on Explosives seem to show that there is little difference in either velocity or pressure in a smooth bore and a rifled gun of the same calibre, and firing the same charge and weight of projectile.

The objects to be attained in the production of an explosive agent for cannon and small-arms are:— <small>Objects to be attained.</small>

1. The maximum of propelling force.
2. The minimum of initial pressure in bore of gun.
3. Uniformity of action.
4. Freedom from fouling (especially in small-arm powders).
5. Durability (i.e.) power to bear transport and to keep well in store.

Of all explosive substances at present known, gunpowder alone can be said to fulfil the first three conditions.

1. The ingredients are easily procured. <small>Advantages of gunpowder.</small>
2. They are comparatively cheap.
3. It is, with proper precautions, safe in manufacture, in store, and in transport; it also keeps well.
4. Its rate of combustion is gradual compared with that of most other explosive compounds, and can be readily modified by the processes of

manufacture so as to suit every description of weapon.

Explosiveness. Powders made from exactly the same materials, mixed in the same proportions, yet differ greatly in "explosiveness," which may be defined as the *rate* at which the powder burns or is converted into gas. This quality will depend chiefly upon the following physical properties :—

(a.) The density of the powder.
(b.) Its hardness.
(c.) Size of the grains or pieces.
(d.) Shape of the grains.
(e.) Amount of glaze imparted to it.

Of these the density is found to have the most effect.

Outline of Manufacture.

The following are the usual processes :—

1. Purification of the ingredients, pulverizing and sifting the charcoal and sulphur.
2. Mixing the ingredients.
3. Incorporation, or "milling."
4. Breaking down the mill cake.
5. Pressing.
6. Granulating.
7. Dusting.
8. Glazing.
9. Stoving, or drying.
10. Finishing.

Purity of ingredients. The ingredients should be absolutely free from impurity, and the greatest care is taken in the processes of refining the saltpetre and sulphur, and burning the charcoal, to prevent the introduction of any particles of foreign substances, however small; this care is continued through all the stages of manufacture.

Charcoal. The quality of the powder is very materially affected by that of the charcoal, and this depends both on the description of wood used, and upon the manner in which it is burnt.

Dogwood charcoal is now generally used in the manufacture of gunpowder for small arms.

The first stage in the manufacture is the purification of the ingredients; upon it depends the regularity of the action, the keeping qualities, and the safety. Purification of ingredients.

The next operation is to mix the materials so thoroughly, that combustion shall be uniform. This mixing is effected 1. By placing the ingredients in proper proportion in a vessel and then stirring them all up together. 2. By subjecting this mixture to a grinding process in huge mortars called incorporating mills; the result is an intimate mechanical mixture in the form of a cake, something like broken oil cake. Mixing of ingredients. Incorporating.

This meal cake is the real powder, but the pieces are irregular in size, varying from dust to comparatively large pieces of cake; the density is also not uniform. Both of these causes would lead to irregularity in the action. To obviate this, it is broken into small pieces, and then pressed uniformly in a machine by hydraulic pressure. After pressing, the powder is in the form of slabs of uniform density, and its after-treatment depends upon the description of powder required; up to this point the manufacture of all grain and cubical powder are practically the same, the only difference being variations in the quality of the charcoal and in the time occupied in incorporating, which is longer in the case of small-arm powders which are thus increased in density. Pressing.

If the powder required is a grain-powder, the press cake is broken up in a machine, and the products sifted through different sieves, so that uniformity in the size of grain can be obtained, but if a pebble-powder is wanted the press cake is cut up in a different machine to pieces of the proper size.

R.F.G. (rifle fine grain) is the powder used for Snider arms.

R.F.G^2. is the powder used with the Martini-Henry; it is denser than R.F.G. The size of the grain in both these powders is the same; they pass through a sieve of 12 meshes to a square inch, and are retained on one of 20 meshes to the inch.

After granulating, R.F.G. and R.F.G^2. are dusted in a

revolving sloping reel, and covered with 24-mesh canvas; this removes the dust.

"Pistol powder" is obtained from the siftings of R.F.G. powder, the grains being of such a size as to pass the 20-mesh sieve, and to be retained on one of 36 mesh.

Glazing. The small-arm powders are next glazed by being revolved in glazing barrels, a fine glaze is imparted merely by the friction of the grains against each other, and the heat generated; they are then ready for drying.

Drying. This is done in a drying room heated by steam-pipes at a heat of 125° F.; the powder is placed in copper trays.

Finishing. The drying process produces in all kinds of powder a small portion of dust which it is necessary to remove, but "finishing" also gives a final glaze, especially to fine-grain powders.

Finishing. R.F.G. and R.F.G^2. are finished by being reeled in a horizontal reel covered with 18-mesh canvas, making 45 revolutions in a minute. These powders when finished have a very glossy appearance, the denser R.F.G^2. taking the higher polish, and are ready to be put in barrels for use.

The following specification to guide the manufacture of R.F.G^2. gunpowder obtained from the contractors, shows the requirements for this nature of powder:—

Sample Barrel.—A sample barrel of powder to be sent from the Royal Gunpowder Factory, Waltham Abbey, as a guide to the Contractor in finishing the powder, and as regards the charcoal to be used.

1. *Ingredients.*—Every hundred parts of the gunpowder should contain 75 parts of pure saltpetre, 10 parts of pure sulphur, and 15 parts of charcoal made from the best selected *dogwood* charred in cylinders.

2. *Analysis.*—Samples may be selected from any portion of the gunpowder supplied and submitted to chemical examination and analysis.

The analysis should show:—

1st. That the saltpetre exists in a proportion of not less than 75 per cent., nor more than 76 per cent., and that not more than 1 part of chlorine, nor more than

4 parts of sodium are contained in 3000 parts of saltpetre.

2nd. That the proportion of sulphur is not less than 9·5 per cent., nor more than 10·5 per cent., and that it has been thoroughly freed from earthy matter and other impurities.

3rd. That the wood has been charred to the same extent, not less nor more than in manufacture at Waltham Abbey. The colour of the ground sample powder will be a guide to the Contractor.

3. *Flashing.*—Samples of the powder must show, on being fired on a clean glass plate, results similar to those given by an equal quantity of the sample.

4. *Size, Shape, and Colour of the Grain.*—The size of the powder to be from 1-12th to 1-20th of an inch.

To ascertain that the different sizes of grain are present in the same proportions as in the Waltham Abbey powder, samples will be sifted by hand on sieves respectively of eleven, sixteen, and twenty meshes to the *linear* inch, made with copper wire of No. 27 gauge.

The whole must pass through the 11-mesh sieve; out of 16 parts, 12 should be retained on the 16-mesh sieve; of the remainder, not less than 3 parts should be retained on the 20-inch sieve; 1 part may be allowed to pass the 20-mesh sieve.

In shape the grains must be compact, not flaky, nor flat.

The colour of the powder must be bright, showing that it has been glazed to the same extent as the sample; *no blacklead* must be used. The appearance of the sample Waltham Abbey powder will be a guide to the Contractor in this respect.

5. *Density.*—The absolute density of the finished powder must not exceed 1·75, nor be less than 1·72.

6. *Hygrometric Test.*—The powder when received must not contain less than ·9 per cent. nor more than 1·2 per cent. of moisture, and when it has been perfectly dried and exposed to an atmosphere saturated with moisture, temperature 62° F., should not absorb more than 2·75 per cent. in 24 hours.

7. *Velocity.*—The muzzle velocity imparted to a 480-grain Service bullet fired from a Martini-Henri rifle,

with the Service cartridge, charge 85 grains, to be proportionate to the amount of moisture it contains according to the following table:—

Percentage of Moisture.   Muzzle Velocity.

·9 to 1·0   not under   1310 f.s.
1·0 to 1·1   ,,   1300 ,,
1·1 to 1·2   ,,   1290 ,,

8. *Firing Proof at Royal Laboratory, Woolwich.*—Targets will be made at 500 yards range, with the powder fired from a Martini-Henry rifle Service cartridge, and it will be required to give *mean* results, as regards "*figure of merit*" of shooting, and *freedom from fouling* the rifle, equal to those afforded by the Waltham Abbey sample powder.

9. The powder to be delivered in barrels of one hundred pounds each.

The margin permitted for this powder on receipt at Woolwich is from 1290 f.s. to 1340 f.s., *i.e.*, a mean velocity of 1315 f.s. In the latest specification there is no high limit laid down

The charcoal used in R.F.G^2. powder is burnt slowly, and absorbs moisture more readily than quickly burnt charcoal; hence the importance of keeping this powder in a dry place.

The following memorandum on the subject of ventilation of magazines is important:—

Memorandum Respecting the Ventilation of Magazines.

1. The dampness complained of in buildings will frequently be found to arise from condensation of the watery vapour of the air which enters the building. Buildings with thick walls and vaulted roofs, and especially those covered with earth, are particularly liable to dampness from this cause.

2. Air always contains some proportion of watery vapour. When the proportion is small the air is said to be dry, and when large the air is said to be damp; when the proportion is the greatest that can be diffused through

air at a given temperature, the air is said to be saturated at that temperature.

3. The proportion of watery vapour which saturated air contains varies with the temperature, being greater for high than for low temperatures. Air containing a particular proportion of moisture is rendered less capable of depositing moisture by its temperature being raised, and the reverse when it is lowered.

4. Air may be brought to a state of saturation by reducing its temperature. If the air contain but little moisture, the reduction of temperature must be considerable; but if it contain much, a slight reduction will bring it to a state of saturation.

5. If air be cooled below the degree of temperature at which it will be in a state of saturation, a portion of the watery vapour contained therein will be deposited on any cold substance with which it may come in contact. The degree of temperature at which air will thus begin to deposit moisture is called its *dew-point*.

6. When warm air enters a comparatively cold building the temperature of the air is reduced by coming in contact with the interior walls and other cold surfaces; and if its temperature be thus reduced below the *dew-point*, condensation will take place. In the latter case it is obvious that the admission of fresh air will not tend to dry a building, but to render it damp.

7. Each magazine used for the permanent storage of powder should be provided with a common thermometer to indicate the temperature of the internal walls.

8. At each station the officer in charge should be supplied with a pair of wet-and-dry-bulb thermometers. These thermometers should be placed, when used for observations, in some spot in the open air protected from the sun and wind, and not exposed to any exceptional influences. The scale attached to the dry bulb will indicate the temperature of the external air. The scale attached to the wet bulb will indicate a temperature more or less below that of the air, in proportion to the quantity of moisture which the air contains, except in the case of its being completely saturated, when both scales will give similar readings. It is necessary for the

wet bulb to be always supplied with water, and its capillary threads and muslin covering kept in order.

The magazine must not be opened for ventilation unless—

(1.) The reading of the dry bulb thermometer is at least 3° higher than that of the wet bulb.
(2.) The reading of the thermometer inside the magazine is higher than the reading of the wet bulb thermometer outside.

Great care should be taken that the magazine is securely closed as soon as the above conditions cease to apply, or when the limit is approached.

Subject to the above direction magazines should be opened as often and for as long a time as possible, and every means should be adopted to secure a thorough circulation of air.

Lead as a Material for Bullets.

In selecting a metal for expanding bullets, there are several conditions to be observed, 1st, the metal should be as non-elastic as possible; 2nd, it should be sufficiently malleable that perfect expansion may be obtained by the action of the gunpowder; 3rd, it should be of sufficient hardness that its form should not be destroyed by the action of the gunpowder, and that it may destroy animal life; 4th, the metal should be of the greatest density possible; 5th, it should be of moderate cost.

Lead, which is a very common metal and easily obtained, is one of the most inelastic substances with which we are acquainted; it requires the least force of all the metals to perfect its expansion, and it makes but little effort to resume its former shape after it has been altered by any force impressed upon it. The mixture of any other metal with lead will affect its property of non-elasticity.

The Martini-Henry bullet is composed of 1 part of tin to 12 of lead, its elasticity and power of resistance to a crushing force is greater than that of pure lead.

In using a hardening material in combination with

lead, care should be taken to use no more of it than is necessary to attain the required object, in order to retain as much density and expanding power as possible. By hardening lead its penetrating power in one sense is increased, but its density and power of expansion are diminished.

The greater the windage and depth of grooving, the greater must necessarily be the expanding property of the metal used in the manufacture of bullets. The windage of the Snider rifle being ·027, pure lead is absolutely necessary for its projectiles.

Chapter VI.

SMALL-ARM AMMUNITION. CARTRIDGE CASES. WADS AND LUBRICATION. SNIDER AND MARTINI-HENRY CARTRIDGES. PROFESSOR BASHFORTH'S GENERAL TABLES, WITH EXAMPLES WORKED OUT BY THEM.

Small-Arm Ammunition.

However perfect in every respect a rifle may be made, it will not shoot accurately unless care is taken to make up suitable ammunition to be used with it.

As many advances have of late years been made in the improvement of cartridges as in the perfecting of breech-loading arms themselves.

When deciding on the nature of a cartridge for a military arm, the points to be considered are :—

1. The weight and form of the bullet.
2. The powder charge.
3. The description of cartridge case, its weight and form.
4. The nature of wads.
5. The lubrication of the bullet.

The weight of the bullet. The weight of the bullet, for a rifle of any given calibre, depends on the twist of rifling and the powder charge to be used; for the longer (*i.e.*, the heavier) the bullet is, the greater must be its velocity of rotation in order that it may fly point foremost.

A low trajectory is also to be desired, and this cannot be obtained if the weight of the bullet is unduly great when compared with that of the powder, producing a low muzzle velocity.

The weight of the bullet also must not be too great, in order that the soldier may be able to carry a sufficient number of rounds.

If the bullet is made very light, a high muzzle velocity

and a low trajectory are obtained at short ranges, but as the sectional density of the bullet is small, the velocity soon decreases, and for long ranges the trajectory becomes very high.

It will therefore be seen that the bullet which will give the best results must have both a good sectional density and a high muzzle velocity.

The weight of the powder charge is regulated by the weight of the rifle and the bullet, as has already been explained when dealing with recoil.

Powder charge.

If the recoil is not excessive, the greater the powder charge is made the better, as the muzzle velocity cannot be too high.

It may be objected that the fouling increases with the amount of the powder charge, but when suitable wads are made use of the fouling need not be feared.

The following table gives the proportion which the weight of the powder charge bears to the weight of the bullet in cartridges fired from various military arms, and the muzzle velocities imparted to the bullets.

TABLE showing relation between Charge and Muzzle Velocity.

Country.	Nature of Rifle.	Calibre.	Weight of Bullet.	Powder Charge.	Proportion of Powder to Bullet.	Muzzle Velocity.
		inch.	grains.	grains.		Feet per second.
America	Springfield	0·45	500	70	1 : 7·143	1301
Austria	Werndl	0·433	370	75	1 : 4·805	1439
Denmark	Remington	0·433	400	75	1 : 5·33	1340
Egypt	Remington	0·433	400	75	1 : 5·33	1340
France	Gras	0·433	386	80	1 : 4·82	1489
Germany	Mauser	0·433	380	75	1 : 5·066	1430
Great Britain	Snider	0·577	480	70	1 : 6·857	1240
" "	Martini-Henry	0·45	480	85	1 : 5·65	1315
Holland	Beaumont	0·433	378	77	1 : 4·9	1332
Italy	Vetterli	0·408	310	60	1 : 5·16	1430
Japan	Murata	0·432	420	83	1 : 5·06	1487
Norway and Sweden	Remington	0·433	400	75	1 : 5·33	1340
Russia	Berdan	0·42	371	77	1 : 4·743	1444
Spain	Remington	0·433	400	75	1 : 5·33	1340
Switzerland	Vetterli (magazine)	0·409	310	55	1 : 5·63	1314
Turkey	Peabody-Martini	0·45	480	85	1 : 5·65	1380

Cartridge Cases.

Cartridge cases.

The cartridge case must combine the qualities of strength and lightness, and be of such a form as to render the operation of extracting the empty case from the chamber of the rifle as easy as possible.

Brass is the alloy which has generally been selected as the most suitable material from which to form the cases, for it is light, ductile, and elastic.

The case must be made sufficiently strong to withstand the strain it is subjected to on ignition of the powder charge, because if the case gives way its extraction may be difficult, or portions of the case may be left in the bore causing a burst or bulged barrel when the next round is fired, or pieces may be blown back and completely jam the breech action.

On the other hand, it is of importance to make the case as light as possible in order that the soldier may have the least amount of unnecessary weight to carry.

Cartridge cases of rolled sheet brass, such as those for the Snider and Martini-Henry rifles, possess ample strength and lightness, but they have the disadvantage of being easily deformed (when they do not completely fill the chamber), and they do not preserve the powder from damp as well as the solid drawn cases.

The following table gives particulars as to various military cartridge cases:—

Country.	Nature of Rifle.	Cartridge Cases.	
		Nature.	Weight, including wads and lubrications.
			grains.
America	Springfield	Central fire, brass, solid drawn, conical	182
Austria	Werndl	Central fire, brass, solid drawn, bottle-shape	269
Denmark	Remington	Central fire, brass, solid drawn, bottle-shape	109
Egypt	Remington	Central fire, brass, solid drawn, bottle-shape	109
France	Gras	Central fire, brass, solid drawn, bottle shape	216
Germany	Mauser	Central fire, brass, solid drawn, bottle-shape	195
Great Britain	Snider	Central fire, brass, rolled, cylindrical	165
" "	Martini-Henry	Central fire, brass, rolled, bottle-shape	193
Holland	Beaumont	Central fire, brass, solid drawn, bottle-shape	216
Italy	Vetterli	Central fire, brass, solid drawn, bottle-shape	103
Japan	Murata	Central fire, brass, solid drawn, bottle-shape	194
Norway and Sweden	Remington	Central fire, brass, solid drawn, bottle-shape	109
Russia	Berdan	Central fire, brass, solid drawn, bottle-shape	163
Spain	Remington	Central fire, brass, solid drawn, bottle-shape	109
Switzerland	Vetterli (magazine)	Rim fire, pinchbeck,* solid drawn, bottle-shape	100
Turkey	Peabody-Martini	Central fire, brass, solid drawn, bottle-shape	237

It will be seen from this table that the Swiss rifle is the only one which has a "*rim-fire*" cartridge, *i.e.*, a cartridge which contains the detonating powder in the rim round the base, instead of in a cap placed in the centre of its base disc. The central fire cartridge is much superior to the rim fire; it requires much less detonating composition, and it is much better protected from accidental explosion. It also permits the reinforcing of the rim internally by a cup, thus strengthening the weakest portion of the cartridge case.

* Pinchbeck is composed of three parts of copper to one part of zinc. Brass is usually composed of two parts of copper to one part of zinc.

The Snider cartridge is the only cylindrical, and the Springfield the only conical form of case, the remainder (except the Martini-Henry cartridge which has a larger base), being all somewhat similar in form to the Gatling case, or what is commonly known as the bottle-shaped cartridge.

(See plates of these four forms of cartridge).

The more conical a cartridge case is made, the easier it will be to extract the empty case after firing, but this form has not been generally adopted owing to difficulties attending its manufacture.

Wads and Lubrication.

Wads.

Most cartridges for military rifles have wads of some kind between the powder charge and the base of the bullet, the use of these wads being two-fold, viz., to prevent any of the powder gas escaping round the bullet on the ignition of the charge and before the bullet has been set up into the grooves, and to partially clear the bore of fouling.

When no wads, or when inferior wads are used, some of the gas invariably escapes round the bullet before it receives the full shock necessary to set it up, the result being that there is a loss of power, and that fouling is deposited on the surface of the bore in front of the bullet. When this happens, the bore soon "*leads*," and accurate shooting is impossible.

It used to be generally supposed that wads of wax or grease lubricated the interior surface of the barrel as they were driven from the breech to muzzle, and in fact were gradually expended as they passed up the bore by being smeared on its surface. That this is not the case can easily be proved by an examination of the wax wads which have been fired from a Martini-Henry rifle. Numbers of these wads can be picked up on any range where these rifles are fired, and they will be found to be of the same weight as similar wads taken from unfired cartridges, and only differing from them in having been set up into the rifling.

The following table gives the nature of wads used in loading cartridges for various military rifles:—

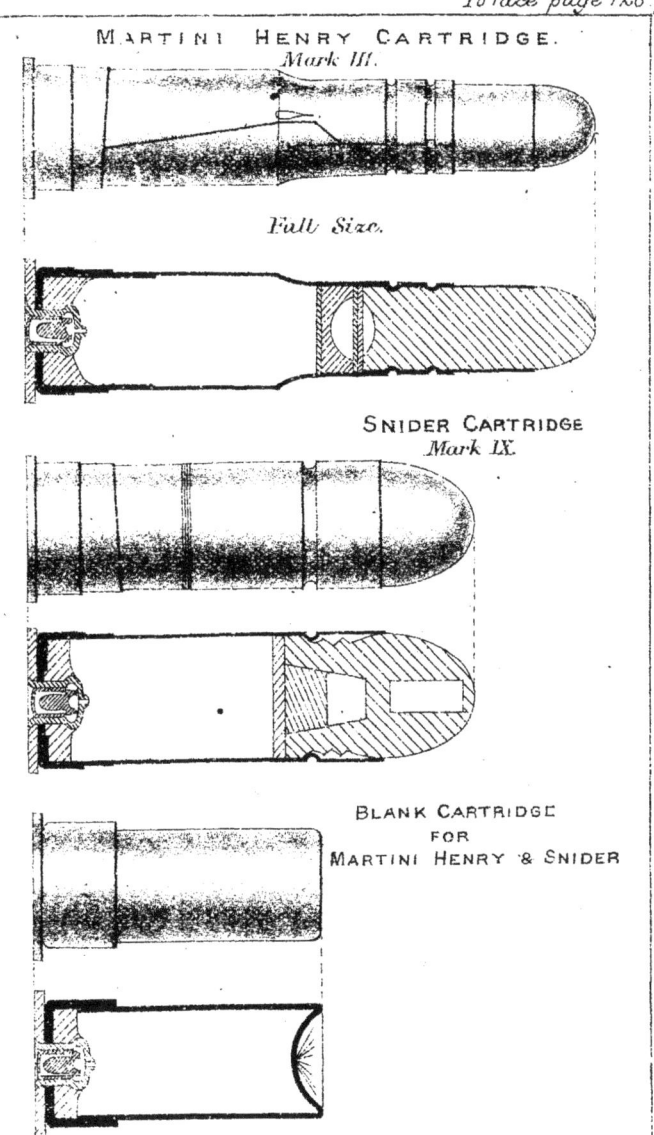

To face page 128.

0".45 GATLING CARTRIDGE.
SOLID DRAWN CASE.

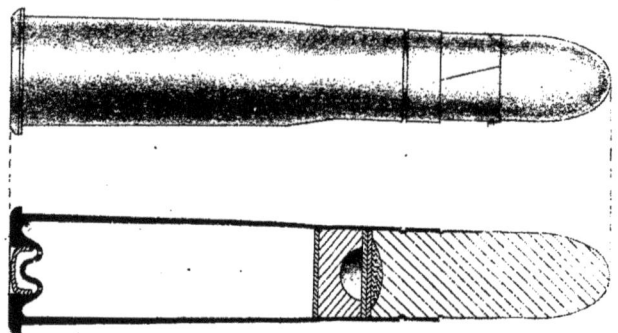

AMERICAN (SPRINGFIELD) CARTRIDGE
SOLID DRAWN TAPER CASE.

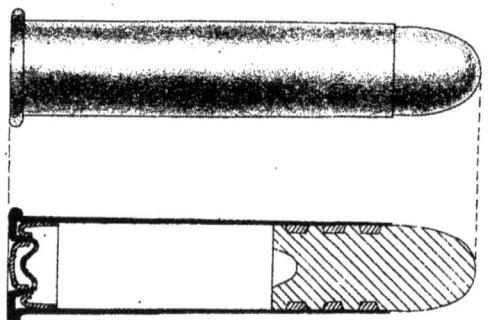

FULL SIZE.

Country.	Nature of Rifle.	Wads.	Lubrication of Bullet.
America	Springfield	None	3 cannelures on bullet filled with wax.
Austria	Werndl	Wax wad between card wads	Papered bullet, tallow on head.
Denmark	Remington	1 millboard, 1 grease, 1 card wad	Bullet papered and greased.
Egypt	Remington	1 millboard, 1 grease, 1 card wad	Bullet papered and greased.
France	Gras	Wax wad between card wads	Papered bullet, tallow on head.
Germany	Mauser	Wax wad between card wads	Papered bullet.
Great Britain	Snider	Cotton between powder and bullet	3 cannelures on bullet filled with wax.
,, ,, {	Martini-Henry	Wax wad, 2 card wads in front and 1 behind	Waxed paper round bullet.
Holland	Beaumont	1 felt and 1 grease wad	Cannelures in bullet filled with wax.
Italy	Vetterli	None	3 cannelures on bullet filled with wax.
Japan	Murata	2 cardboard wads	Wax in cannelures and over head.
Norway and Sweden	Remington	1 millboard, 1 grease, 1 card	Bullet papered and greased.
Russia	Berdan	Grease wad in paper envelope	Bullet papered and greased.
Spain	Remington	1 millboard, 1 grease, 1 card	Bullet papered and greased.
Switzerland {	Vetterli (magazine)	None	Bullet papered and greased.
Turkey {	Peabody-Martini	Wax wad between card wads	Waxed paper round bullet.

It will be seen from this table that with the Snider, the Springfield, the Vetterli, and the Vetterli magazine rifles, no wads are used.

As already stated, the wads do not lubricate the surface of the bore, but rather tend to remove the fouling by their scouring action.

The lubrication is effected by some substance such as grease, wax, or a mixture of them, which is either smeared on the paper round the bullet, or in the case of a naked bullet fills one or more cannelures, which encircle the cylindrical portion.

Lubrication.

Wax is a better lubricant than grease, as the latter melts at a low temperature, and corrodes lead when in contact with it. Lubrication is of advantage, as it prevents the fouling from taking a firm hold on the surface of the bore, and so renders its removal easier.

Papering the cylindrical portion of the bullet tends to

prevent the grooves and surface of the bore from becoming "*leaded*," but if there is much fouling in the bore it is certain, after a time, to become leaded, even though the bullet is papered.

Some idea may be formed of the great necessity for reducing the weight of the cartridge as much as possible, without injuring its efficiency, from an examination of the following table:—

TABLE comparing the Weight of Rifle and 70 Rounds of Ammunition in British and Foreign Armies.

Country.	Nature of Rifle.	Calibre.	Weight the Soldier has to Carry.		
			Rifle without Bayonet.	70 rounds Ammunition.	Total.
		inch.	lbs. oz.	lbs. oz.	lbs. ozs.
America ...	Springfield ...	0·45	9 5¼	7 8	16 13¼
Austria .	Werndl ...	0·433	9 13½	6 8	16 5½
Denmark ...	Remington ...	0·433	9 5½	6 11	16 0
Egypt	Remington ...	0·433	9 5½	6 11	16 0
France ...	Gras	0·433	9 11	6 13	16 8
Germany ...	Mauser ...	0·433	10 4	6 8	16 12
Great Britain	Snider ...	0·577	9 0¾	7 2¼	16 2¼
" "	Martini-Henry ...	0·45	9 0	7 9¼	16 9¼
Holland ...	Beaumont ...	0·433	9 11	6 11	16 6
Italy	Vetterli ...	0·408	9 9	5 1½	14 10½
Japan	Murata ...	0·432	9 10	6 15½	16 9½
Norway and Sweden	Remington ...	0·433	9 5½	6 11	16 0
Russia	Berdan ...	0·42	9 12½	6 1½	15 14
Spain	Remington ...	0·433	9 5½	6 11	16 0
Switzerland	Vetterli (magazine)	0·409	10 6	4 10¼	15 0
Turkey	Peabody-Martini ...	0·45	9 10	8 0½	17 10½

Description of the Snider Cartridge.

The same description of cartridge is used for all the B.L. small-arms with Snider action in the Service. The diameter of the bore is ·577 inch, the diameter of the bullet is ·573 inch, small enough to drop through the bore, and, depending on expansion for its fit; the length of the bullet is about 1 inch (1·04 inch in present pattern), and the length of the cartridge is a very little under 2½ inches. The charge is 70 grs. (very nearly 2¼ drs.) of R.F.G. Each packet of ten rounds weighs about 1 lb.

The bullet is made from pure lead, weight 480 grs.; the hollow in the head is closed by having the lead spun over it, the hollow parts are necessary in order to get the bullet of a sufficient length for good shooting, without unduly incraesing its weight, and to get its centre of gravity in the proper place; the hollow in the base is also used to give the expansive action to the bullet; the plug, made of clay, and soaked in beeswax, closes the rear cavity, and on firing expands the bullet, which has three cannelures; the sides of the bullet as far as the front cannelure are coated with beeswax, the cannelures holding a sufficient supply of the lubricant in their recesses; by the expansion of the bullet the lubricant is squeezed out, and the bore is thoroughly cleaned out by the bullets passing through it. As many as 4000 rounds have been fired without fouling sufficiently to injure the shooting.

The case is formed of sheet brass covered with brown paper. It is lined with shellac and thin white paper to prevent corrosion from the powder. The case overlaps by about ¼ inch, and is cemented together with shellac and glue. It is attached to the bullet by being choked into the rear cannelure; the base is strengthened by two cups, and the bottom closed by an iron disc; inside, a paper pellet is pressed against the bottom of the cartridge, a brass cap chamber pierced with a fire-hole passes through the base and rivets the bottom of the cartridge to the case, the top being bulged out over the paper pellet, and the base of the cap chamber being flanged to fit the recess in the iron base disc; the cap chamber holds a brass anvil, on the shoulders of which rests the copper cap, which is primed with cap composition (fulminate of mercury, sulphide of antimony, and chlorate of potash) and varnished. A little wool is placed over the powder to keep it from touching the bullet.

On firing, the cap composition is forced against the point of the anvil, and the flash reaches the charge through the hole in the chamber; the case unwinds, and being pressed firmly against the sides of the bore prevents the gas from escaping in the direction of the breech; after firing, the cartridge contracts to its original proportions making extraction easy.

The base of the cartridge is very strong owing to its base cups and disc, and it is at the base that strength is essential; indeed if the base is perfect, a very faulty cartridge may be fired without throwing any undue strain on the breech.

The cartridge is found to stand rough usage and wet well; what tries it most is a moist hot climate; it is almost impossible to prevent the moist air from penetrating when aided by great variations of temperature. Experiments have shown that it is impossible to explode these cartridges in a mass, thus firing $\frac{1}{4}$ lb. of powder along with a number of cartridges in an iron cylinder hardly exploded any rounds.

The same blank ammunition suits either Snider or Martini-Henry rifles.

Buck-shot cartridges. A special cartridge containing buck-shot has been issued to convict prisons; it is adapted for the Snider Enfield. Mark I, charge in a pellet and shot embedded in plaster of Paris; Mark II, charge loose and shot in bone-dust; the latter is far superior. It is effective to about 50 yards.

Martini-Henry Ammunition.

The bore of the Martini-Henry rifle is ·45 inch; the bullet is made of lead hardened with tin, 1·27 inch long, weight 480 grs. (12 lead to 1 tin), its diameter increases from ·439 inch at the shoulder to ·45 inch at the base; the small hollow in the base of the bullet tends to expand it, and the great length of the bullet causes it to set up in the bore and fill the grooves; two cannelures allow the cartridges to be secured to the bullet by choking. The charge is 85 grs. of R.F.G^2.

In general construction the cartridge resembles the Snider. The case consists of two turns and an overlap of ·5 inch of ·004 inch brass, and in addition to the two base cups has a strip of brass ·004 inch thick inserted between the folds of the case at the base of the cartridge.* The cartridge is made of a bottle-necked shape by crimping in the upper part so as to make it fit into the short chamber of the rifle; before this change was made the cartridge was found to be inconveniently long. The bullet has two turns of fine white parchment paper wrapped round it from right to left, and lubricated at the base for about half its length in beeswax; the object of the paper is to prevent leading, and it untwists in passing through the bore.

Over the powder in the cartridge a cardboard disc is placed, then a wad of beeswax,† and then two more cardboard discs; the bullet is choked in the usual manner into the case; the cartridge is a little over 3 inches in length.

Packing.—In tens, packed heads and tails, in brown paper; 10 rounds weigh a little over 1 lb.

The comparative accuracy of the Snider and Martini-Henry is shown by the figure of merit obtained in firing new ammunition from a fixed rest at a range of 500 yards; the figure of merit of the Snider is about 14 inches, and that of the Martini-Henry about 9 inches; the latter having also the advantage of a flatter trajectory.

Martini-Henry Carbine Ammunition.—The same ammunition serves for the Martini-Henry cavalry carbine and for the Artillery carbine. The chambers for the Martini-Henry rifles and carbines being alike, the cartridge for the carbine is the same in construction and dimensions as that for the rifle, except in the following particulars. The bullet is ·12 inch shorter, and only weighs 410 grains. The charge of powder is 70 grains R.F.G^2. The total length of the cartridge is 2·98 inches $\pm$ ·05 inch.

In the Mark I cartridge the vacant space in the case was filled by introducing ·7 grain of carded cotton immediately on top of the powder; but the use of this cotton-wool having been found to cause irregular shooting, Mark II was introduced, in which the brass strip forming the body of the case was lined with brown

---

* To enable the examiner to see that this strip is in proper position, a small "sight-hole" is punched in the outer fold of the case.

† The beeswax wad is hollowed out to ensure its expanding in cold weather.

paper, so as to fill up a space equivalent to that which was occupied by the wool. Occasional misses still occurred with this ammunition, owing to the length of the carbine barrel being insufficient always to detach the paper from the bullet, and Mark III ammunition was consequently introduced, in which the disengagement of the paper is ensured by three longitudinal cuts, made through the paper after being lubricated.

The rifle ammunition might be used from the carbine, or *vice versâ*, on an emergency, but the sighting of course would not in either case be correct. For ready distinction the paper round the bullet of the carbine cartridge will in future be red.

Packing.—The same as for the rifle. The bundle of 10 rounds weighs 1 lb.

Two cartridges have been made for the Gatling guns, one for the ·45 bore, and one for the ·65 bore.

The ·45 cartridge is a solid case, lacquered inside, and containing the same powder charge, wads, and bullet as the Martini-Henry rifle cartridge. The cartridge case is too small for the Martini-Henry rifle.

No anvil is used; the cap is fired by being driven against a nipple in the base, pierced to allow the flash to pass into the charge.

Ammunition for Enfield Pistol.—The cartridge case is of solid drawn brass; the bullet of lead and tin, weight 265 grains; and the powder charge 18 grains of pistol powder.

Muzzle Velocity.

The Le Boulengé chronograph is the apparatus which is now generally used for determining the velocity of bullets, though many other instruments have been invented for this purpose.

The chronograph merely records the velocity of the bullet at a point midway between the wire screens used in conjunction with the instrument, or gives the "*observed velocity,*" and Bashforth's general tables are required in order to find the amount of velocity lost by the bullet while passing from the muzzle to this point. When this is added to the observed velocity, the muzzle velocity is obtained. The use of the Bashforth general tables is explained by problems which are worked out with their aid.

The Application of Professor Bashforth's General Tables to Problems on the Flight of Rifle Bullets.

These general tables are applicable to any elongated bullet with an ogival head, when its weight and diameter are known.

If d = diameter of the bullet in inches,
  w = weight of the bullet in lbs.,
  s = range in feet,
  t = time of flight in seconds.

Then $\dfrac{d^2}{w} \times s = $ reduced range (Table II),

and $\dfrac{d^2}{w} \times t = $ reduced time (Table I).

Examples.

1. With what velocity would a Martini-Henry bullet strike a target at 1000 yards range? (The muzzle velocity is 1315 feet per second.)

d = the diameter of the bullet in inches = 0·45 inch.

w = the weight of the bullet in lbs. = $\dfrac{480}{7000}$

s = range = 1000 yards = 3000 feet.

Reduced range = $\dfrac{d^2}{w} \times s = 2\cdot953 \times 3000 = 8859$ ft.

Now, corresponding to velocity 1315 in Table II, is found—

42259·8 feet.
Subtracting reduced range 8859·0 ,,
───────
33400·8 ,,

which, by an inverse process in the same table, corresponds to a velocity of 664 feet per second nearly.

Therefore, the striking velocity at 1000 yards is 664 feet per second.

2. With what velocity will a Martini-Henry bullet be travelling at the end of 3 seconds? (Muzzle velocity = 1315 feet per second.)

$$Reduced\ time = \frac{d^2}{w} \times t = 2{\cdot}953 \times 3 = 8{\cdot}859\ secs.$$

Corresponding to velocity 1315 in Table I, is found—

231·6690 seconds
Subtracting reduced time,   8·859   ,,
_____
222·8100 ,,

which, by an inverse process in the same table, corresponds to a velocity of 701 feet per second, nearly.

Therefore, the remaining velocity after 3 seconds' time of flight, is about 701 feet per second.

3. What would be the time of flight of a Martini-Henry bullet over a range of 2000 yards? (Muzzle velocity = 1315 feet per second.)

We must first find the remaining velocity at 2000 yds., as in example 1.

$$Reduced\ range = \frac{d^2}{w} \times s = 2{\cdot}953 \times 6000 = 17718\ ft.$$

Corresponding to velocity 1315 in Table II, is found—

42259·8 feet
Subtracting reduced range 17718·0 ,,
_____
24541·8 ,,

which, by an inverse process in the same table, corresponds to a velocity of 389 feet per second, nearly.

Therefore the remaining velocity at 2000 yards is 389 feet per second.

The question now resolves itself to this:—In what time will the velocity of the Martini-Henry bullet be reduced from 1315 to 389 feet per second?

Now, $reduced\ time = \frac{d^2}{w} \times t = 2{\cdot}953t.$

Corresponding to velocity 1315 in Table I, is found—

231·6690 seconds,
and corresponding to } 203·835   ,,
  velocity 389   = }
_____
Subtracting   27·8340 ,,   = *reduced time.*
Therefore, $2{\cdot}953t$ = 27·8340 ,,
    and t = 9·42 ,,

4. In what range would the velocity of a Snider bullet be reduced from 1240 to 500 feet per second? $d = 0.577$ inch, $w = 480$ grains.

$Reduced\ range = \dfrac{d^2}{w} \times s = 4.855 \times s.$

Corresponding to velocity 1240 in Table II, is found—

41837·5 feet

and corresponding to velocity 500 } 28704·3 ,,

Subtracting .. 13133·2 ,, = *reduced range*.
Therefore $4.855s = 13133.2$,,
and $s = 2705.087$ feet $= 901.695$ yards.

5. The time of flight of a Snider bullet is observed to be 3 seconds; the muzzle velocity is known to be 1240 feet per second. Find the striking velocity and range.

$Reduced\ time = \dfrac{d^2}{w} t = 4.855 \times 3 = 14.565$ seconds.

Corresponding to velocity 1240 in Table I, we find—

231·3381 seconds
Subtracting *reduced time*   14·565   ,,
───────────
216·7731   ,,

which corresponds to a velocity in the same table of 559 feet per second, nearly.

Therefore the striking velocity = 559 feet per second.

Now to find the range,

$Reduced\ range = \dfrac{d^2}{w} \times s = 4.855 \times s.$

Corresponding to velocity 1240 in Table II, is found—

41837·5 feet,

and corresponding to velocity 559 } 30534·3 ,,

Subtracting .. 11303·2 ,, = *reduced range*.
Therefore $4.855\ s =$ 11303·2 ,,
and $s =$ 2328·15 ,, $= 776.05$ yards.

6. The range of a Snider bullet is observed to be

138

900 yards. What is its striking velocity and time of flight? (Muzzle velocity = 1240 feet per second.)

$$\text{Reduced range} = \frac{d^2}{w} s = 4\cdot 855 \times 900 \times 3 = 13108\cdot 5 \text{ feet.}$$

Corresponding to velocity 1240 in Table II, is found—

41837·5 feet
Subtract reduced range   13108·5 „
——————
28729·0 „

which corresponds to 501 feet per second, nearly.

Therefore the striking velocity is 501 feet per second

$$\text{Reduced time} = \frac{d^2}{w} t = 4\cdot 855 t.$$

In Table I, corresponding to velocity 1240, is .. } 231·3381 secs.
And corresponding to velocity 501 is .. } 213·3814 „

Subtracting .. ..   17·9567 reduced time.
Therefore $4\cdot 855 t = 17\cdot 9567$ seconds,
     and $t = 3\cdot 69$ „

Approximate Method of Finding Trajectories.

Find the trajectory of the Martini-Henry rifle bullet at 500 yards range. Muzzle velocity = 1315 feet per second. Weight of bullet = 480 grains. Diameter of bullet = 0·45 inch.

The height of points on the trajectory at any desired intervals may be found; but for sake of example they will only be found at intervals of every 100 yards.

First, by Table II, the remaining velocity must be found at every 100 yards.

$$\text{Reduced range} = \frac{d^2}{w} \times s = 2\cdot 953 \times 100 \times 3 = 885\cdot 9 \text{ feet.}$$

In Table II for velocity 1315 = } 42259·8
Subtracting reduced range for 100 yards= } 885·9
―――――
41373·9 = 1167 vel. at 100 yds.
885·9
―――――
40488·0 = 1053 ,, 200 ,,
885·9
―――――
39602·1 = 982 ,, 300 ,,
885·9
―――――
38716·2 = 922 ,, 400 ,,
885·9
―――――
37830·3 = 869 ,, 500 ,,

We must now find the time of flight over these intervals.

1. To find the time per 100 yards range; velocity = 1167 f.s.

$Reduced\ time = \dfrac{d^2}{w}t = 2·953t.$

Table I for vel. 1315 = 231·6690
,, 1167 = 230·9548
―――――
0·7142

$\therefore t = \dfrac{0·7142}{2·953} = 0·24186$ second.

2. Time over 200 yards; vel. = 1053 f.s.
for vel. 1315 = 231·6690
,, 1053 = 230·1520
―――――
1·5170

$t = \dfrac{1·5170}{2·953} = 0·51372$ second.

3. Time over 300 yards; vel. = 982 f.s.
for vel. 1315 = 231·6690
,, 982 = 229·2737
―――――
2·3953

$$t = \frac{2\cdot3953}{2\cdot953} = 0\cdot81114 \text{ second.}$$

4. Time over 400 yards; vel. = 922 f.s.
for vel. 1315 = 231·6690
,,   922 = 228·3432
─────────
3·3258

$$t = \frac{3\cdot3258}{2\cdot953} = 1\cdot1262 \text{ seconds.}$$

5. Time over 500 yards; vel. = 869 f.s.
for vel. 1315 = 231·6690
,,   869 = 227·3549
─────────
4·3141

$$t = \frac{4\cdot3141}{2\cdot953} = 1\cdot4609 \text{ seconds.}$$

The following results have now been obtained:—

Range.	Remaining velocity.	Time of flight.
yards.	feet per second.	seconds.
0	1315	0·0000
100	1167	0·24186
200	1053	0·51372
300	982	0·81114
400	922	1·1262
500	869	1·4609

When the time over a given range is known, the corresponding height of trajectory is given by the equation

$$y = \frac{g}{2} t (T - t);$$

where T is the whole time of flight, and t the time over given range.

Thus, at 100 yards $t = 0\cdot24186$ second.

$y_{100} = 16\cdot1 \times 0\cdot24186 \times 1\cdot2190 = 4\cdot7466$ feet.
$y_{200} = 16\cdot1 \times 0\cdot51372 \times 0\cdot9472 = 7\cdot8341$,,
$y_{300} = 16\cdot1 \times 0\cdot81114 \times 0\cdot6498 = 8\cdot4860$,,
$y_{400} = 16\cdot1 \times 1\cdot1262 \times 0\cdot3347 = 6\cdot069$,,
$y_{500} = 16\cdot1 \times 1\cdot4609 \times 0 = 0$,,

141

Greatest height of trajectory $= \dfrac{g}{8} T^2 = \dfrac{32 \cdot 2}{8}(1 \cdot 4609)^2$
$= 8 \cdot 594$ feet.

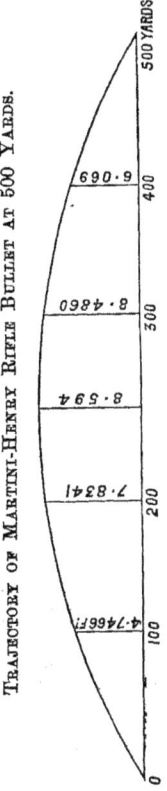

For low angles of elevation, trajectories computed on this principles are very approximately correct.

Table I.

A General Table of Values of $\dfrac{d^2}{w}t$ for Ogival-headed Bullets.

v.	0	1	2	3	4	5	6	7	8	9	Diff.
f.s.	secs.	secs.	secs.	secs.	secs.	secs.	secs.	secs.	secs.	secs.	+
10	75·399	77·111	78·790	80·437	82·052	83·636	85·190	86·715	88·212	89·682	1·584
11	91·125	92·542	93·934	95·301	96·644	97·964	99·261	*00·536	*01·789	*03·021	1·320
12	1 04·232	05·423	06·595	07·748	08·883	09·999	11·097	12·178	13·243	14·291	1·116
13	1 15·323	16·389	17·340	18·326	19·297	20·254	21·196	22·124	23·039	23·941	·957
14	24·830	25·706	26·570	27·422	28·262	29·091	29·908	30·714	31·509	32·294	·829
15	33·068	33·832	34·586	35·331	36·066	36·792	37·508	38·215	38·913	39·602	·726
16	1 40·283	40·955	41·618	42·273	42·920	43·559	44·190	44·813	45·429	46·038	·639
17	46·640	47·235	47·823	48·404	48·978	49·546	50·107	50·662	51·211	51·754	·568
18	52·291	52·822	53·347	53·867	54·381	54·890	55·393	55·890	56·382	56·869	·509
19	1 57·351	57·828	58·300	58·767	59·229	59·686	60·138	60·586	61·029	61·468	·457
20	61·902	62·332	62·758	63·180	63·598	64·012	64·422	64·828	65·230	65·628	·414
21	66·022	66·412	66·798	67·181	67·560	67·936	68·308	68·676	69·041	69·403	·376
22	1 69·762	70·118	70·470	70·819	71·165	71·508	71·848	72·185	72·519	72·850	·343
23	73·179	73·505	73·828	74·148	74·465	74·780	75·092	75·401	75·708	76·012	·315
24	76·314	76·613	76·909	77·203	77·494	77·783	78·070	78·354	78·636	78·916	·289
25	1 79·194	79·470	79·743	80·014	80·283	80·550	80·815	81·078	81·339	81·598	·267
26	81·855	82·110	82·363	82·614	82·863	83·110	83·355	83·598	83·839	84·079	·247
27	84·317	84·553	84·787	85·020	85·251	85·481	85·709	85·935	86·160	86·382	·230
28	1 86·604	86·824	87·042	87·259	87·474	87·688	87·900	88·111	88·320	88·528	·214
29	88·734	88·939	89·143	89·345	89·546	89·745	89·943	90·140	90·335	90·529	·199
30	90·721	90·912	91·102	91·291	91·478	91·664	91·849	92·033	92·216	92·397	·186
31	1 92·577	92·756	92·934	93·111	93·287	93·461	93·634	93·806	93·971	94·147	·174
32	94·316	94·484	94·651	94·817	94·982	95·146	95·309	95·471	95·632	95·792	·164
33	95·951	96·109	96·266	96·422	96·577	96·731	96·884	97·036	97·187	97·338	·154
34	1 97·488	97·637	97·785	97·932	98·078	98·223	98·367	98·510	98·652	98·794	·145
35	98·935	99·075	99·214	99·352	99·490	99·627	99·763	99·898	*00·032	*00·166	·137
36	2 00·299	00·431	00·562	00·692	00·822	00·951	01·079	01·206	01·333	01·459	·129
37	2 01·585	01·710	01·834	01·957	02·080	02·202	02·323	02·443	02·563	02·682	·122
38	02·801	02·919	03·036	03·152	03·268	03·383	03·497	03·610	03·723	03·835	·115
39	03·947	04·058	04·168	04·278	04·387	04·496	04·604	04·711	04·818	04·924	·109
40	20 5·0299	5·1349	5·2393	5·3432	5·4466	5·5494	5·6517	5·7534	5·8546	5·9553	·1028
41	6·0554	6·1550	6·2540	6·3525	6·4505	6·5480	6·6450	6·7414	6·8373	6·9327	·0975
42	7·0276	7·1220	7·2159	7·3093	7·4022	7·4947	7·5867	7·6782	7·7693	7·8599	·0925
43	20 7·9501	8·0398	8·1291	8·2179	8·3063	8·3942	8·4817	8·5687	8·6553	8·7415	·0879
44	8·8272	8·9125	8·9974	9·0819	9·1660	9·2497	9·3330	9·4159	9·4984	9·5805	·0837
45	9·6622	9·7435	9·8244	9·9050	9·9852	*0·0651	*0·1446	*0·2237	*0·3025	*0·3809	·0799
46	21 0·4590	0·5367	0·6140	0·6910	0·7677	0·8440	0·9200	0·9956	1·0709	1·1459	·0763
47	1·2205	1·2948	1·3687	1·4423	1·5156	1·5886	1·6613	1·7336	1·8056	1·8773	·0730
48	1·9487	2·0198	2·0906	2·1611	2·2313	2·3012	2·3708	2·4401	2·5091	2·5779	·0699
49	21 2·6464	2·7146	2·7825	2·8501	2·9174	2·9845	3·0513	3·1178	3·1841	3·2501	·0671
50	3·3159	3·3814	3·4466	3·5116	3·5763	3·6608	3·7050	3·7689	3·8326	3·8960	·0645
51	3·9592	4·0221	4·0848	4·1472	4·2094	4·2713	4·3330	4·3944	4·4556	4·5165	·0619

TABLE I.—continued.

A General Table of Values of $\dfrac{d^2}{w}t$ for Ogival-headed Bullets.

v	0	1	2	3	4	5	6	7	8	9	Diff.
f.s.	secs.	secs.	secs.	secs.	secs.	secs.	secs.	secs.	secs.	secs.	+
52	21 4·5772	4·6377	4·6979	4·7579	4·8177	4·8773	4·9367	4·9958	5·0547	5·1134	·0596
53	5·1719	5·2302	5·2882	5·3460	5·4036	5·4610	5·5182	5·5752	5·6320	5·6886	·0574
54	5·7450	5·8012	5·8572	5·9130	5·9686	6·0240	6·0792	6·1342	6·1890	6·2436	·0554
55	21 6·2980	6·3522	6·4062	6·4600	6·5136	6·5670	6·6202	6·6732	6·7260	6·7786	·0534
56	6·8311	6·8834	6·9355	6·9874	7·0391	7·0907	7·1421	7·1933	7·2444	7·2953	·0516
57	7·3460	7·3965	7·4469	7·4971	7·5471	7·5970	7·6467	7·6962	7·7456	7·7948	·0499
58	21 7·8438	7·8928	7·9417	7·9904	8·0389	8·0873	8·1356	8·1837	8·2316	8·2793	·0483
59	8·3271	8·3746	8·4220	8·4692	8·5163	8·5632	8·6100	8·6566	8·7031	8·7494	·0468
60	8·7957	8·8417	8·8877	8·9334	8·9791	9·0246	9·0700	9·1152	9·1603	9·2052	·0454
61	21 9·2501	9·2947	9·3393	9·3837	9·4280	9·4721	9·5161	9·5600	9·6037	9·6473	·0441
62	9·6908	9·7341	9·7773	9·8204	9·8633	9·9062	9·9489	9·9914	*0·0338	*0·0761	·0428
63	22 0·1183	0·1604	0·2023	0·2441	0·2858	0·3273	0·3687	0·4100	0·4512	0·4922	·0415
64	22 0·5332	0·5740	0·6147	0·6552	0·6957	0·7360	0·7762	0·8163	0·8563	0·8962	·0403
65	0·9359	0·9755	1·0151	1·0544	1·0937	1·1328	1·1718	1·2107	1·2495	1·2881	·0391
66	1·3267	1·3651	1·4034	1·4416	1·4797	1·5177	1·5555	1·5933	1·6309	1·6684	·0379
67	22 1·7059	1·7432	1·7804	1·8175	1·8545	1·8914	1·9281	1·9648	2·0014	2·0378	·0368
68	2·0742	2·1105	2·1466	2·1827	2·2186	2·2545	2·2902	2·3259	2·3614	2·3968	·0358
69	2·4322	2·4675	2·5027	2·5377	2·5727	2·6076	2·6424	2·6771	2·7117	2·7462	·0348
70	22 2·7806	2·8150	2·8492	2·8833	2·9174	2·9513	2·9852	3·0189	3·0526	3·0862	·0339
71	3·1196	3·1530	3·1863	3·2195	3·2526	3·2856	3·3185	3·3513	3·3840	3·4167	·0330
72	3·4492	3·4816	3·5140	3·5462	3·5784	3·6105	3·6424	3·6743	3·7061	3·7378	·0320
73	22 3·7694	3·8009	3·8323	3·8636	3·8949	3·9260	3·9571	3·9881	4·0189	4·0497	·0311
74	4·0804	4·1110	4·1416	4·1720	4·2024	4·2326	4·2628	4·2929	4·3230	4·3529	·0302
75	4·3828	4·4125	4·4422	4·4719	4·5014	4·5308	4·5602	4·5895	4·6187	4·6478	·0294
76	22 4·6769	4·7058	4·7347	4·7635	4·7922	4·8208	4·8493	4·8777	4·9060	4·9343	·0286
77	4·9624	4·9905	5·0195	5·0464	5·0742	5·1020	5·1296	5·1572	5·1847	5·2121	·0277
78	5·2394	5·2666	5·2937	5·3208	5·3478	5·3747	5·4015	5·4282	5·4549	5·4814	·0268
79	22 5·5079	5·5343	5·5606	5·5869	5·6130	5·6391	5·6652	5·6911	5·7170	5·7428	·0261
80	5·7685	5·7941	5·8197	5·8452	5·8706	5·8959	5·9212	5·9463	5·9714	5·9965	·0253
81	6·0214	6·0463	6·0711	6·0959	6·1205	6·1451	6·1696	6·1941	6·2184	6·2427	·0245
82	22 6·2669	6·2910	6·3151	6·3390	6·3629	6·3867	6·4104	6·4340	6·4576	6·4810	·0237
83	6·5044	6·5277	6·5509	6·5740	6·5971	6·6201	6·6430	6·6658	6·6885	6·7111	·0229
84	6·7337	6·7562	6·7786	6·8009	6·8232	6·8454	6·8675	6·8895	6·9114	6·9333	·0221
85	22 6·9551	6·9768	6·9984	7·0200	7·0415	7·0629	7·0842	7·1055	7·1267	7·1478	·0214
86	7·1688	7·1898	7·2107	7·2315	7·2522	7·2729	7·2935	7·3140	7·3345	7·3549	·0206
87	7·3752	7·3954	7·4156	7·4357	7·4558	7·4757	7·4956	7·5155	7·5353	7·5550	·0199
88	22 7·5746	7·5942	7·6137	7·6332	7·6526	7·6719	7·6912	7·7104	7·7295	7·7486	·0193
89	7·7677	7·7866	7·8055	7·8244	7·8431	7·8618	7·8805	7·8991	7·9176	7·9360	·0187
90	7·9544	7·9727	7·9909	8·0091	8·0272	8·0452	8·0632	8·0812	8·0990	8·1168	·0180
91	22 8·1346	8·1523	8·1699	8·1875	8·2050	8·2225	8·2399	8·2573	8·2746	8·2918	·0174
92	8·3090	8·3261	8·3432	8·3602	8·3772	8·3941	8·4109	8·4277	8·4445	8·4611	·0169
93	8·4778	8·4943	8·5109	8·5273	8·5437	8·5601	8·5764	8·5927	8·6089	8·6250	·0163

TABLE I.—*continued*.

A General Table of Values of $\dfrac{d^2}{w} t$ for Ogival-headed Bullets.

v.	0	1	2	3	4	5	6	7	8	9	Diff.
f.s.	secs.	secs.	secs.	secs.	secs.	secs.	secs.	secs.	secs.	secs.	+
94	22 8·6411	8·6572	8·6732	8·6892	8·7051	8·7209	8·7367	8·7525	8·7682	8·7838	·0158
95	8·7994	8·8150	8·8305	8·8459	8·8613	8·8767	8·8920	8·9073	8·9225	8·9376	·0153
96	8·9528	8·9678	8·9828	8·9978	9·0128	9·0276	9·0425	9·0573	9·0720	9·0867	·0149
97	22 9·1014	9·1160	9·1306	9·1451	9·1595	9·1740	9·1884	9·2027	9·2170	9·2312	·0144
98	9·2454	9·2596	9·2737	9·2878	9·3018	9·8158	9·3298	9·3437	9·3575	9·3713	·0140
99	9·3851	9·3989	9·4126	9·4262	9·4398	9·4534	9·4670	9·4805	9·4939	9·5073	·0136
100	22 9·5207	9·5340	9·5473	9·5606	9·5738	9·5869	9·6001	9·6132	9·6262	9·6392	·0132
101	9·6522	9·6651	9·6780	9·6908	9·7036	9·7164	9·7291	9·7418	9·7544	9·7670	·0127
102	9·7796	9·7921	9·8046	9·8170	9·8294	9·8417	9·8540	9·8662	9·8783	9·8904	·0123
103	22 9·9024	9·9144	9·9262	9·9380	9·9496	9·9612	9·9727	9·9841	9·9954	*0·0066	·0115
104	23 0·0177	0·0287	0·0396	0·0504	0·0610	0·0716	0·0820	0·0923	0·1025	0·1126	·0105
105	0·1226	0·1325	0·1423	0·1520	0·1615	0·1710	0·1804	0·1897	0·1988	0·2079	·0094
106	23 0·2170	0·2259	0·2347	0·2435	0·2522	0·2609	0·2694	0·2780	0·2864	0·2948	·0086
107	0·3031	0·3114	0·3196	0·3278	0·3359	0·3439	0·3520	0·3599	0·3678	0·3757	·0080
108	0·3835	0·3913	0·3990	0·4067	0·4143	0·4219	0·4295	0·4370	0·4445	0·4519	·0076
109	23 0·4593	0·4667	0·4740	0·4813	0·4885	0·4958	0·5030	0·5101	0·5172	0·5243	·0072
110	0·5314	0·5384	0·5454	0·5524	0·5593	0·5662	0·5731	0·5800	0·5868	0·5936	·0069
111	0·6004	0·6071	0·6139	0·6206	0·6272	0·6339	0·6405	0·6471	0·6537	0·6603	·0066
112	23 0·6668	0·6733	0·6798	0·6863	0·6928	0·6992	0·7056	0·7120	0·7184	0·7248	·0064
113	0·7311	0·7374	0·7437	0·7500	0·7563	0·7625	0·7688	0·7750	0·7812	0·7874	·0062
114	0·7936	0·7997	0·8059	0·8120	0·8181	0·8242	0·8303	0·8364	0·8424	0·8484	·0061
115	23 0·8545	0·8605	0·8665	0·8726	0·8787	0·8847	0·8906	0·8965	0·9024	0·9083	·0059
116	0·9142	0·9200	0·9259	0·9317	0·9375	0·9433	0·9490	0·9548	0·9605	0·9663	·0058
117	0·9720	0·9777	0·9833	0·9890	0·9947	1·0003	1·0059	1·0115	1·0171	1·0227	·0056
118	23 1·0283	1·0338	1·0394	1·0449	1·0504	1·0559	1·0614	1·0669	1·0723	1·0778	·0055
119	1·0832	1·0886	1·0940	1·0994	1·1048	1·1101	1·1154	1·1208	1·1261	1·1314	·0054
120	1·1367	1·1420	1·1473	1·1525	1·1578	1·1630	1·1682	1·1734	1·1786	1·1838	·0052
121	23 1·1889	1·1941	1·1992	1·2043	1·2095	1·2146	1·2196	1·2247	1·2298	1·2348	·0051
122	1·2399	1·2449	1·2499	1·2549	1·2599	1·2649	1·2698	1·2748	1·2797	1·2847	·0050
123	1·2896	1·2945	1·2994	1·3043	1·3091	1·3140	1·3188	1·3237	1·3285	1·3333	·0049
124	23 1·3381	1·3429	1·3477	1·3524	1·3572	1·3619	1·3667	1·3714	1·3761	1·3808	·0047
125	1·3855	1·3902	1·3948	1·3995	1·4041	1·4088	1·4134	1·4180	1·4226	1·4272	·0046
126	1·4318	1·4364	1·4410	1·4455	1·4501	1·4546	1·4591	1·4636	1·4681	1·4726	·0045
127	23 1·4771	1·4816	1·4860	1·4905	1·4949	1·4993	1·5038	1·5082	1·5126	1·5170	·0044
128	1·5214	1·5257	1·5301	1·5345	1·5388	1·5431	1·5475	1·5518	1·5561	1·5604	·0043
129	1·5647	1·5690	1·5732	1·5775	1·5818	1·5860	1·5902	1·5945	1·5987	1·6029	·0042
130	23 1·6071	1·6113	1·6155	1·6196	1·6238	1·6280	1·6321	1·6362	1·6404	1·6445	·0042
131	1·6486	1·6527	1·6568	1·6609	1·6650	1·6690	1·6731	1·6772	1·6812	1·6852	·0041
132	1·6893	1·6933	1·6973	1·7013	1·7053	1·7093	1·7133	1·7173	1·7212	1·7252	·0040
133	23 1·7291	1·7331	1·7370	1·7410	1·7449	1·7488	1·7527	1·7566	1·7605	1·7644	·0039
134	1·7682	1·7721	1·7760	1·7798	1·7837	1·7875	1·7913	1·7952	1·7990	1·8028	·0038
135	1·8066	1·8104	1·8142	1·8179	1·8217	1·8255	1·8292	1·8330	1·8367	1·8405	·0038

TABLE I.—continued.

A General Table of Values of $\dfrac{d^2}{w} t$ for Ogival-headed Bullets.

v.	0	1	2	3	4	5	6	7	8	9	Diff.
f.s.	secs.	secs.	secs.	secs.	secs.	secs.	secs.	secs.	secs.	secs.	+
136	23 1·8442	1·8479	1·8517	1·8554	1·8591	1·8628	1·8665	1·8702	1·8738	1·8775	·0037
137	1·8812	1·8848	1·8885	1·8921	1·8958	1·8994	1·9030	1·9067	1·9103	1·9139	·0036
138	1·9175	1·9211	1·9247	1·9282	1·9318	1·9354	1·9890	1·9425	1·9461	1·9496	·0036
139	23 1·9532	1·9567	1·9602	1·9638	1·9673	1·9708	1·9743	1·9778	1·9813	1·9848	·0035
140	1·9883	1·9918	1·9952	1·9987	2·0022	2·0056	2·0091	2·0125	2·0160	2·0194	·0035
141	2·0228	2·0263	2·0297	2·0331	2·0365	2·0399	2·0433	2·0467	2·0501	2·0535	·0034
142	23 2·0569	2·0602	2·0636	2·0670	2·0703	2·0737	2·0770	2·0804	2·0837	2·0870	·0034
143	2·0904	2·0937	2·0970	2·1003	2·1036	2·1069	2·1102	2·1135	2·1168	2·1201	·0033
144	2·1234	2·1267	2·1299	2·1332	2·1364	2·1397	2·1430	2·1462	2·1494	2·1627	·0033
145	23 2·1559	2·1591	2·1624	2·1656	2·1688	2·1720	2·1752	2·1784	2·1816	2·1848	·0032
146	2·1880	2·1912	2·1944	2·1975	2·2007	2·2039	2·2071	2·2102	2·2134	2·2165	·0032
147	2·2197	2·2228	2·2260	2·2291	2·2322	2·2354	2·2385	2·2416	2·2447	2·2478	·0031
148	23 2·2509	2·2540	2·2571	2·2602	2·2633	2·2664	2·2695	2·2726	2·2757	2·2787	·0031
149	2·2818	2·2849	2·2879	2·2910	2·2940	2·2971	2·3001	2·3032	2·3062	2·3093	·0030
150	2·3123	2·3153	2·3183	2·3214	2·3244	2·3274	2·3304	2·3334	2·3364	2·3394	·0030
151	23 2·3424	2·3454	2·3484	2·3514	2·3543	2·3573	2·3603	2·3633	2·3662	2·3692	·0030
152	2·3722	2·3751	2·3781	2·3810	2·3840	2·3869	2·3899	2·3928	2·3958	2·3987	·0029
153	2·4016	2·4046	2·4075	2·4104	2·4133	2·4162	2·4192	2·4221	2·4250	2·4279	·0029
154	23 2·4308	2·4337	2·4366	2·4395	2·4424	2·4453	2·4481	2·4510	2·4539	2·4568	·0029
155	2·4597	2·4625	2·4654	2·4683	2·4711	2·4740	2·4768	2·4797	2·4825	2·4854	·0029
156	2·4882	2·4911	2·4939	2·4967	2·4996	2·5024	2·5052	2·5080	2·5108	2·5137	·0028
157	23 2·5165	2·5193	2·5221	2·5249	2·5277	2·5305	2·5333	2·5361	2·5389	2·5416	·0028
158	2·5444	2·5472	2·5500	2·5528	2·5555	2·5583	2·5611	2·5638	2·5666	2·5693	·0028
159	2·5721	2·5748	2·5776	2·5803	2·5831	2·5858	2·5885	2·5913	2·5940	2·5967	·0027
160	23 2·5994	2·6022	2·6049	2·6076	2·6103	2·6130	2·6157	2·6184	2·6211	2·6238	·0027
161	2·6265	2·6292	2·6319	2·6346	2·6373	2·6400	2·6426	2·6453	2·6480	2·6506	·0027
162	2·6533	2·6560	2·6586	2·6613	2·6640	2·6666	2·6693	2·6719	2·6745	2·6772	·0027
163	23 2·6798	2·6825	2·6851	2·6877	2·6903	2·6930	2·6956	2·6982	2·7008	2·7034	·0026
164	2·7061	2·7087	2·7113	2·7139	2·7165	2·7191	2·7217	2·7243	2·7268	2·7294	·0026
165	2·7320	2·7346	2·7372	2·7398	2·7423	2·7449	2·7475	2·7500	2·7526	2·7552	·0026
166	23 2·7577	2·7603	2·7628	2·7654	2·7679	2·7705	2·7730	2·7756	2·7781	2·7806	·0025
167	2·7832	2·7857	2·7882	2·7908	2·7933	2·7958	2·7983	2·8008	2·8034	2·8059	·0025
168	2·8084	2·8109	2·8134	2·8159	2·8184	2·8209	2·8234	2·8258	2·8283	2·8308	·0025
169	23 2·8333	2·8358	2·8383	2·8407	2·8432	2·8457	2·8481	2·8506	2·8531	2·8555	·0025
170	2·8580	2·8604	2·8629	2·8653	2·8678	2·8702	2·8726	2·8751	2·8775	2·8799	·0024
171	2·8824	2·8848	2·8872	2·8896	2·8921	2·8945	2·8969	2·8993	2·9017	2·9041	·0024
172	23 2·9065	2·9089	2·9113	2·9137	2·9161	2·9185	2·9209	2·9233	2·9257	2·9281	·0024
173	2·9304	2·9328	2·9352	2·9376	2·9399	2·9423	2·9447	2·9470	2·9494	2·9518	·0024
174	2·9541	2·9565	2·9588	2·9612	2·9635	2·9659	2·9682	2·9705	2·9729	2·9752	·0023
175	23 2·9776	2·9799	2·9822	2·9845	2·9869	2·9892	2·9915	2·9938	2·9961	2·9985	·0023
176	3·0008	3·0031	3·0054	3·0077	3·0100	3·0123	3·0146	3·0169	3·0192	3·0215	·0023
177	3·0237	3·0260	3·0283	3·0306	3·0329	3·0351	3·0374	3·0397	3·0420	3·0442	·0023

(S.A.)

Table I.—continued.

A General Table of Values of $\dfrac{d^2}{w}t$ for Ogival-headed Bullets.

v.	0	1	2	3	4	5	6	7	8	9	Diff.
f.s.	secs.	secs.	secs.	secs.	secs.	secs.	secs.	secs.	secs.	secs.	+
178	23 3·0465	3·0488	3·0510	3·0533	3·0555	3·0578	3·0600	3·0623	3·0645	3·0668	·0023
179	3·0690	3·0713	3·0735	3·0757	3·0780	3·0802	3·0824	3·0847	3·0869	3·0891	·0022
180	3·0913	3·0935	3·0958	3·0980	3·1002	3·1024	3·1045	3·1068	3·1090	3·1112	·0022
181	23 3·1134	3·1156	3·1178	3·1200	3·1222	3·1244	3·1266	3·1287	3·1309	3·1331	·0022
182	3·1353	3·1375	3·1396	3·1418	3·1440	3·1461	3·1483	3·1505	3·1526	3·1548	·0022
183	3·1569	3·1591	3·1613	3·1634	3·1656	3·1677	3·1698	3·1720	3·1741	3·1763	·0021
184	23 3·1784	3·1805	3·1827	3·1848	3·1869	3·1891	3·1912	3·1933	3·1954	3·1975	·0021
185	3·1997	3·2018	3·2039	3·2060	3·2081	3·2102	3·2123	3·2144	3·2165	3·2186	·0021
186	3·2207	3·2228	3·2249	3·2270	3·2291	3·2312	3·2333	3·2353	3·2374	3·2395	·0021
187	23 3·2416	3·2437	3·2457	3·2478	3·2499	3·2520	3·2540	3·2561	3·2582	3·2602	·0021
188	3·2623	3·2643	3·2664	3·2685	3·2705	3·2726	3·2746	3·2767	3·2787	3·2808	·0021
189	3·2828	3·2848	3·2869	3·2889	3·2909	3·2930	3·2950	3·2970	3·2991	3·3011	·0020
190	23 3·3031	3·3051	3·3072	3·3092	3·3112	3·3132	3·3152	3·3172	3·3192	3·3212	·0020
191	3·3233	3·3253	3·3273	3·3293	3·3313	3·3333	3·3353	3·3372	3·3392	3·3412	·0020
192	3·3432	3·3452	3·3472	3·3492	3·3511	3·3531	3·3551	3·3571	3·3590	3·3610	·0020
193	23 3·3630	3·3649	3·3669	3·3689	3·3708	3·3728	3·3747	3·3767	3·3786	3·3806	·0020
194	3·3825	3·3845	3·3864	3·3884	3·3903	3·3922	3·3942	3·3961	3·3980	3·4000	·0019
195	3·4019	3·4038	3·4057	3·4077	3·4096	3·4115	3·4134	3·4153	3·4172	3·4192	·0019
196	23 3·4211	3·4230	3·4249	3·4268	3·4287	3·4306	3·4325	3·4344	3·4362	3·4381	·0019
197	3·4400	3·4419	3·4438	3·4457	3·4476	3·4494	3·4513	3·4532	3·4550	3·4569	·0019
198	3·4588	3·4606	3·4625	3·4644	3·4662	3·4681	3·4699	3·4718	3·4736	3·4755	·0019
199	23 3·4773	3·4791	3·4810	3·4828	3·4846	3·4865	3·4883	3·4901	3·4920	3·4938	·0018
200	3·4956	3·4974	3·4992	3·5010	3·5028	3·5047	3·5065	3·5083	3·5101	3·5119	·0018
201	3·5137	3·5155	3·5172	3·5190	3·5208	3·5226	3·5244	3·5262	3·5280	3·5297	·0018
202	23 3·5315	3·5333	3·5351	3·5368	3·5386	3·5404	3·5421	3·5439	3·5456	3·5474	·0018
203	3·5492	3·5509	3·5527	3·5544	3·5561	3·5579	3·5596	3·5614	3·5631	3·5648	·0017
204	3·5666	3·5683	3·5700	3·5717	3·5735	3·5752	3·5769	3·5786	3·5803	3·5820	·0017
205	23 3·5837	3·5854	3·5871	3·5888	3·5905	3·5922	3·5939	3·5956	3·5973	3·5990	·0017
206	3·6007	3·6024	3·6040	3·6057	3·6074	3·6091	3·6107	3·6124	3·6141	3·6157	·0017
207	3·6174	3·6191	3·6207	3·6224	3·6240	3·6257	3·6273	3·6290	3·6306	3·6323	·0016
208	23 3·6339	3·6355	3·6372	3·6388	3·6404	3·6420	3·6437	3·6453	3·6469	3·6485	·0016
209	3·6502	3·6518	3·6534	3·6550	3·6566	3·6582	3·6598	3·6614	3·6630	3·6646	·0016
210	3·6662	3·6678	3·6694	3·6710	3·6726	3·6741	3·6757	3·6773	3·6789	3·6805	·0016
211	23 3·6820	3·6836	3·6852	3·6867	3·6883	3·6899	3·6914	3·6930	3·6946	3·6961	·0016
212	3·6977	3·6992	3·7008	3·7023	3·7039	3·7054	3·7070	3·7085	3·7100	3·7116	·0015
213	3·7131	3·7146	3·7162	3·7177	3·7192	3·7207	3·7223	3·7238	3·7253	3·7268	·0015
214	23 3·7283	3·7298	3·7313	3·7329	3·7344	3·7359	3·7374	3·7389	3·7404	3·7419	·0015
215	3·7434	3·7448	3·7463	3·7478	3·7493	3·7508	3·7523	3·7538	3·7552	3·7567	·0015
216	3·7582	3·7597	3·7612	3·7626	3·7641	3·7656	3·7670	3·7685	3·7700	3·7714	·0015
217	23 3·7729	3·7743	3·7758	3·7772	3·7787	3·7801	3·7816	3·7830	3·7845	3·7859	·0014
218	3·7874	3·7888	3·7902	3·7917	3·7931	3·7945	3·7960	3·7974	3·7988	3·8002	·0014
219	3·8016	3·8031	3·8045	3·8059	3·8073	3·8087	3·8101	3·8115	3·8129	3·8144	·0014

147

Table I.—continued.

A General Table of Values of $\dfrac{d^2}{w}t$ for Ogival-headed Bullets.

v.	0	1	2	3	4	5	6	7	8	9	Diff.
f.s.	secs.	secs.	secs.	secs.	secs.	secs.	secs.	secs.	secs.	secs.	+
220	23 3·8158	3·8172	3·8186	3·8200	3·8214	3·8227	3·8241	3·8255	3·8269	3·8283	·0014
221	3·8297	3·8311	3·8325	3·8338	3·8352	3·8366	3·8380	3·8394	3·8407	3·8421	·0014
222	3·8435	3·8448	3·8462	3·8476	3·8489	3·8503	3·8517	3·8530	3·8544	3·8557	·0014
223	23 3·8571	3·8584	3·8598	3·8611	3·8625	3·8638	3·8651	3·8665	3·8678	3·8692	·0013
224	3·8705	3·8718	3·8732	3·8745	3·8758	3·8772	3·8785	3·8798	3·8811	3·8824	·0013
225	3·8838	3·8851	3·8864	3·8877	3·8890	3·8903	3·8916	3·8930	3·8943	3·8956	·0013
226	23 3·8969	3·8982	3·8995	3·9008	3·9021	3·9034	3·9047	3·9059	3·9072	3·9085	·0013
227	3·9098	3·9111	3·9124	3·9137	3·9150	3·9162	3·9175	3·9188	3·9201	3·9214	·0013
228	3·9226	3·9239	3·9252	3·9264	3·9277	3·9290	3·9303	3·9315	3·9328	3·9341	·0013
229	23 3·9353	3·9366	3·9378	3·9391	3·9404	3·9416	3·9429	3·9441	3·9454	3·9467	·0013
230	3·9479	3·9492	3·9504	3·9517	3·9529	3·9542	3·9554	3·9567	3·9579	3.9592	·0013
231	3·9604	3·9617	3·9629	3·9642	3·9654	3·9667	3·9679	3·9692	3·9704	3·9716	·0012
232	23 3·9729	3·9741	3·9754	3·9766	3·9779	3·9791	3·9803	3·9816	3·9828	3·9841	·0012
233	3·9853	3·9866	3·9878	3·9890	3·9903	3·9915	3·9927	3·9940	3·9952	3·9965	·0012
234	3·9977	3·9989	4·0002	4·0014	4·0026	4·0039	4·0051	4·0063	4·0076	4·0088	·0012
235	23 4·0100	4·0113	4·0125	4·0137	4·0150	4·0162	4·0174	4·0186	4·0199	4·0211	·0012
236	4·0223	4·0236	4·0248	4·0260	4·0272	4·0284	4·0297	4·0309	4·0321	4·0334	·0012
237	4·0346	4·0358	4·0370	4·0383	4·0395	4·0407	4·0419	4·0431	4·0444	4·0456	·0012
238	23 4·0468	4·0480	4·0492	4·0505	4·0517	4·0529	4·0541	4·0553	4·0566	4·0578	·0012
239	4·0590	4·0602	4·0614	4·0626	4·0639	4·0651	4·0663	4·0675	4·0687	4·0699	·0012
240	4·0711	4·0724	4·0736	4·0748	4·0760	4·0772	4·0784	4·0796	4·0809	4·0821	·0012
241	23 4·0833	4·0845	4.0857	4·0869	4·0881	4·0893	4·0905	4·0917	4·0930	4·0942	·0012
242	4·0954	4·0966	4·0978	4·0990	4·1002	4·1014	4·1026	4·1038	4·1050	4·1062	·0012
243	4·1074	4·1087	4·1099	4·1111	4·1123	4·1135	4·1147	4·1159	4·1171	4·1183	·0012
244	23 4·1195	4·1207	4·1219	4·1231	4·1243	4·1255	4·1267	4·1279	4·1291	4·1303	·0012
245	4·1315	4·1327	4·1339	4·1351	4·1363	4·1375	4·1387	4·1399	4·1411	4·1423	·0012
246	4·1435	4·1447	4·1459	4·1471	4·1483	4·1495	4·1506	4·1518	4·1530	4·1542	·0012
247	23 4·1554	4·1566	4·1578	4·1590	4·1602	4·1614	4·1626	4·1638	4·1649	4·1661	·0012
248	4·1673	4·1685	4·1697	4·1709	4·1721	4·1733	4·1744	4·1756	4·1768	4·1780	·0012
249	4·1792	4·1804	4·1815	4·1827	4·1839	4·1851	4·1863	4·1874	1·1886	4·1898	·0012
250	23 4·1910	4·1922	4·1933	4·1945	4·1957	4·1969	4·1980	4·1992	4·2004	4·2015	·0012
251	4·2027	4·2039	4·2051	4·2062	4·2074	4·2086	4·2097	4·2109	4·2121	4·2132	·0012
252	4·2144	4·2156	4·2167	4·2179	4·2190	4·2202	4·2214	4·2225	4·2237	4·2248	·0012
253	23 4·2260	4·2272	4·2283	4·2295	4·2306	4·2318	4·2329	4·2341	4·2352	4·2364	·0012
254	4·2375	4·2387	4·2398	4·2410	4·2421	4·2433	4·2444	4·2455	4·2467	4·2478	·0011
255	4·2490	4·2501	4·2513	4·2524	4·2535	4·2547	4·2558	4·2569	4·2581	4·2592	·0011
256	23 4·2603	4·2615	4·2626	4·2637	4·2648	4·2660	4·2671	4·2682	4·2693	4·2705	·0011
257	4·2716	4·2727	4·2738	4·2749	4·2760	4·2772	4·2783	4·2794	4·2805	4·2816	·0011
258	4·2827	4·2838	4·2849	4·2860	4·2871	4·2882	4·2893	4·2904	4·2915	4·2926	·0011
259	23 4·2937	4·2948	4·2959	4·2970	4·2981	4·2992	4·3003	4·3014	4·3025	4·3036	·0011
260	4·3046	4·3057	4·3068	4·3079	4·3090	4·3101	4·3111	4·3122	4·3133	4·3144	·0011
261	4·3154	4·3165	4·3176	4·3187	4·3197	4·3208	4·3219	4·3229	4·3240	4·3250	·0011

(S.A.)

TABLE I.—continued.

A General Table of Values of $\dfrac{d^2}{w}t$ for Ogival-headed Bullets.

u.	0	1	2	3	4	5	6	7	8	9	Diff.
f.s.	secs.	secs.	secs.	secs.	secs.	secs.	secs.	secs.	secs.	secs.	+
262	23 4·3261	4·3272	4·3282	4·3293	4·3303	4·3314	4·3325	4·3335	4·3346	4·3356	·0011
263	4·3367	4·3377	4·3388	4·3398	4·3409	4·3419	4·3429	4·3440	4·3450	4·3461	·0010
264	4·3471	4·3482	4·3492	4·3502	4·3513	4·3523	4·3533	4·3544	4·3554	4·3564	·0010
265	23 4·3574	4·3585	4·3595	4·3605	4·3615	4·3626	4·3636	4·3646	4·3656	4·3667	·0010
266	4·3677	4·3687	4·3697	4·3707	4·3717	4·3728	4·3738	4·3748	4·3758	4·3768	·0010
267	4·3778	4·3788	4·3798	4·3808	4·3818	4·3828	4·3838	4·3848	4·3858	4·3868	·0010
268	23 4·3878	4·3888	4·3898	4·3908	4·3918	4·3928	4·3938	4·3948	4·3958	4·3968	·0010
269	4·3977	4·3987	4·3997	4·4007	4·4017	4·4027	4·4036	4·4046	4·4056	4·4066	·0010
270	4·4075	4·4085	4·4095	4·4105	4·4114	4·4124	4·4134	4·4143	4·4153	4·4163	·0010
271	23 4·4172	4·4182	4·4192	4·4201	4·4211	4·4220	4·4230	4·4240	4·4249	4·4259	·0010
272	4·4268	4·4278	4·4287	4·4297	4·4307	4·4316	4·4326	4·4335	4·4344	4·4354	·0010
273	4·4363	4·4373	4·4382	4·4392	4·4401	4·4411	4·4420	4·4429	4·4439	4·4448	·0009
274	23 4·4457	4·4467	4·4476	4·4485	4·4495	4·4504	4·4513	4·4523	4·4532	4·4541	·0009
275	4·4551	4·4560	4·4569	4·4578	4·4587	4·4597	4·4606	4·4615	4·4624	4·4633	·0009
276	4·4643	4·4652	4·4661	4·4670	4·4679	4·4688	4·4697	4·4706	4·4715	4·4725	·0009
277	23 4·4734	4·4743	4·4752	4·4761	4·4770	4·4779	4·4788	4·4797	4·4806	4·4815	·0009
278	4·4824	4·4833	4·4842	4·4850	4·4859	4·4868	4·4877	4·4886	4·4895	4·4904	·0009
279	4·4913	4·4922	4·4930	4·4939	4·4948	4·4957	4·4966	4·4975	4·4983	4·4992	·0009
280	23 4·5001	4·5010	4·5018	4·5027	4·5036	4·5045	4·5053	4·5062	4·5071	4·5080	·0009
281	4·5088	4·5097	4·5105	4·5114	4·5123	4·5131	4·5140	4·5148	4·5157	4·5166	·0009
282	4·5174	4·5183	4·5191	4·5200	4·5208	4·5217	4·5226	4·5234	4·5243	4·5251	·0009
283	23 4·5260	4·5268	4·5277	4·5285	4·5293	4·5302	4·5310	4·5319	4·5327	4·5336	·0008
284	4·5344	4·5352	4·5361	4·5369	4·5378	4·5386	4·5394	4·5403	4·5411	4·5419	·0008
285	4·5427	4·5436	4·5444	4·5452	4·5461	4·5469	4·5477	4·5485	4·5494	4·5502	·0008
286	23 4·5510	4·5518	4·5527	4·5535	4·5543	4·5551	4·5559	4·5567	4·5576	4·5584	·0008
287	4·5592	4·5600	4·5608	4·5616	4·5624	4·5632	4·5641	4·5648	4·5657	4·5665	·0008
288	4·5673	4·5681	4·5689	4·5697	4·5705	4·5713	4·5721	4·5729	4·5737	4·5745	·0008
299	23 4·5753	4·5761	4·5769	4·5777	4·5785	4·5793	4·5800	4·5808	4·5816	4·5824	·0008
290	4·5832										

149

TABLE II.

A General Table of Values of $\dfrac{d^2}{w}s$ for Ogival-headed Bullets.

v	0	1	2	3	4	5	6	7	8	9	Diff.
f.s.	feet.	feet.	feet.	feet.	feet.	feet.	feet.	feet.	feet.	feet.	+
10	1066	1238	1409	1578	1745	1910	2074	2236	2397	2557	166
11	2715	2871	3026	3180	3333	3484	3633	3782	3929	4075	151
12	4220	4363	4506	4647	4787	4926	5064	5200	5336	5471	139
13	5604	5737	5866	5999	6129	6257	6385	6511	6637	6762	129
14	6886	7009	7132	7253	7373	7493	7612	7730	7847	7964	120
15	8079	8194	8309	8422	8535	8647	8758	8868	8978	9087	112
16	9196	9304	9411	9517	9623	9728	9833	9937	10040	10142	105
17	10244	10346	10447	10546	10645	10743	10841	10939	11037	11134	98
18	11230	11326	11421	11516	11610	11704	11797	11890	11982	12074	94
19	12165	12256	12346	12436	12525	12614	12703	12791	12878	12966	89
20	13052	13139	13224	13310	13395	13460	13564	13648	13731	13814	85
21	13896	13979	14060	14142	14223	14303	14384	14463	14543	14622	81
22	14701	14779	14857	14935	15013	15090	15167	15244	15319	15395	77
23	15470	15545	15620	15694	15768	15842	15916	15989	16061	16134	74
24	16206	16278	16350	16421	16492	16563	16633	16703	16773	16843	71
25	1 6912·1	6981·2	7050·0	7118·5	7186·7	7254·7	7322·4	7389·8	7457·0	7523·9	68·0
26	7590·6	7657·0	7723·2	7789·1	7854·7	7920·1	7985·3	8050·2	8114·8	8179·3	65·4
27	8243·5	8307·5	8371·2	8434·7	8498·0	8561·0	8623·9	8686·4	8748·8	8810·9	63·0
28	1 8872·8	8934·5	8996·0	9057·2	9118·3	9179·1	9239·7	9300·1	9360·3	9420·3	60·8
29	. 9480·0	9539·6	9598·9	9658·1	9717·0	9775·8	9834·3	9892·6	9950·8	*0008·7	58·7
30	2 0066·5	0124·0	0181·4	0238·5	0295·5	0352·3	0409·0	0465·4	0521·7	0577·7	56·8
31	2 0633·6	0689·3	0744·8	0800·1	0855·3	0910·2	0965·0	1019·6	1074·0	1128·3	55·0
32	1182·4	1236·3	1290·0	1343·5	1396·9	1450·2	1503·2	1556·1	1608·8	1661·4	53·2
33	1713·8	1766·0	1818·1	1870·0	1921·7	1973·3	2024·7	2076·0	2127·1	2178·1	51·6
34	2 2228·9	2279·6	2330·0	2380·4	2430·6	2480·6	2530·5	2580·2	2629·7	2679·1	50·0
35	2728·4	2777·5	2826·4	2875·2	2923·8	2972·3	3020·7	3068·8	3116·9	3164·7	48·5
36	3212·5	3260·1	3307·5	3354·8	3402·0	3449·0	3495·9	3542·6	3589·2	3635·6	47·0
37	2 3682·0	3728·1	3774·2	3820·0	3865·8	3911·4	3956·9	4002·2	4047·4	4092·5	45·6
38	4137·4	4182·2	4226·8	4271·4	4315·7	4360·0	4404·1	4448·1	4491·9	4535·7	44·3
39	4579·2	4622·7	4666·0	4709·2	4752·3	4795·2	4838·1	4880·8	4923·3	4965·7	42·9
40	2 5008·0	5050·2	5092·3	5134·2	5176·0	5217·6	5259·2	5300·6	5341·9	5383·0	41·7
41	5424·0	5464·9	5505·7	5546·4	5586·9	5627·3	5667·6	5707·8	5747·8	5787·8	40·4
42	5827·6	5867·3	5906·9	5946·4	5985·8	6025·0	6064·2	6103·3	6142·2	6181·0	39·3
43	2 6219·8	6258·4	6296·9	6335·3	6373·6	6411·8	6449·9	6487·9	6525·8	6563·6	38·2
44	6601·3	6638·9	6676·4	6713·7	6751·0	6788·2	6825·3	6862·3	6899·3	6936·1	37·2
45	6972·8	7009·4	7046·0	7082·4	7118·8	7155·0	7191·2	7227·3	7263·3	7299·2	36·3
46	2 7335·1	7370·8	7406·5	7442·1	7477·6	7513·0	7548·3	7583·6	7618·8	7653·9	35·4
47	7688·9	7723·8	7758·7	7793·5	7828·2	7862·8	7897·3	7931·8	7966·2	8000·5	34·6
48	8034·7	8068·9	8103·0	8137·0	8170·9	8204·8	8238·6	8272·3	8305·9	8339·5	33·9
49	2 8373·0	8406·5	8439·8	8473·1	8506·4	8539·5	8572·6	8605·6	8638·6	8671·5	33·2
50	8704·3	8737·1	8769·8	8802·4	8835·0	8867·5	8900·0	8932·3	8964·7	8996·9	32·5
51	9029·1	9061·2	9093·2	9125·2	9157·1	9189·0	9220·8	9252·5	9284·2	9315·8	31·9

Table II.—continued.

A General Table of Values of $\dfrac{d^2}{w}s$ for Ogival-headed Bullets.

v.	0	1	2	3	4	5	6	7	8	9	Diff.
f.s.	feet.	feet.	feet.	feet.	feet.	feet.	feet.	feet.	feet.	feet.	+
52	2 9347·3	9378·8	9410·3	9441·6	9472·9	9504·2	9535·4	9566·5	9597·6	9628·7	31·3
53	9659·6	9690·6	9721·4	9752·2	9783·0	9813·7	9844·3	9874·9	9905·4	9935·9	30·7
54	9966·3	9996·7	*0027·0	*0057·3	*0087·5	*0117·7	*0147·8	*0177·8	*0207·8	*0237·8	30·2
55	3 0267·6	0297·5	0327·3	0357·0	0386·7	0416·3	0445·9	0475·4	0504·9	0534·3	29·6
56	0563·6	0592·9	0622·2	0651·4	0680·6	0709·7	0738·7	0767·7	0796·7	0825·6	29·1
57	0854·5	0883·3	0912·1	0940·9	0969·6	0998·2	1026·8	1055·4	1083·9	1112·4	28·6
58	3 1140·8	1169·2	1197·6	1226·0	1254·3	1282·5	1310·8	1339·0	1367·1	1395·2	28·3
59	1423·3	1451·3	1479·3	1507·3	1535·2	1563·0	1590·9	1618·7	1646·4	1674·2	27·9
60	1701·8	1729·5	1757·1	1784·6	1812·2	1839·6	1867·1	1894·5	1921·9	1949·2	27·5
61	3 1976·5	2003·7	2031·0	2058·1	2085·3	2112·4	2139·4	2166·4	2193·4	2220·4	27·1
62	2247·3	2274·2	2301·0	2327·8	2354·5	2381·3	2407·9	2434·6	2461·2	2487·7	26·7
63	2514·3	2540·8	2567·2	2593·6	2620·0	2646·3	2672·6	2698·9	2725·1	2751·3	26·3
64	3 2777·5	2803·6	2829·7	2855·7	2881·7	2907·7	2933·7	2959·6	2985·4	3011·2	26·0
65	3037·0	3062·8	3088·5	3114·2	3139·8	3165·4	3191·0	3216·5	3242·0	3267·4	25·6
66	3292·8	3318·2	3343·5	3368·8	3394·1	3419·3	3444·5	3469·6	3494·7	3519·8	25·2
67	3 3544·8	3569·8	3594·8	3619·8	3644·7	3669·5	3694·3	3719·1	3743·9	3768·6	24·8
68	3793·3	3818·0	3842·6	3867·2	3891·7	3916·2	3940·7	3965·2	3989·6	4014·0	24·5
69	4038·4	4062·7	4087·0	4111·3	4135·6	4159·8	4184·0	4208·1	4232·2	4256·3	24·2
70	3 4280·4	4304·5	4328·5	4352·4	4376·4	4400·3	4424·1	4448·0	4471·8	4495·5	23·9
71	4519·3	4543·0	4566·6	4590·2	4613·8	4637·4	4660·9	4684·4	4707·8	4731·3	23·5
72	4754·7	4777·9	4801·3	4824·6	4847·9	4871·1	4894·2	4917·4	4940·5	4963·6	23·2
73	3 4986·6	5009·6	5032·6	5055·5	5078·4	5101·3	5124·1	5146·9	5169·6	5192·4	22·8
74	5215·1	5237·7	5260·3	5282·9	5305·5	5328·0	5350·5	5373·0	5395·4	5417·8	22·5
75	5440·2	5462·5	5484·8	5507·1	5529·3	5551·5	5573·7	5595·8	5617·9	5640·0	22·2
76	3 5662·1	5684·1	5706·0	5728·0	5749·9	5771·7	5793·5	5815·3	5837·0	5858·7	21·8
77	5880·4	5902·0	5923·6	5945·1	5966·6	5988·1	6009·5	6030·9	6052·2	6073·6	21·5
78	6094·8	6116·1	6137·3	6158·4	6179·6	6200·7	6221·7	6242·7	6263·7	6284·6	21·1
79	3 6305·5	6326·4	6347·2	6368·0	6388·8	6409·5	6430·2	6450·8	6471·4	6492·0	20·7
80	6512·6	6533·1	6553·6	6574·0	6594·4	6614·8	6635·1	6655·4	6675·7	6695·9	20·4
81	6716·1	6736·3	6756·4	6776·5	6796·5	6816·5	6836·5	6856·4	6876·3	6896·1	20·0
82	3 6916·0	6935·7	6955·5	6975·1	6994·8	7014·4	7033·9	7053·4	7072·9	7092·3	19·6
83	7111·7	7131·0	7150·3	7169·6	7188·8	7207·9	7227·1	7246·1	7265·2	7284·1	19·1
84	7303·1	7322·0	7340·8	7359·6	7378·4	7397·1	7415·8	7434·4	7453·0	7471·5	18·7
85	3 7490·0	7508·5	7526·9	7545·3	7563·6	7581·8	7600·0	7618·2	7636·3	7654·4	18·2
86	7672·4	7690·5	7708·4	7726·4	7744·2	7762·0	7779·9	7797·6	7815·4	7833·0	17·8
87	7850·6	7868·2	7885·8	7903·3	7920·8	7938·2	7955·6	7973·0	7990·3	8007·6	17·4
88	3 8024·8	8042·0	8059·2	8076·3	8093·4	8110·4	8127·4	8144·4	8161·3	8178·2	17·0
89	8195·0	8211·9	8228·6	8245·4	8262·1	8278·7	8295·4	8312·0	8328·5	8345·0	16·6
90	8361·5	8377·9	8394·3	8410·7	8427·0	8443·3	8459·6	8475·8	8492·0	8508·2	16·3
91	3 8524·3	8540·4	8556·6	8572·4	8588·4	8604·3	8620·3	8636·1	8652·0	8667·8	15·9
92	8683·5	8699·3	8715·0	8730·7	8746·3	8761·9	8777·5	8793·0	8808·5	8824·0	15·6
93	8839·4	8854·8	8870·2	8885·5	8900·8	8916·1	8931·3	8946·5	8961·7	8976·8	15·3

TABLE II.—continued.

A General Table of Values of $\dfrac{d^2}{w}s$ for Ogival-headed Bullets.

v.	0	1	2	3	4	5	6	7	8	9	Diff. +
f.s.	feet.	feet.	feet.	feet.	feet.	feet.	feet.	feet.	feet.	feet.	
94	3 8991·9	9007·0	9022·0	9037·0	9052·0	9066·9	9081·9	9096·7	9111·6	9126·4	15·0
95	9141·2	9156·0	9170·7	9185·4	9200·1	9214·7	9229·3	9243·9	9258·4	9272·9	14·6
96	9287·4	9301·9	9316·3	9330·7	9345·0	9359·4	9373·7	9387·9	9402·2	9416·4	14·3
97	3 9430·6	9444·7	9458·9	9473·0	9487·0	9501·1	9515·1	9529·1	9543·0	9557·0	14·0
98	9570·8	9584·7	9598·6	9612·4	9626·1	9639·9	9653·6	9667·3	9681·0	9694·6	13·7
99	9708·3	9721·9	9735·4	9749·0	9762·5	9775·9	9789·4	9802·8	9816·2	9829·6	13·5
100	3 9842·9	9856·3	9869·6	9882·9	9896·1	9909·3	9922·5	9935·3	9948·8	9961·9	13·2
101	9975·0	9988·1	*0001·1	*0014·1	*0027·1	*0040·0	*0052·9	*0065·8	*0078·7	*0091·5	12·9
102	4 0104·3	0117·1	0129·8	0142·5	0155·2	0167·8	0180·4	0192·9	0205·4	0217·8	12·6
103	4 0230·1	0242·4	0254·6	0266·8	0278·8	0290·8	0302·7	0314·5	0326·2	0337·8	11·9
104	0349·4	0360·8	0372·2	0383·4	0394·5	0405·6	0416·5	0427·3	0438·1	0448·7	11·0
105	0459·2	0469·6	0479·9	0490·0	0500·1	0510·1	0520·0	0529·8	0539·5	0549·2	9.9
106	4 0558·7	0568·2	0577·6	0586·9	0596·2	0605·4	0614·5	0623·6	0632·6	0641·6	9·2
107	0650·5	0659·3	0668·1	0676·9	0685·6	0694·2	0702·8	0711·4	0719·9	0728·4	8·6
108	0736·8	0745·2	0753·6	0761·9	0770·2	0778·4	0786·6	0794·8	0802·9	0811·0	8·2
109	4 0819·0	0827·1	0835·0	0843·0	0850·9	0858·9	0866·7	0874·6	0882·4	0890·2	7·9
110	0897·9	0905·7	0913·4	0921·1	0928·7	0936·4	0944·0	0951·5	0959·1	0966·6	7·6
111	0974·2	0981·6	0989·1	0996·6	1004·0	1011·4	1018·8	1026·2	1033·5	1040·9	7·4
112	4 1048·2	1055·5	1062·8	1070·0	1077·3	1084·5	1091·7	1099·0	1106·1	1113·3	7·2
113	1120·5	1127·6	1134··	1141·9	1149·0	1156·1	1163·2	1170·2	1177·3	1184·4	7·1
114	1191·4	1198·4	1205·4	1212·4	1219·4	1226·4	1233·3	1240·3	1247·2	1254·1	6·9
115	4 1261·0	1267·9	1274·8	1281·7	1288·6	1295·4	1302·3	1309·1	1315·9	1322·7	6·8
116	1329·5	1336·3	1343·1	1349·8	1356·6	1363·3	1370·0	1376·7	1383·4	1390·1	6·7
117	1396·8	1403·5	1410·1	1416·8	1423·4	1430·0	1436·6	1443·2	1449·8	1456·4	6·6
118	4 1462·9	1469·5	1476·0	1482·6	1489·1	1495·6	1502·1	1508·6	1515·1	1521·5	6·5
119	1528·0	1534·4	1540·9	1547·3	1553·7	1560·1	1566·5	1572·9	1579·2	1585·6	6·4
120	1591·9	1598·3	1604·6	1610·9	1617·2	1623·5	1629·8	1636·1	1642·3	1648·5	6·3
121	4 1654·8	1661·1	1667·3	1673·5	1679·7	1685·9	1692·1	1698·2	1704·4	1710·5	6·2
122	1716·7	1722·8	1728·9	1735·0	1741·1	1747·2	1753·3	1759·4	1765·4	1771·5	6·1
123	1777·5	1783·6	1789·6	1795·6	1801·6	1807·6	1813·6	1819·6	1825·6	1831·5	6·0
124	4 1837·5	1843·4	1849·4	1855·3	1861·2	1867·1	1873·0	1878·9	1884·8	1890·6	5·9
125	1896·5	1902·3	1908·2	1914·0	1919·8	1925·6	1931·5	1937·3	1943·0	1948·8	5.8
126	1954·6	1960·4	1966·1	1971·9	1977·6	1983·3	1989·0	1994·8	2000·5	2006·2	5.7
127	4 2011·8	2017·5	2023·2	2028·9	2034·5	2040·2	2045·8	2051·4	2057·0	2062·7	5·6
128	2068·3	2073·9	2079·5	2085·0	2090·6	2096·2	2101·8	2107·3	2112·9	2118·4	5·5
129	2123·9	2129·4	2135·0	2140·5	2146·0	2151·5	2157·0	2162·4	2167·9	2173·4	5·5
130	4 2178·8	2184·3	2189·7	2195·1	2200·6	2206·0	2211·4	2216·8	2222·2	2227·6	5·4
131	2233·0	2238·4	2243·7	2249·1	2254·5	2259·8	2265·1	2270·5	2275·8	2281·1	5·3
132	2286·4	2291·8	2297·1	2302·4	2307·6	2312·9	2318·2	2323·5	2328·7	2334·0	5·3
133	4 2339·2	2344·5	2349·7	2355·0	2360·2	2365·4	2370·6	2375·8	2381·0	2386·2	5·2
134	2391·4	2396·6	2401·8	2406·9	2412·1	2417·3	2422·4	2427·6	2432·7	2437·8	5·2
135	2443·0	2448·1	2453·2	2458·3	2463·4	2468·5	2473·6	2478·7	2483·8	2488·9	5·1

152

TABLE II.—*continued.*

A General Table of Values of $\dfrac{d^2}{w}s$ for Ogival-headed Bullets.

v.	0	1	2	3	4	5	6	7	8	9	Diff.
f.s.	secs.	secs.	secs.	secs.	secs.	secs.	secs.	secs.	secs.	secs.	+
136	4 2493·9	2499·0	2504·1	2509·1	2514·2	2519·2	2524·3	2529·3	2534·3	2539·4	5·0
137	2544·4	2549·4	2554·4	2559·4	2564·4	2569·4	2574·4	2579·4	2584·3	2589·3	5·0
138	2594·3	2599·2	2604·2	2609·1	2614·1	2619·0	2624·0	2628·9	2633·8	2638·8	4·9
139	4 2643·7	2648·6	2653·5	2658·4	2663·3	2668·2	2673·1	2678·0	2682·9	2687·8	4·9
140	2692·6	2697·5	2702·4	2707·2	2712·1	2717·0	2721·8	2726·7	2731·5	2736·3	4·9
141	2741·2	2746·0	2750·8	2755·7	2760·5	2765·3	2770·1	2774·9	2779·7	2784·5	4·8
142	4 2789·3	2794·1	2798·9	2803·7	2808·5	2813·2	2818·0	2822·8	2827·5	2832·3	4·8
143	2837·1	2841·8	2846·6	2851·3	2856·0	2860·8	2865·5	2870·2	2875·0	2879·7	4·7
144	2884·4	2889·1	2893·8	2898·6	2903·3	2908·0	2912·7	2917·4	2922·1	2926·7	4·7
145	4 2931·4	2936·1	2940·8	2945·5	2950·1	2954·8	2959·5	2964·1	2968·8	2973·5	4·7
146	2978·1	2982·8	2987·4	2992·1	2996·7	3001·3	3006·0	3010·6	3015·2	3019·9	4·6
147	3024·5	3029·1	3033·7	3038·4	3043·0	3047·6	3052·2	3056·8	3061·4	3066·0	4·6
148	4 3070·6	3075·2	3079·8	3084·4	3089·0	3093·5	3098·1	3102·7	3107·3	3111·8	4·6
149	3116·4	3121·0	3125·6	3130·1	3134·7	3139·2	3143·8	3148·3	3152·9	3157·4	4·6
150	3162·0	3166·5	3171·0	3175·6	3180·1	3184·6	3189·2	3193·7	3198·2	3202·7	4·5
151	4 3207·2	3211·8	3216·3	3220·8	3225·3	3229·8	3234·3	3238·8	3243·3	3247·8	4·5
152	3252·3	3256·8	3261·3	3265·8	3270·3	3274·8	3279·3	3283·8	3288·3	3292·8	4·5
153	3297·2	3301·7	3306·2	3310·6	3315·1	3319·6	3324·1	3328·5	3333·0	3337·5	4·5
154	4 3342·0	3346·4	3350·9	3355·3	3359·8	3364·3	3368·7	3373·2	3377·6	3382·1	4·5
155	3386·5	3391·0	3395·4	3399·9	3404·3	3408·7	3413·2	3417·6	3422·0	3426·5	4·4
156	3430·9	3435·3	3439·8	3444·2	3448·6	3453·0	3457·4	3461·9	3466·3	3470·7	4·4
157	4 3475·1	3479·5	3483·9	3488·3	3492·7	3497·1	3501·5	3505·9	3510·3	3514·7	4·4
158	3519·1	3523·5	3527·9	3532·3	3536·7	3541·1	3545·4	3549·8	3554·2	3558·6	4·4
159	3563·0	3567·3	3571·7	3576·1	3580·4	3584·8	3589·1	3593·5	3597·9	3602·2	4·4
160	4 3606·6	3610·9	3615·3	3619·6	3624·0	3628·3	3632·6	3637·0	3641·2	3645·7	4·3
161	3650·0	3654·3	3658·7	3663·0	3667·3	3671·6	3676·0	3680·3	3684·6	3688·9	4·3
162	3693·3	3697·6	3701·9	3706·1	3710·5	3714·8	3719·1	3723·4	3727·7	3732·0	4·3
163	4 3736·3	3740·6	3744·9	3749·2	3753·5	3757·8	3762·1	3766·4	3770·6	3774·9	4·3
164	3779·2	3783·5	3787·8	3792·0	3796·3	3800·6	3804·9	3809·1	3813·4	3817·6	4·3
165	3281·9	3826·2	3830·4	3834·7	3838·9	3843·2	3847·4	3851·7	3855·9	3860·2	4·3
166	4 3864·4	3868·7	3872·9	3877·2	3881·4	3885·6	3889·9	3894·1	3898·3	3902·5	4·2
167	3906·8	3911·0	3915·2	3919·5	3923·7	3927·9	3932·1	3936·3	3940·5	3944·7	4·2
168	3949·0	3953·2	3957·4	3961·6	3965·8	3970·0	3974·2	3978·4	3982·6	3986·7	4·2
169	4 3990·9	3995·1	3999·3	4003·5	4007·7	4011·9	4016·0	4020·2	4024·4	4028·6	4·2
170	4032·7	4036·9	4041·1	4045·2	4049·4	4053·6	4057·7	4061·9	4066·0	4070·2	4·2
171	4074·3	4078·5	4082·6	4086·8	4090·9	4095·1	4099·2	4103·3	4107·5	4111·6	4·1
172	4 4115·7	4119·9	4124·0	4128·1	4132·3	4136·4	4140·5	4144·6	4148·7	4152·9	4·1
173	4157·0	4161·1	4165·2	4169·3	4173·4	4177·5	4181·6	4185·7	4189·8	4193·9	4·1
174	4198·0	4202·1	4206·2	4210·3	4214·4	4218·5	4222·6	4226·7	4230·8	4234·8	4·1
175	4 4238·9	4243·0	4247·1	4251·2	4255·3	4259·3	4263·4	4267·5	4271·5	4275·6	4·1
176	4279·6	4283·7	4287·8	4291·8	4295·9	4300·0	4304·0	4308·0	4312·1	4316·1	4·1
177	4320·2	4324·2	4328·3	4332·3	4336·4	4340·4	4344·4	4348·5	4352·5	4356·5	4·0

Table II.—continued.

A General Table of Values of $\frac{d^2}{w}s$ for Ogival-headed Bullets.

v.	0	1	2	3	4	5	6	7	8	9	Diff.
f.s.	feet.	feet.	feet.	feet.	feet.	feet.	feet.	feet.	feet.	feet.	+
178	4 4360·5	4364·6	4368·6	4372·6	4376·6	4380·7	4384·7	4388·7	4392·7	4396·7	4·0
179	4400·7	4404·7	4408·8	4412·8	4416·8	4420·8	4424·8	4428·8	4432·8	4436·8	4·0
180	4440·8	4444·7	4448·7	4452·7	4456·7	4460·7	4464·7	4468·7	4472·6	4476·6	4·0
181	4 4480·6	4484·6	4488·5	4492·5	4496·5	4500·5	4504·4	4508·4	4512·4	4516·3	4·0
182	4520·3	4524·2	4528·2	4532·2	4536·1	4540·1	4544·0	4548·0	4551·9	4555·9	4·0
183	4559·8	4563·7	4567·7	4571·0	4575·6	4579·5	4583·4	4587·4	4591·3	4595·2	3·9
184	4 4599·2	4603·1	4607·0	4610·9	4614·9	4618·8	4622·7	4626·6	4630·5	4634·4	3·9
185	4638·4	4642·3	4646·2	4650·1	4654·0	4657·9	4661·8	4665·7	4669·6	4673·5	3·9
186	4677·4	4681·3	4685·2	4689·1	4693·0	4696·9	4700·8	4704·6	4708·5	4712·4	3·9
187	4 4716·3	4720·2	4724·1	4727·9	4731·8	4735·7	4739·6	4743·4	4747·3	4751·2	3·9
188	4755·0	4758·9	4762·8	4766·7	4770·5	4774·4	4778·2	4782·1	4786·0	4789·8	3·9
189	4793·7	4797·5	4801·4	4805·2	4809·1	4812·9	4816·8	4820·6	4824·5	4828·3	3·8
190	4 4832·2	4836·0	4839·8	4843·7	4847·5	4851·4	4855·2	4859·0	4862·8	4866·7	3·8
191	4870·5	4874·3	4878·1	4882·0	4885·8	4889·6	4893·4	4897·3	4901·1	4904·9	3·8
192	4908·7	4912·5	4916·3	4920·1	4923·9	4927·7	4931·5	4935·3	4939·1	4942·9	3·8
193	4 4946·7	4950·5	4954·3	4958·1	4961·9	4965·7	4969·4	4973·2	4977·0	4980·7	3·8
194	4984·5	4988·3	4992·1	4995·8	4999·6	5003·4	5007·1	5010·9	5014·7	5018·4	3·8
195	5022·2	5025·9	5029·7	5033·4	5037·2	5040·9	5044·7	5048·4	5052·1	5055·9	3·7
196	4 5059·6	5063·4	5067·1	5070·8	5074·6	5078·3	5082·0	5085·7	5089·4	5093·1	3·7
197	5096·9	5100·6	5104·3	5108·0	5111·7	5115·4	5119·1	5122·8	5126·5	5130·2	3·7
198	5133·9	5137·5	5141·2	5144·9	5148·6	5152·3	5156·0	5159·6	5163·3	5166·9	3·7
199	4 5170·6	5174·3	5177·9	5181·6	5185·2	5188·9	5192·5	5196·2	5199·8	5203·4	3·6
200	5207·1	5210·7	5214·3	5218·0	5221·6	5225·2	5228·8	5232·5	5236·1	5239·7	3·6
201	5243·3	5246·9	5250·5	5254·1	5257·7	5261·3	5264·9	5268·5	5272·1	5275·7	3·6
202	4 5279·2	5282·8	5286·4	5290·0	5293·6	5297·2	5300·7	5304·3	5307·8	5311·4	3·6
203	5314·9	5318·5	5322·0	5325·6	5329·1	5332·7	5336·2	5339·7	5343·3	5346·8	3·5
204	5350·3	5353·8	5357·3	5360·9	5364·4	5367·9	5371·4	5374·9	5378·4	5381·9	3·5
205	4 5385·4	5388·9	5392·4	5395·9	5399·4	5402·9	5406·4	5409·8	5413·3	5416·7	3·5
206	5420·2	5423·7	5427·1	5430·6	5434·1	5437·5	5441·0	5444·5	5447·8	5451·3	3·5
207	5454·7	5458·1	5461·6	5465·0	5468·4	5471·9	5475·3	5478·7	5482·1	5485·5	3·4
208	4 5488·9	5492·3	5495·7	5499·1	5502·5	5505·9	5509·3	5512·7	5516·1	5519·4	3·4
209	5522·8	5526·2	5529·6	5532·9	5536·3	5539·7	5543·0	5546·4	5549·7	5553·1	3·4
210	5556·4	5559·8	5563·1	5566·4	5569·8	5573·1	5576·5	5579·8	5583·1	5586·4	3·3
211	4 5589·7	5593·0	5596·4	5599·7	5603·0	5606·3	5609·6	5612·9	5616·2	5619·5	3·3
212	5622·8	5626·1	5629·3	5632·6	5635·9	5639·2	5642·5	5645·7	5649·0	5652·3	3·3
213	5655·5	5658·8	5662·0	5665·3	5668·6	5671·8	5675·1	5678·3	5681·5	5684·8	3·2
214	4 5688·0	5691·2	5694·5	5697·7	5700·9	5704·2	5707·4	5710·6	5713·8	5717·0	3·2
215	5720·2	5723·4	5726·6	5729·9	5733·1	5736·3	5739·5	5742·6	5745·8	5749·0	3·2
216	5752·2	5755·4	5758·6	5761·8	5764·9	5768·1	5771·3	5774·4	5777·6	5780·8	3·2
217	4 5783·9	5787·1	5790·2	5793·4	5796·6	5799·7	5802·9	5806·0	5809·1	5812·2	3·1
218	5815·4	5818·5	5821·6	5824·8	5827·9	5831·0	5834·1	5837·3	5840·4	5843·5	3·1
219	5846·6	5849·7	5852·8	5855·9	5859·0	5862·1	5865·2	5868·3	5871·4	5874·4	3·1

TABLE II.—continued.

A General Table of Values of $\dfrac{d^2}{w}s$ for Ogival-headed Bullets.

v.	0	1	2	3	4	5	6	7	8	9	Diff.
f.s.	feet.	feet.	feet.	feet.	feet.	feet.	feet.	feet.	feet.	feet.	+
220	4 5877·5	5880·6	5883·7	5886·8	5889·9	5893·0	5896·0	5899·1	5902·1	5905·2	3·1
221	5908·3	5911·3	5914·4	5917·4	5920·5	5923·6	5926·6	5929·6	5932·7	5935·7	3·0
222	5938·7	5941·8	5944·8	5947·8	5950·9	5953·9	5956·9	5959·9	5963·0	5966·0	3·0
223	4 5969·0	5972·0	5975·0	5978·0	5981·0	5984·0	5987·0	5990·0	5993·0	5996·0	3·0
224	5999·0	6002·0	6004·9	6007·9	6010·9	6013·9	6016·9	6019·8	6022·8	6025·8	3·0
225	6028·7	6031·7	6034·6	6037·6	6040·5	6043·5	6046·5	6049·4	6052·4	6055·3	3·0
226	4 6058·3	6061·2	6064·1	6067·1	6070·0	6072·9	6075·9	6078·8	6081·7	6084·7	2·9
227	6087·6	6090·5	6093·4	6096·3	6099·3	6102·2	6105·1	6108·0	6110·9	6113·8	2·9
228	6116·7	6119·6	6122·5	6125·4	6128·3	6131·2	6134·1	6137·0	6139·9	6142·8	2·9
229	4 6145·7	6148·6	6151·5	6154·4	6157·3	6160·2	6163·1	6166·0	6168·8	6171·7	2·9
230	6174·6	6177·5	6180·4	6183·3	6186·2	6189·1	6191·9	6194·8	6197·7	6200·6	2·9
231	6203·5	6206·4	6209·3	6212·1	6215·0	6217·9	6220·8	6223·7	6226·6	6229·5	2·9
232	4 6232·3	6235·2	6238·1	6241·0	6243·9	6246·8	6249·7	6252·6	6255·4	6258·3	2·9
233	6261·2	6264·1	6267·0	6269·9	6272·8	6275·7	6278·6	6281·5	6284·3	6287·2	2·9
234	6290·1	6293·0	6295·9	6298·8	6301·7	6304·6	6307·5	6310·4	6313·3	6316·2	2·9
235	4 6319·0	6322·0	6324·9	6327·7	6330·6	6333·5	6336·4	6339·3	6342·2	6345·1	2·9
236	6348·0	6350·9	6353·8	6356·7	6359·6	6362·5	6365·4	6368·3	6371·2	6374·1	2·9
237	6377·0	6379·9	6382·8	6385·7	6388·6	6391·5	6394·4	6397·3	6400·2	6403·1	2·9
238	4 6406·0	6408·9	6411·8	6414·8	6417·7	6420·6	6423·5	6426·4	6429·3	6432·2	2·9
239	6435·1	6438·0	6440·9	6443·8	6446·8	6449·7	6452·6	6455·5	6458·4	6461·3	2·9
240	6464·2	6467·1	6470·1	6473·0	6475·9	6478·8	6481·7	6484·6	6487·6	6490·5	2·9
241	4 6493·4	6496·3	6499·2	6502·2	6505·1	6508·0	6510·9	6513·8	6516·8	6519·7	2·9
242	6522·6	6525·6	6528·5	6531·4	6534·3	6537·3	6540·2	6543·1	6546·1	6549·0	2·9
243	6551·9	6554·9	6557·8	6560·7	6563·7	6566·6	6569·5	6572·5	6575·4	6578·3	2·9
244	4 6581·3	6584·2	6587·2	6590·1	6593·0	6596·0	6598·9	6601·8	6604·8	6607·7	2·9
245	6610·6	6613·6	6616·5	6619·5	6622·4	6625·3	6628·3	6631·2	6634·2	6637·1	2·9
246	6640·1	6643·0	6645·9	6748·9	6651·8	6654·8	6657·7	6660·6	6663·6	6666·5	2·9
247	4 6669·5	6672·4	6675·4	6678·3	6681·3	6684·2	6687·2	6690·1	6693·0	6696·0	2·9
248	6698·9	6701·9	6704·8	6707·8	6710·7	6713·7	6716·6	6719·6	6722·5	6725·5	2·9
249	6728·4	6731·3	6734·3	6737·2	6740·2	6743·1	6746·1	6749·0	6752·0	6754·9	2 9
250	4 6757·8	6760·7	6763·7	6766·7	6769·6	6772·6	6775·5	6778·4	6781·4	6784·3	2·9
251	6787·3	6790·2	6793·1	6796·1	6799·0	6802·0	6804·9	6807·8	6810·8	6813·7	2·9
252	6816·6	6819·6	6822·5	6825·4	6828·4	6831·3	6834·2	6837·1	6840·1	6843·0	2·9
253	4 6845·9	6848·8	6851·8	6854·7	6857·6	6860·5	6863·5	6866·4	6869·3	6872·2	2·9
254	6875·1	6878·1	6881·0	6883·9	6886·8	6889·7	6892·6	6895·6	6898·5	6901·4	2·9
255	6904·3	6907·2	6910·1	6913·0	6915·9	6918·8	6921·7	6924·6	6927·5	6930·4	2·9
256	4 6933·3	6936·2	6939·1	6942·0	6944·9	6947·8	6950·6	6953·5	6956·4	6959·3	2·9
257	6962·2	6965·0	6967·9	6970·8	6973·7	6976·5	6979·4	6982·3	6985·1	6988·0	2·9
258	6990·9	6993·7	6996·6	6999·4	7002·3	7005·1	7008·0	7010·8	7013·7	7016·5	2·9
259	4 7019·4	7022·2	7025·0	7027·9	7030·7	7033·5	7036·4	7039·2	7042·0	7044·8	2·8
260	7047·7	7050·5	7053·3	7056·1	7058·9	7061·7	7064·5	7067·4	7070·2	7073·0	2·8
261	7075·8	7078·6	7081·4	7084·2	7087·0	7089·7	7092·5	7095·3	7098·1	7100·9	2·8

TABLE II.—continued.

A General Table of Values of $\dfrac{d^2}{w} s$ for Ogival-headed Bullets.

v.	0	1	2	3	4	5	6	7	8	9	Diff.
f.s.	feet.	feet.	feet.	feet.	feet.	feet.	feet.	feet.	feet.	feet.	+
262	4 7103·7	7106·5	7109·2	7112·0	7114·8	7117·6	7120·3	7123·1	7125·9	7128·6	2·8
263	7131·4	7134·2	7136·9	7139·7	7142·4	7145·2	7147·9	7150·7	7153·4	7156·2	2·8
264	7158·9	7161·7	7164·4	7167·1	7169·9	7172·6	7175·4	7178·1	7180·8	7183·5	2·7
265	4 7186·3	7189·0	7191·7	7194·4	7197·1	7199·9	7202·6	7205·3	7208·0	7210·7	2·7
266	7213·4	7216·1	7218·8	7221·5	7224·2	7226·9	7229·6	7232·3	7235·0	7237·7	2·7
267	7240·4	7243·1	7245·8	7248·5	7251·2	7253·8	7256·5	7259·2	7261·9	7264·5	2·7
268	4 7267·2	7269·9	7272·5	7275·2	7277·9	7280·5	7283·2	7285·9	7288·5	7291·2	2·7
269	7293·8	7296·5	7299·1	7301·8	7304·4	7307·1	7309·7	7312·3	7315·0	7317·6	2·6
270	7320·2	7322·9	7325·5	7328·1	7330·8	7333·4	7336·0	7338·6	7341·2	7343·9	2·6
271	4 7346·5	7349·1	7351·7	7354·3	7356·9	7359·5	7362·1	7364·7	7367·3	7369·9	2·6
272	7372·5	7375·1	7377·7	7380·3	7382·9	7385·5	7388·1	7390·7	7393·3	7395·8	2·6
273	7398·4	7401·0	7403·6	7406·2	7408·7	7411·3	7413·9	7416·4	7419·0	7421·6	2·6
274	4 7424·1	7426·7	7429·3	7431·8	7434·4	7436·9	7439·5	7442·0	7444·6	7447·1	2·6
275	7449·7	7452·2	7454·8	7457·3	7459·8	7462·4	7464·9	7467·4	7470·0	7472·5	2·5
276	7475·0	7477·5	7480·1	7482·6	7485·1	7487·6	7490·1	7492·7	7495·2	7497·7	2·5
277	4 7500·2	7502·7	7505·2	7507·7	7510·2	7512·7	7515·2	7517·7	7520·2	7522·7	2·5
278	7525·2	7527·7	7530·1	7532·6	7535·1	7537·6	7540·1	7542·6	7545·0	7547·5	2·5
279	7550·0	7552·4	7554·9	7557·4	7559·9	7562·3	7564·8	7567·2	7569·7	7572·2	2·5
280	4 7574·6	7577·1	7579·5	7582·0	7584·4	7586·8	7589·3	7591·7	7594·2	7596·6	2·4
281	7599·0	7601·5	7603·9	7606·4	7608·8	7611·2	7613·6	7616·1	7618·5	7620·9	2·4
282	7623·3	7625·7	7628·2	7630·6	7633·0	7635·4	7637·8	7640·2	7642·6	7645·0	2·4
283	4 7647·4	7649·8	7652·2	7654·6	7657·0	7659·4	7661·8	7664·2	7666·6	7669·0	2·4
284	7671·3	7673·7	7676·1	7678·5	7680·9	7683·3	7685·6	7688·0	7690·4	7692·7	2·4
285	7695·1	7697·5	7699·8	7702·2	7704·6	7706·9	7709·3	7711·6	7714·0	7716·4	2·4
286	4 7718·7	7721·1	7723·4	7725·8	7728·1	7730·4	7732·8	7735·1	7737·5	7739·8	2·3
287	7742·1	7744·5	7746·8	7749·1	7751·5	7753·8	7756·1	7758·4	7760·8	7763·1	2·3
288	7765·4	7767·7	7770·0	7772·4	7774·7	7777·0	7779·3	7781·6	7783·9	7786·2	2·3
289	4 7788·5	7790·8	7793·1	7795·4	7797·7	7800·0	7802·3	7804·6	7806·9	7809·2	2·3
290	7811·5										

Chapter VII.

HISTORY OF SMALL ARMS TO THE ADOPTION OF BREECH-LOADERS.

Arms.

The word *arms*, in a general sense, includes every description of warlike weapon, whether for offence or defence; the following history will show, as far as can be ascertained, the time and place of their invention, and when introduced into England.

Clubs.

It is supposed that the first artificial arms of offence were of wood, and that the *club* was the first weapon of the kind.

Arms of stone, of bone, and of brass, appear to have been used before recourse was had to those of iron or steel.

Josephus assures us that the patriarch Joseph taught the use of iron arms in Egypt among the troops of Pharaoh.

Speaking generally, the leading nations of Europe have adopted improved weapons, whether invented in their own country or not. This policy contributed, in a great measure, to render the Romans masters of the world; for, having successively warred against all nations, they constantly renounced their own methods of warfare, arms, &c., whenever they met with better.

In England we have adopted continually the inventions of other nations; whatever arm we refer to, we cannot trace its origin to the conceptions of our own countrymen, although, after its adoption, we have generally improved and perfected it.

Spears.

Arms of the *spear* kind reach into the past far beyond our powers of tracing.

Swords.

Swords have also been known from time immemorial.

Bows and arrows.

Bows and arrows are likewise of ancient date, for we read of them in Scripture, as early as 1892 B C., in

Genesis xxi, in which it is said of Ishmael, "and God "was with the lad; and he grew, and dwelt in the "wilderness, and became an archer."

Until the Second Punic War the Romans had no archers in their armies, except among their auxiliaries; afterwards they had them as mercenaries only.

ANCIENT BRITONS.

The arms of the inhabitants of Britain previous to 1100 B.C. 1100 B.C. were *bows*, with *arrows* of reed headed with flint or pointed bone;—*spears* and *javelins* made of long bones ground to a point and inserted in oaken shafts;—*battle-axes* of flint; and *clubs* of four points or edges called "cats," made of oak.

Ancient British Stone Arms (reduced size).

Battle axe head of marl containing silex.

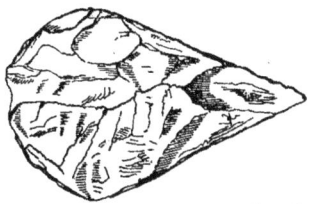

Stone blade of spear let into wooden shaft.

A kind of Tomahawk, blow given by point, of brown or black silex.

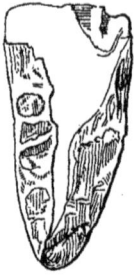
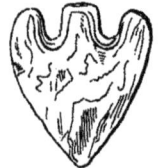

Battle axe head. Silician stone, broad end sharpened to an edge.

Flint arrow head inserted in reed.

Ancient British Bronze Arms.

Blade weapon, the prototype of the Welsh glaive.

Battle-axe, improved form, found in Ireland.

Battle-axe of earliest form, found in Cardiganshire.

Improved style of spear blade, found in Ireland.

[Early style of spear blades.

Upwards of 11 centuries before the Christian Era 1100 B.C. Phœnician merchants were attracted to the south-western coasts of Britain, and especially towards the Scilly Islands, by the abundant supply of tin, which was extensively used abroad in the manufacture of bronze, both for weapons of war and for implements of peace.

From the Phœnicians the Britons learnt the art of manufacturing warlike implements of metal.

In the Tower Armoury may be seen several ancient stone weapons, which have been found in Norfolk, in Ireland, and in various parts of the world; also bronze weapons, ancient British swords, ancient Irish swords, daggers, bronze spear heads, and celts, found in England, Ireland, and abroad.

ROMAN PERIOD.

The Romans first invaded Britain under Julius Cæsar, 55 B.C. 55 B.C. The arms of the British at this time were the *spear* or *lance*, the *sword*, *dagger*, *battle-axe*, and *bows* and *arrows*, the latter being made of reed, with flint, bone, or metal heads. The metal used in the construction of arms was bronze.

On the Romans obtaining a footing in England, the A.D. 78 to British exchanged their bronze weapons for steel. 400.

The Roman cavalry and infantry were armed with swords, shields, and javelins, pointed at both ends.

Ancient Roman Arms.

Broken blade of a Roman iron lance, found in Suffolk.

Roman spear head of iron, found in Lincolnshire.

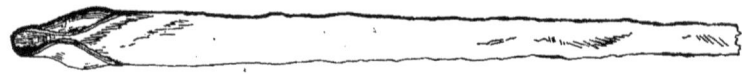

Broken blade of Roman javelin, found in Roman entrenchment in Gloucestershire.

THE SAXONS.

A.D. 450 to 1066.

During the Anglo-Saxon period, the Saxons, who were all soldiers, used the sword, the spear, and the axe, which were all formed of iron.

The Saxon military force consisted principally of heavy and light infantry, the former carried large shields armed with spikes, long broad swords, and spears; the latter, swords and spears only. Some of the spears were "barbed," and others broad and "leaf shaped." They had, moreover, men armed with clubs, and others with battle-axes and javelins. Axes were hurled about this time.

In the early part of this period the Saxons may have used bows and arrows in war; if so, in the latter part they had discontinued their use except in the chase, for Henry of Huntingdon makes William the Conqueror speak of the Saxons as a nation not even having arrows; they were, however, celebrated for their expertness with the *mace* and *battle-axe*.

There was a severe penance prescribed in the ancient canons for going unarmed, and the sword consequently was almost generally worn.

Harold II. having observed that the heavy armour of the Saxons prevented them from pursuing the Welsh into their recesses, commanded them to use lighter weapons, and armour made of leather only.

At the battle of Hastings the Saxons used the battle-axe, javelin, sling spear, and lance.

NORMAN PERIOD.

William the Conqueror.

A.D. 1066 to 1087.

Under the Normans the archers were a most important body; they did the Conqueror invaluable service at the battle of Hastings, which was decided by them.

The bow from this time, and for many centuries after, was the chief arm of the English. Archers were both mounted and on foot.

The weapons carried by the infantry from the time of the Conquest were bows and arrows, half pikes, spears, halberds, maces, various kinds of battle-axes, swords, daggers, and piles, *i.e.*, pieces of wood smaller at one end than the other; these arms continued in use, with little variation, to the close of the 12th century. Piles and maces were the arms of the serfs; lances and swords the arms of the freemen. The bow does not appear to have been among the arms of the noblemen.

William Rufus.

William II.—It appears that in the first Crusade in 1097 the Turks used the bow, and by the rapidity of their fire caused great havoc among the crusaders.

A.D. 1097 to 1100.

The Welsh in this reign used arrows and javelins as missile weapons; the Irish used javelins only.

Henry I.

In the reign of Henry I., archery was much cultivated, and great numbers of bowmen were brought into the field; and to encourage practice with the bow, a law, the first of its kind, was passed freeing from the charge of murder anyone who, in practising with arrows or darts, should kill a person standing near.

A.D. 1100 to 1135.

The cross-bow appears to have been used in the chase in this reign.

Stephen.

Stephen.—No improvement in arms appears to have been made in this reign.

A.D. 1135 to 1154.

Henry II.

Henry II.—The Irish at this period were still without the bow, and the English conquests in Ireland were due to its use.

A.D. 1154 to 1189.

The Welsh were celebrated for expertness in the use of their bow, which was made very stout and of wild unpolished elm; their arrows inflicted severe wounds at close quarters.

Richard I.

A.D. 1189 to 1199.

To the sword, the spear, the battle-axe, and the bow, we have to add the *arbalest* or cross-bow, which was adopted as a weapon of war in England during the reign of Richard I.

The cross-bow was not a new invention, for by some it is said to have been of Sicilian origin, by others of Cretan, and that it had been previously introduced into England by the Saxons at the time of Hengist and Horsa, about A.D. 457. The cross-bow, however, does not appear on any of the early Roman monuments.

The use of the cross-bow was forbidden by the second Lateran Council, A.D. 1139, as fatal and cruel, and again by Pope Innocent III., about A.D. 1200.

The bow of the cross-bow was fixed crosswise on the top of a sort of staff or stock of wood, and was commonly made of steel, although at first, and occasionally at a later period, it was made of hazel and other wood; the cord or string of the bow when undrawn crossed the stock at right angles; the bow was bent at first by the foot being placed on it to keep it down, whilst the string was drawn up to the catch on the stock by the hand; the cord was double, with a loop in the centre on which the projectile rested.

The stock of the cross-bow was often hollowed out on its upper surface with a view to direct the arrow. In filling up the channel thus made with a tube split laterally to receive the string of the bow, an arm was obtained which threw round pebbles, stone or metal bullets; it consequently received the name of the pebble bow or "arc-a-buse," *i.e.*, a bow which conducts or directs. The term harquebus is the same as applied later to one of the early fire-arms.

About the end of the 13th century the stock of the cross-bow had affixed to it a moveable wheel of steel with two notches, the one above to hold the string, and the other below to catch the trigger; the bow was held down by the foot while the cord was drawn up to the notch with the aid of a lever, such as the "goat's foot":—the cord of the stronger bows was drawn back by a mechanical appliance called the "moulinet," a series of pulleys, and sometimes by a kind of windlass.

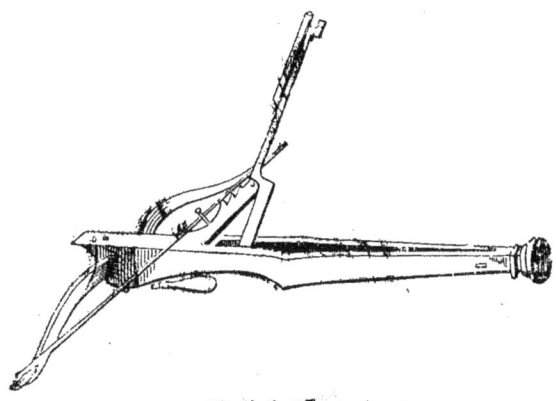

Goat's Foot Lever.

Windlass.

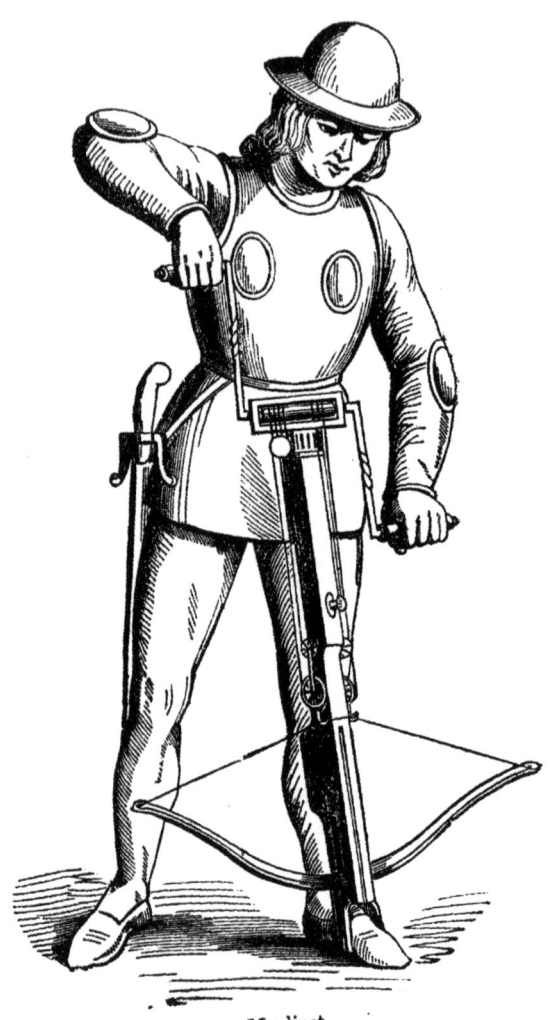

Moulinet.

Many of the cross-bows were provided with sights.

The cross-bow continued in use until small arms superseded it, and the cross-bowmen were some mounted and some on foot, and their place in battle was in the van.

The long bow for infantry was of the most simple construction, and a far superior weapon to the crossbow, inasmuch as half a dozen arrows could be discharged from it in the time taken to wind up the cross-bow and fix its projectile.

The long-bow was lighter than the cross-bow, and being held vertically, the soldier required but little space to work in. It however required the most careful training to use the long-bow dexterously, whereas the cross-bow could be charged and discharged by a boy, or without training.

Barbed arrows were in general use, and were the most fatal.

A captain was in charge of 20 archers, who became daily of more importance in the field; archers usually commenced the battle. They were sometimes intermixed with cavalry, and, when with infantry, were generally placed on the flanks, as well as the cross-bowmen.

Archers were preferred as infantry, and cross-bowmen as cavalry.

Richard I. established the corps of serjeants-at-arms, the original number being 24; they were appointed for life, and were armed with the mace, sword, and bows and arrows.

John.

John.—No change in arms made in this reign.   A.D. 1199 1216.

Henry III.

In the reign of Henry III., the *martel-de-fer*, a pointed hammer or small pick-axe, was added to the offensive weapons; it made sad havoc with the mail or armour, and left fatal openings for the passage of the sword or lance.   A.D. 1216 to 1272.

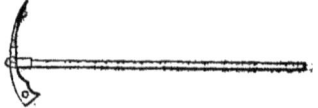

Martel-de-fer, time of Henry III.

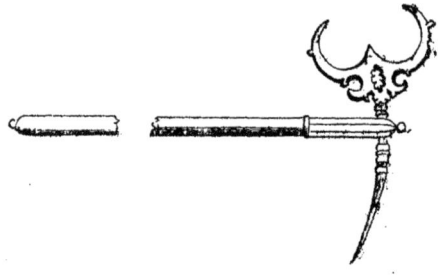

Martel-de-fer, time of Edward VI.

The infantry were of three kinds, viz., the men at arms or dismounted knights; the spearmen; the light armed, having light spears or axes: and besides these there were the slingers, the archers, and the cross-bowmen.

The archers at this period carried their arrows for immediate use in a belt or girdle.

Edward I.

A.D. 1272 to 1307.

During the reign of Edward I., the *falchion*, a peculiarly shaped broad bladed sword; the *estoc*, a small stabbing sword; the *anelas*, a broad dagger tapering to a small point; and the *cuttelas* (whence cutlass), a military knife, were added to the offensive weapons.

Edward I. commanded every man to be armed according to his property; some to have sword, knife, bow and arrows; some, other weapons; and those having less than 40s., in land, if able, to have a bow and arrows.

Edward II.

In the reign of Edward II. a kind of pole-axe, *i.e.*, an axe at the end of a pole, and so called to distinguish it from the battle-axe, was introduced.

A.D. 1307 to 1327.

Edward III.

During the reign of Edward III. the weapons of the knights were chiefly lances, swords, maces, and battle-axes.

A.D. 1327 to 1377.

Although Edward III. found it necessary to enjoin practice with the long-bow by two mandates, in consequence of its superiority over the cross-bow in length of range and rapidity of fire, he having observed the great exactness of the shot discharged from the cross-bow, and the convenience with which it was used on horseback, wrote to the sheriffs of London to encourage its use; it does not, however, appear that crossbowmen were raised in England in this reign; those in the English service were mercenaries.

The Genoese were the most celebrated cross-bowmen in Europe, and were employed by the English and the French at various periods.

The English archers did great execution at, and may be said to have gained the battle of Cressy in 1346, at which the French had 15000 Genoese cross-bowmen, the greatest number of these troops ever known to have been in the field at one time. The English archers did great havoc also at the battle of Poictiers in 1356.

While the long-bow was the chief arm of the English, the cross-bow was that of foreign powers: and our great successes in war at this period may be attributed, in a great measure, to the very rapid fire of the long-bow; the cross-bow, however, was constantly used by the English in the defence of places, and various missiles were propelled by it.

In this century archery was at its zenith; a painted bow sold for 1s. 6d.; a white bow for 1s.; arrows, with sharpened points, 1s. 2d. per sheaf of 24; if blunt headed, 1s. per sheaf.

Infantry were employed in preference to cavalry,

in consequence of the great slaughter of horses, &c., by the archers and cross-bowmen.

The knights often performed their chief service in the field when dismounted, and then mounted to pursue the enemy.

The cavalry in this and the previous reign were composed of men-at-arms (heavy cavalry), hobilers (light cavalry), and mounted archers. The hobilers were in great repute at this time; they were armed with a sword, knife, and lance; the infantry consisted of spearmen, archers, and cross-bowmen.

Pavisers, men carrying pavises or shields, were employed about this period; they were of three kinds, viz., those who fought on horseback, those who fought on foot, and those who carried pavises in front of archers or cross-bowmen, to defend and shield them from the enemy.

Fire-arms were introduced in this reign. Authors differ in their statements as regards the exact year and country in which they were invented; the actual date, &c., of the first portable fire-arm, the *hand gun*, is involved in obscurity.

An inquisition taken at Huntercombe in Yorkshire, in 1375, the record being in the Chapterhouse, Westminster, mentions the attack on the manor house of Huntercombe by 40 men armed, among other weapons, with " gonnes," supposed to be the hand gun.

We read of the "*Arquebuse à Mèche*" in Germany in 1378, so that the invention probably occurred some years earlier.

Gunpowder having been first manufactured in England in 1346, it is not probable that the actual introduction of cannon and hand guns could be of a later date.

Cannon are said to have been used in the English expedition against Scotland in 1327, and at the battle of Cressy in 1346. In 1360 there were four copper guns in the tower. Cannon were first used for siege purposes, but were rarely used, even at the end of this century, in the field.

Cannon balls were chiefly of stone, but sometimes of iron or lead.

Stones thrown by hand were used in the defence of places, in the field, and on board ship in this reign.

Richard II

Richard II. commanded the practice of archery on Sundays and holidays by servants, labourers, &c., and the leaving off by them of games of quoits, ball, &c. A.D. 1377 to 1399.

In the excavation of the castle of Tannenberg, dismantled in 1399, there was found a hand gun of brass, with part of the wooden stock remaining, and the iron rammer belonging to it.

Henry IV.

By an Act of Parliament in the reign of Henry IV. it was enacted that the heads of arrows and quarrels should be boiled, or brazed and hardened at the points with steel, and that every arrow head or quarrel should bear the name of the maker under pain of imprisonment. A quarrel was an arrow with a four-sided or pyramidal head; they were sometimes feathered with wood or brass. A.D. 1399 to 1415.

The archers did great execution at the battle of Shrewsbury in 1403, at which cannon were used.

Henry V.

Henry V., in order that there might be no want of arrows, ordered the sheriffs of the several counties to procure feathers from the wings of geese by picking six from each goose. A.D. 1413 to 1422.

The bows were of great strength, and the arrows a yard in length besides the head; and every archer had a good bow, a sheaf of arrows, and a sword.

The victory of Agincourt in 1415, where cannon were used both by the French and English, is in a great measure ascribed to the English archers, who at this time bore on their shoulders a stake six feet in length, sharpened at both ends, to be fixed in the ground before them in a slanting direction, as a defence against cavalry.

Cross-bowmen, who had a paviser in attendance, carried their bolts or quarrels in a case at the right hip;

Cross-bowman with paviser.

at this period, and for some time previously, the English had but little confidence in the cross-bow, so much so, that with the force of 10000 men which left England in 1415, there were not more than 98 cross-bowmen.

Hand guns are mentioned as having been first used at the siege of Arras, in 1414.

Henry VI.

Hand Guns.

Henry VI.—In 1430 hand guns were used at the siege of Lucca; this is mentioned by some authors as the most reliable date of the first use of small arms in the field. In 1446 they came into more general use. A.D. 1422 to 1461.

Spanish historians state that Spain was the first power which armed the foot soldier with hand guns.

The hand gun was of very rude construction; it consisted of a simple iron or brass tube with a touch hole at the top; this tube was fixed in a straight stock of wood, about a cubit and a half long, called the frame of the "gonne;" it had no lock, and, when about to be fired, the end of the stock passed under the right armpit.

The hand gun used by the horse soldier was similar to that above described; it had a ring at the end of the stock, by which it was suspended by a cord round

Hand Guns.

Hand gun and axe combined.

Hand gun being fired.

the neck; a *forked rest*, fitted by a ring to the saddle bow, served to steady the gun, which, when not in use, hung down in front of the right leg.

A match and ammunition of very inferior quality formed the appurtenances of the hand gun.

The match was made of cotton or hemp spun slack, and boiled in a strong solution of saltpetre, or in the lees of wine.

It was soon found that the priming fell off the touch hole by being on the top of the tube or barrel of the hand gun; a hole was therefore made at the side, and a small pan placed under it to hold the priming, with a cover moving on a pivot to turn off or on with the hand. The hand gun was thus used in England as early as 1446.

The English continued to encourage archery, for in 1453 the Parliament voted an army of 20000 bowmen for service in France.

The battle of St. Albans, in 1455, during the wars of the Roses (York and Lancaster), seems to have been won entirely by archers.

Cross-bow stocks in this reign were made of hard wood; they were ornamented with ivory, and were 3 ft. 3 in. in length, and the steel bow was 2 ft. 8 in. from end to end, all weighing 15 lbs.

Edward IV.

An Act was passed in the reign of Edward IV., A.D. 1461 to ordering every Englishman to have a bow of his own 1483. height, and butts to be erected in every township for the inhabitants to shoot at on feast days; also that bows of yew were to be sold for 3s. 4d.

Bows became so scarce and dear that all vessels bringing merchandise to England were compelled by law to land four bow staves with every ton of goods.

The landing of Edward IV. at Ravenspur, in Yorkshire, in 1471, with 300 Flemings armed with hand "gonnes," has been quoted by authors as the first instance of a force having been landed in England armed with hand guns, it cannot be received as proving that this description of warlike weapon only made its first appearance in this conntry in 1471.

Edward V.

A.D. 1483.
No changes in small arms were made during this short period.

Richard III.

A.D. 1483 to 1485.
In consequence of a seditious conspiracy of the Lombards, by which the bow staves were raised from 2*l*. the 100, the usual price, to the outrageous sum of 8*l*. the 100, it was enacted in the reign of Richard III. that 10 bow staves should be imported with every butt of Malmsey or Tyre wines brought from Venice, under a penalty of 13*s*. 4*d*. for every butt of the said wines in case of neglect.

Henry VII.

The Matchlock.

A.D. 1485 to 1509.
An improvement in fire-arms took place in the first year of the reign of Henry VII., or, as some say, perhaps at the close of Edward IV., by fixing a cock on the hand gun to hold the *match*, which was brought down to the priming by a trigger, whence the term matchlock, or *arc-a-bouche*, a bow with a mouth, which was afterwards corrupted to harquebus, the same name that was occasionally applied to the cross-bow.

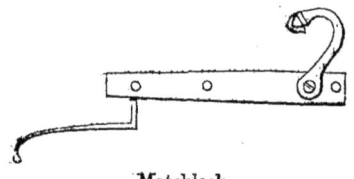

Matchlock.

It is supposed that the harquebus or matchlock was invented in Italy. The weapon is still in use among the Chinese, Tartars, Sikhs, Persians, and Turks.

Henry VII., in establishing his body guard of 50 men (now the yeomen of the guard) in 1485, armed them with swords, and half with bows and arrows, and the other half with the harquebus. This was the first

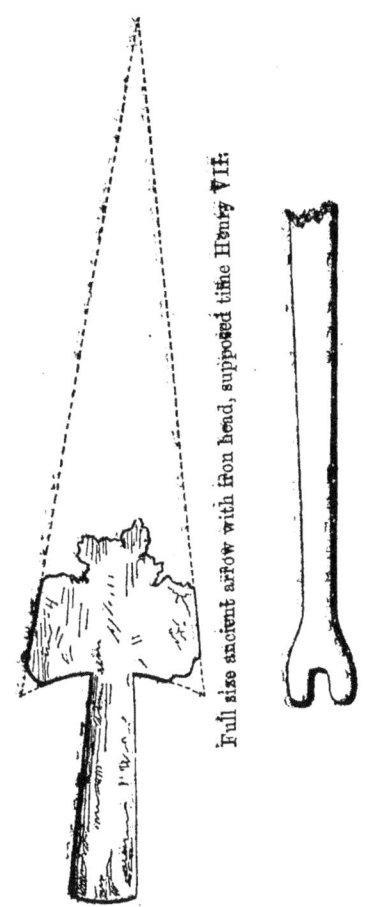

Full size ancient arrow with iron head, supposed time Henry VII.

regular standing force in England, with the exception of the corps of serjeant-at-arms established by Richard I.

The cross-bow of this reign was of two kinds, the *latch* with its grooved stock for quarrels, and the *prodd* for bullets, which latter was in use by the Genoese at this period. The service cross-bow would kill point blank at from 40 to 60 yards, and when elevated at from 120 to 160 yards.

At the battle of Fornone, in 1495, there were German harquebusiers mounted, and on foot.

The harquebus underwent an improvement during this period; hitherto, like the cross-bow, it had a straight stock, but now it was formed with a wide butt end which might be placed against the right breast. Subsequently the stock was bent or crooked, a German invention, when the arm was called a hackbutt, or hagbut, and the smaller sort demihags.

By a statute of Henry VII., in 1508, the use of the cross-bow was forbidden, except among the nobility, the object being to induce the more frequent practice of archery.

Henry VIII.

A.D. 1509 to 1547.

Henry VIII., to enforce the practice of archery, enacted "that every man under the age of 60, not "labouring under some bodily incapacity (ecclesiastics "and judges excepted) should use the exercise of "shooting in the long-bow, that fathers, governors, and "masters should instruct and bring up their sons and "youths under their charge in the knowledge of shoot-"ing, and that every man having a boy or boys in his "house should provide for each of them of the age of "seven years, and until he came to that of 17, a bow "and two shafts to induce him to learn archery;" also, "that the young archer might acquire an accurate "eye and a strength of arm-bone, none under 24 years "of age might shoot at a standing mark . . . . . under "the penalty of 4d. for each shot made contrary to this "regulation," and that "no person above the said age "should shoot at any mark that was not above eleven "score yards (220) distance under pain of forfeiting for "every shot 6s. 8d." The range of the bow is said to have been from 320 to 400 yards.

The statute of Henry VII. (1508) was renewed for prohibiting the cross-bow, and another was enacted some 20 years later inflicting a fine of 20l. on every person who kept a cross-bow in his house.

The best wood for bows was yew; but as this was not very plentiful, they were ordered to be made of witch-hazel, ash, or elm; for people from seven to 17 years of age, bowyers were bound to keep a supply of bows at 6d. and not exceeding 1s. each; a yew wood bow was not to be sold for more than 3s. 4d.

The strings of bows were made of hemp, or of the best silk; the string ought to be the height of a man, and the arrow half the length of the string.

Arrows (which were carried in a quiver at the right side, or at the back) were made of different kinds of wood; ash was considered the best for warfare; their heads were of the best iron pointed with steel, and were of different forms and denominations; some were barbed, which rendered it impossible to withdraw them without laceration; they were feathered with goose feathers, and some were tipped with combustible matter for setting fire to houses, ships, &c.

The latch cross-bow in this century had a windlass let into the stock to draw up the string to save the trouble of putting it on and taking it off, as was the case with the "moulinet;" as this measure, however, weakened the handle or stock, recourse was had to the "goat's foot lever."

In the reign of Henry VIII. the infantry were chiefly archers, cross-bowmen, halberdiers, pikemen, and harquebusiers. Pikemen formed the principal portion of the English army from this reign to that of William III.

The Pistol.

The pistol, invented by Camillo Vitelli, an Italian, and so named from having been made at Pistoia, with its variety the "dag" or "tache," is of this period, and was first used by cavalry in England in 1544.

(S.A.)

The Wheel Lock.

The wheel lock, an improvement on the matchlock or harquebus, was invented at Nuremberg in 1517; was first used at the siege of Parma in 1521; was brought

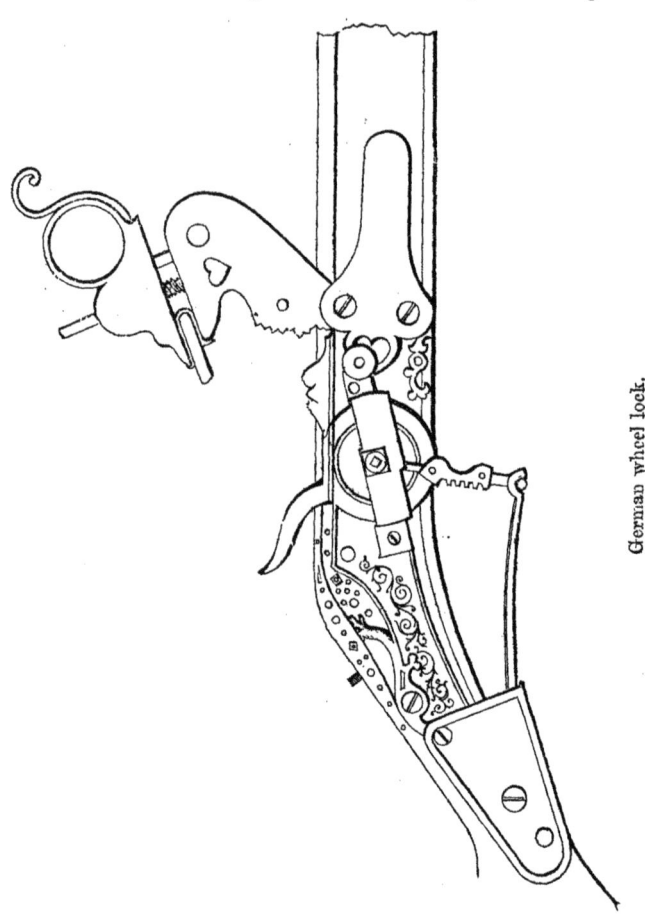

German wheel lock.

to England in 1530, and continued in use in this country, although not generally, until the time of Charles II.

The wheel lock consisted of a steel wheel rasped at the edge, which protruded into the priming pan; a strong spring, and a cock which was fixed on the square end of an axle or spindle, into which fitted a piece of pyrites (sulphuret of iron); the wheel and the spring were connected by a chain swivel; and the cock was so fitted that it could be moved backwards or forwards at pleasure, a strong spring being connected with it to keep it firm in its position. When it was required to discharge the gun, the lock was wound up by means of a key or spanner, which fitted on the axle or spindle, and the cock was let down to the priming pan, the pyrites resting on the wheel; on the trigger being pressed the wheel was released and put in motion, when sparks were emitted which set fire to the powder in the pan.

The wheel lock frequently missed fire, as the pyrites, which is of a friable nature, broke in the pan, and impeded the free action of the wheel, hence the match was usually retained to be ready for use when required; it was complicated it its construction, and difficult to repair, and the priming was exposed to the wet and wind when the pan was uncovered to wind up the lock previous to the gun being fired; these defects and its expense prevented, no doubt, its general adoption.

The small arms of this period were the hand gun or harquebus, hackbutt, and demihague; and it was enacted in this reign that no hand gun should be used of less dimensions than one yard in length, barrel and stock included, and no hackbutt under three-quarters of a yard.

The harquebus and hackbutt do not appear originally to have been of any particular length or bore. Hewitt's Ancient Armour and Weapons in Europe, p. 624, vol. iii., speaking of the harquebus of the 16th century, says, "The barrels are of several varieties; breech-
"loading and muzzle-loading, bell-mouthed and cylin-
"drical. Two examples of the breech-loading arm,
"both of which appear to have belonged to King Henry

"VIII., are in the Tower collection. One of these, "No. $\frac{1}{1}$ of the catalogue, has the royal initials, H.R., "and a rose crowned, supported by lions, chased on "the barrel, where also is the date 1537. The No. $\frac{1}{3}$ "has the rose and fleur-de-lis carved "on the stock, and it is remarkable "that the moveable chamber which "carries the cartridge has exactly "the form of that in vogue at the "present day. These two examples "appear to be the arms named in the "Tower inventory of 1679:—'car- "'bine, 1, and fowling-piece, 1, said "'to be King Henry the VIII.'s.'"
The invention of breech-loading small arms has likewise been attributed to Henry II. of France in 1540, who applied it also to the harquebus. The demihagues were in size and bore smaller, and were probably about half the weight, and gave rise to pistols.

The Musket.

In this reign the Spaniards, in consequence of the small calibre and power of the hand gun and harquebus, were induced to construct heavier and larger fire arms, carrying a larger ball, supposed to be 10 to the lb., which were called muskets, and which were introduced into England before the middle of the 16th century, and came into general use throughout Europe, having been first extensively used at the battle of Pavia in 1525.

The term musket is properly a firearm borne on the shoulder; it was applied to the matchlock, and the term firelock to the wheel lock in this century, to the flint lock towards the end of the 17th century; latterly both terms seem to have been applied indifferently.

Rest from which the musket was fired.

Edward VI.

In Edward VI.'s reign archery began to decline. It is not surprising that the long bow, which was the chief and favourite weapon of England, and which in the hands of trained men was most accurate and capable of being used rapidly, should have been reluctantly given up for fire-arms, which were, for a long time, exceedingly heavy, clumsy, slow in loading, troublesome in cleaning, and without any accuracy in shooting

A.D. 1547 to 1553.

In this reign the cavalry changed the mace for the pistol.

Mary.

In Queen Mary's reign the bow and arrows, pike, bill, harquebus, and hackbutt were the arms in use. The rulers of this reign do not appear to have been anxious to introduce fire-arms into general use, as they left it to the choice of the people whether they should find a long bow and a sheaf of arrows, or a hackbutt, in every case where they were by law charged with the latter; they apparently considered the long bow equal to the harquebus.

A.D. 1553 to 1558.

Elizabeth.

In the reign of Elizabeth a second pistol was given to the cavalry in place of the estoc; and carabines, petronels with wheel lock, and dragons appeared.

A.D. 1558 to 1603.

The Carbine.

The carabine or carbine was a kind of small fire-arm about 3½ feet in length, and so called from a description of light cavalry denominated "carabins," from Spain, probably of Moorish origin, and first mentioned in 1559. These troops were armed with a carabine and pistol. The derivation of the term "carabine," however, is disputed.

The petronel was the medium between the harquebus and pistol, having a broad butt so as to rest in its position with firmness on the chest, against which it was held when firing, whence its name. It was of French origin, and was first used, it is said, by banditti in the Pyrenees.

The dragon was a small kind of blunderbuss, a short hand gun of great bore to carry several pistol or carabine balls or small slugs, and so called from the fact of its having a dragon's head at the muzzle.

The pistol was occasionally combined with other weapons, such as the axe and mace, and was sometimes made with two barrels, placed one above the other.

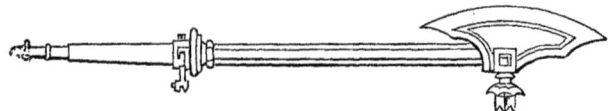

Battle-axe with matchlock pistol, time of Henry VIII.

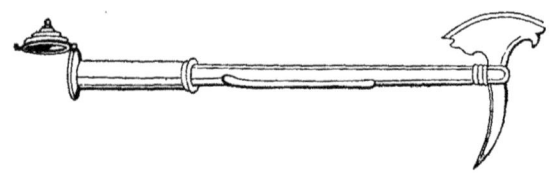

Martel-de-fer with pistol, time of Elizabeth.

The cross-bow was still in our army in this reign, for in 1572 Queen Elizabeth engaged to furnish Charles IX. of France with 6000 men, part of them to be armed with long bows, and part with cross-bows. It seems, however, to have been discontinued in warfare during this reign, and retained only for the chase.

In 1578 there were in the Tower 7000 calivers, 500 pistols, 8000 bows, 16000 sheaves of arrows and other weapons. The caliver, so called because the "bore" was of a fixed size, in order that the common stock of bullets might fit every piece in a regiment, was of greater calibre than the harquebus; was lighter than the musket; was fired without a rest, and could be discharged more quickly than a musket; the shot from the latter, however, did the greatest damage.

In 1580, one of the most remarkable men of the time, Michael Montaigne, in speaking of small arms, writes as follows :—" Except the noise in our ears, to which we " will henceforth be accustomed, I think that it is an " arm of very little effect, and I hope that we shall one " day give up its use;" and somewhat later other writers deplored the gradual abandonment of ancient arms, and predicted the infallible ruin of old England, whose degenerate sons only knew how to use fire-arms.

In 1594 grenades were invented, which were, at first, projected from hand mortars; they gave origin in France to the troops denominated grenadiers, who were soldiers trained in the art of throwing hand grenades in the attack of trenches, or in the covertway.

Queen Elizabeth, in a proclamation dated 1596, directed the bows of all footmen to be changed for muskets, and their bills into pikes. It is from this period that portable fire-arms as weapons of war made decided progress.

The *snaphaunce* appears to have been invented about this period in Germany, and, from its comparative cheapness, was much used afterwards in England, France, and Holland. It was so called, it is said by some authors, from its having been invented by a set of Dutch marauders, designated "snaphans," or poultry stealers, who, finding the light of the match betrayed them in

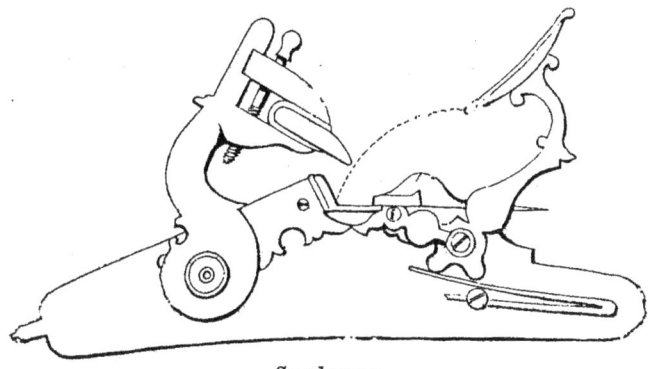

Snaphaunce.

their marauding trips, and the wheel lock too expensive, used a lock consisting of a piece of steel furrowed like the wheel of the wheel lock set on a steel post, and which moved on a pivot, and a cock in which was fixed a flint instead of a piece of pyrites; the priming pan was provided with a cover, which, when it was required to fire the arm, was pushed on one side, and the steel bent down over the pan; on the trigger being pressed, the cock with the flint fell on the steel, and forced it back from the pan, evolving at the same time sparks, which fired the priming.

There were three kinds of locks applied to the harquebus at different times; the exact period of their invention, however, cannot be ascertained.

1st. The cock was fixed on the far side of the priming pan, and was made to move towards the firer.

2nd. The cock was fixed between the priming pan and the firer, and was made to move from the latter.

3rd. The cock was propelled forward by a snap.

In this reign each company of infantry usually consisted of men armed in five different ways.

"Men-at-arms" 40 { 10 halberdiers or battle-axe men.
                  { 30 pike men, pikes 14 to 18 ft. long.
"Shot"   - 60 { 20 archers.
                   { 20 harquebusiers.
                   { 20 musketeers.

Each man carried, in addition, a sword and a dagger.

There existed a law at this time against shooting with hand guns and harquebuses; but those appointed by the authorities to be harquebusiers were to use their weapons without danger from this law.

James I.

A.D. 1603 to 1625.

In the reign of James I. the increasing use of fire-arms brought armour into disrepute, and before the close of it that of the heaviest cavalry terminated at the knees.

As bows and arrows fell into disuse, the infantry became reduced to two classes, viz., musketeers (armed with matchlock musket, sword and dagger), and pikemen.

The musketeer in England in this and the following reign carried his powder in small wooden, tin, or leather

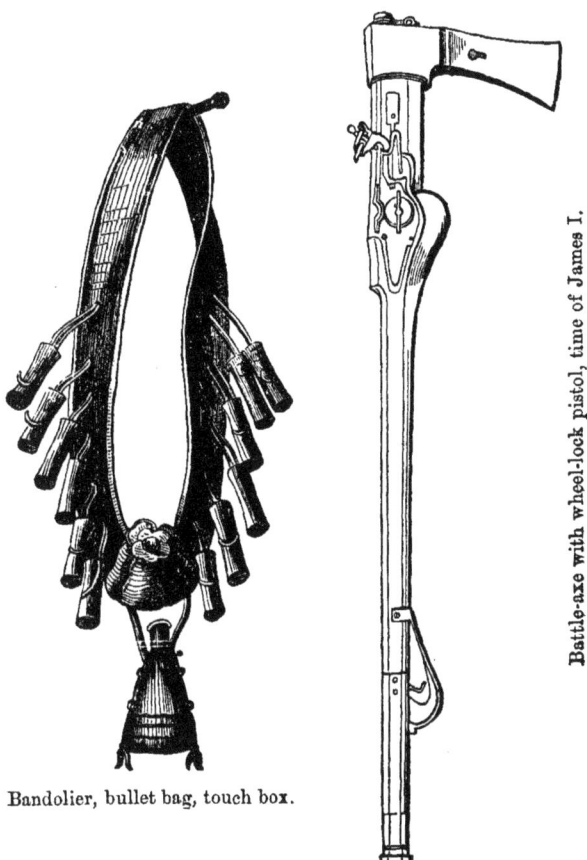

Bandolier, bullet bag, touch box.

Battle-axe with wheel-lock pistol, time of James I.

cylindrical cases, each containing a charge; twelve of these were fixed to a belt, worn over the left shoulder, and were called bandoliers, to which was also attached a bag for bullets; they also had two flasks, a small one, called touch-box, containing powder of a fine description for a priming, which was carried in front, and a larger one, which contained the reserve of loading powder. The musket was carried on the left shoulder, and the rest in the right hand.

In 1621 the length of the barrel of the musket was 4 ft., and the size of the bore 12, *i.e.*, 12 bullets to the pound.

To prevent the match from being seen in the night, small tubes of tin or copper pierced full of holes were invented by a Prince of Orange. Walhuysen describes them, and says, " it is necessary that every "musketeer " know how to carry his match dry in moist and rainy " weather, that is in his pocket or in his hat, by putting " the lighted match between his head and hat, or by " some other means to guard it from the weather; the " musketeer should also have a tin tube, about a foot " long, big enough to admit a match, and pierced full of " little holes, that he may not be disturbed by his match " when he stands sentinel." This was the origin of the match boxes carried by grenadiers.

The caliver now became prominent, and the troops armed with it generally carried their loading powder in large flasks, their powder for priming in small ones (touch boxes), and their bullets in a bag. Sometimes they had bandoliers instead of a flask.

Muskets and calivers were generally match-locks; the wheel-lock was too expensive for the common soldiery, and was confined to cavalry, who carried carbines, pistols, the butts of which were now elongated, and swords.

The musket rest underwent a change in the latter part of this reign; instead of a wooden shaft it was made of a thin tube of iron covered with leather; it had a tuck, *i.e.*, a thin rapier blade enclosed in it, which on touching a spring to open a small valve, flew out. Rests thus armed were said to contain Swedish or swine's feathers, and were used as a defence against cavalry, like archers' stakes. Sometimes instead of swine's feathers a spike projected from one of the prongs of the fork of the rest.

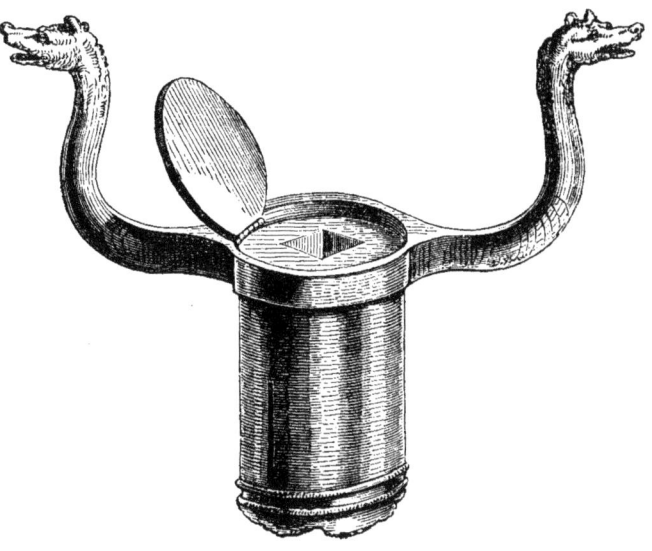

Musket rest, armed with tuck; valve open (full size).

Spike on prong of fork.

Cartridges.

In the early part of the 17th century Gustavus Adolphus, King of Sweden (1611-33), caused the gunpowder, which had hitherto been carried in flasks or bandoliers, to be made up into cartridges and carried in pouches.

Charles I.

A.D. 1625 to 1649.

During the reign of Charles I. the harquebus, matchlock musket, caliver (until about 1635), dragon, carbine, and pike were in use. Great reliance was placed on the pikemen, whose pikes were now 18 feet in length.

In 1629 we hear of the "tricker lock," which appears to imply the hair trigger. A tricker wheel lock of Charles I., a tricker matchlock of Charles II., and a tricker firelock of James II., with hair triggers, are in the collection at Goodrich Court.

In this reign there was an additional case added to the bandoliers, which hung down lower than the rest, to hold the fine powder for priming, supplying the place of the touch-box, and called by the French la pulverain.

The following dimensions of arms at this period are given by Hewitt:—

	Length of barrel.	No. of bullets to the pound.	Nature of lock.
Harquebus	2½ ft.	17	Wheel
Musket	4 ft.	10	Match
Carbine	2½ ft.	24	Flint

The dragoons in 1632 carried short muskets hung at their backs; in 1645 they carried dragons of musket bore, barrel 16 in. long, having wheel, or flint locks; and in 1649 a caliver; they also carried a flask, a priming flask (touch-box), bullet bag, and sword; they served on foot as well as on horseback.

In 1632 the cuirassier is said to have carried two wheel-lock pistols, barrel 18 in. long and 20 bore, *i.e.*, 20 bullets to the pound, and a sword; and the harquebusier the same kind of pistol, in addition to his own weapon, and of whom it is also recorded, that he "had "his purse and his mouth for his bullets, and in his "left hand his match and harquebus."

In the directions for the arming of the Scots in defence of the King in 1643, the cavalry were ordered to be armed with pistols and swords; the infantry with muskets and swords, or pikes and swords, and failing these weapons, they were to have halberds and lockaber axes.

In 1625 the stocks of guns were made of beech and walnut, and about this period browning barrels was in practice.

The Flint Lock.

The modern firelock, the *flint lock*, was invented about 1635, suggested, no doubt, from the snaphaunce already described, and from which it only differed by the cover of the pan forming part of the steel or hammer, which retained its furrows until the 18th century. Before the invention of the flint lock, the wheel lock was frequently called the firelock.

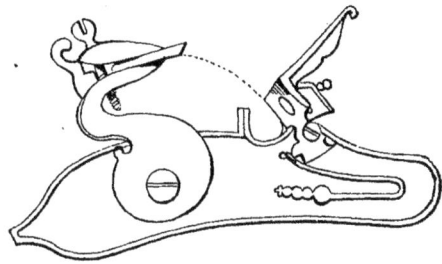

Flint lock.

Cromwell.

During Cromwell's protectorate, or shortly after, the musket rest fell into disuse.

A.D. 1649 to 1660.

Charles II.

Bayonet.

In the reign of Charles II. the swine's feathers and rest were laid aside, and the infantry soldier was armed with a dagger, which he stuck in the muzzle of his gun or firelock to serve as a pike; this appears to have been the origin of the bayonet, which is said to have been invented at Bayonne, and called by the French "bayonet à manche." Although said to have been used abroad as early as 1646, it was not introduced into our

A.D. 1660 to 1685.

army until 1672. The bayonet at first consisted of a wooden handle 8 or 9 in. long, to fix in the muzzle of the gun or firelock, with a two-edged blade 1 ft. in length and a "broad inch" in breadth. This invention was considered a great improvement, as it gave the musket a second means of offence.

In 1673 the infantry were armed by statute as follows: the musketeer had a matchlock musket, the barrel not less than 3 ft. in length, carrying 12 bullets to the pound, a sword, and bandolier; he was ordered to bring with him at every muster ½ lb. of powder, ¼ lb. of bullets, and three yards of match. The musket was occasionally furnished with a flint lock. The tallest men were chosen for pikemen, who carried a pike 16 ft. in length, head and foot included.

In 1678 each company of 100 men consisted of 30 pikemen, 60 musketeers, and 10 men armed with lighter firelocks, supposed to be the fusil, a firelock lighter than the musket invented in France about 1635, and deriving its name from the Italian word "focile," a flint. In 1678 a British regiment was armed with the fusil, and the King added a company of men armed with hand grenades to each of the old British regiments, which was designated the grenadier company. The grenadier had a pouch of grenades, match firelock with bayonet to fit into the barrel, cartridges and primer.

Previous to 1670 the use of the bandolier began to decline; it was found impossible in wet weather, without a cloak, to keep the cases attached to the bandoliers dry, hence the powder very often became spoiled; besides which, the noise occasioned by these cases knocking against each other betrayed those who carried them in all surprises, onslaughts, and sudden enterprises.

Cartridges and cartridge boxes, *i.e.*, pouches, appear to have taken the place of bandoliers in this reign, and were brought into general use about the same time as the introduction of the flint lock. They are said to have been invented by Gustavus Adolphus, King of Sweden, and to have added very much to the efficiency of the soldier, who was enabled thereby to fire three times the number of shots he could discharge when loading from bandoliers. Their use at first was chiefly confined to dragoons and grenadiers.

The flint lock does not appear to have been employed in England until 1677, although used in the French army about seven years earlier.

The Earl of Orrery, in 1677, describes the superiority of the flint lock over the matchlock in the following words:—" First, it is exceedingly more ready; for "with the firelock you have only to cock, and you are "prepared to shoot; but with your matchlock you "have several motions, the least of which is as long a "performing, as but that one of the other, and oftentimes "much more hazardous; besides, if you fire not the "matchlock musket as soon as you have blown your "match (which often, especially in hedge fights and "sieges, you cannot do), you must a second time blow "your match, or the ashes it gathers hinders it from "firing. Secondly, the match is very dangerous, either "where bandeleers are used, or where soldiers run "hastily in fight to the budge-barrel, to refil their "bandeleers; I have often seen sad instances thereof. "Thirdly, marching in the nights, to avoid an enemy, or "to surprize one, or to assault a fortress, the matches "often discover you, and inform the enemy where you "are, whereby you suffer much, and he obtains much. "Fourthly, in wet weather, the pan of the musket being "made wide open, for a while the rain often deads the "powder, and the match too; and in windy weather, "blows away the powder, ere the match can touch the "pan; nay, often in very high winds, I have often seen "the sparks blown from the match, fire the musket ere "the soldier meant it; and either thereby lose his shot, "or wound or kill some one before him. Whereas in the "firelock, the motion is so sudden, that what makes the "cock fall on the hammer, strikes the fire, and opens the "pan at once. Lastly, to omit many other reasons, the "quantity of match used in an army, does much add to "the baggage, and being of a very dry quality, naturally

"draws the moisture of the air, which makes it relax,
"and consequently less fit, though carried in close
"waggons: but if you march without waggons, the
"match is the more exposed; and without being dried
"again in ovens, is but of half the use which otherwise
"it would be of: and which is full as bad, the skeans
"you give the corporals, and the links you give the
"private soldiers (of which near an enemy, or on the
"ordinary guard duty, they must never be unfurnished),
"if they lodge in huts or tents; or if they keep guard
"in the open field (as most often it happens) all the
"match for instant service is too often rendered
"uncertain or useless; nothing of all which can be said
"of the flint, but much of it to the contrary. And then
"the soldiers generally wearing their links of match near
"the bottom of the belt, on which their bandeleers are
"fastened, in wet weather generally spoil the match
"they have, and if they are to fight on a sudden, and
"in the rain, you lose the use of your small shot which
"is sometimes of irreparable prejudice."

The dragoon in 1682 carried a flint lock fusil, bayonet to fit into the barrel, sword, cartridges, and primer.

Archery was still continued for amusement, but in England, at this period, archers seem to have disappeared from the national force.

James II.

A.D. 1865 to 1688.

In James II.'s reign two regiments of dragoon guards were raised, which were armed with firelocks and bayonets, in addition to swords and pistols, and were trained to act either or foot or on horseback.

The pike, in the last half of this century, was falling into disuse, and by the end of it appears to have been discontinued, the musket having become by the addition of the bayonet a weapon of the pike kind.

In 1686 the grenadiers appear to have changed their matchlocks for firelocks or snaphaunce muskets.

William and Mary.

A.D. 1688 to 1702.

In William and Mary's reign most of the troops were armed with muskets or firelocks in the place of matchlocks; the bayonet was still a kind of dagger, but the ring added to the guard or handle, at first for defence, was brought into great use at this time on the continent.

In one of the campaigns in Flanders the British 25th regiment, whose bayonets were made to screw into the muzzle of their firelocks, was attacked by a French regiment which, having their bayonets fitted by a ring over the muzzle, fired a volley and immediately charged them, greatly to their astonishment.

Original bayonet with two rings.

Macaulay states that at the battle of Killiecrankie, fought in 1689, between the forces of William III. under General Mackay, and the adherents of James II. under Graham of Claverhouse, Viscount Dundee, "When only "a space was left between the armies, the Highlanders "suddenly flung away their firelocks, drew their broad-"swords, and rushed forward with a fearful yell. The "Lowlanders prepared to receive the shock: but this "was then a long and awkward process: and the soldiers "were still fumbling with the muzzles of their guns and "the handles of their bayonets when the whole flood of "Macleans, Macdonalds, and Camerons came down. In "two minutes the battle was lost and won." The English were completely defeated, the immediate cause of which was mainly to be attributed to the difficulty of fixing bayonets, or of converting the firelock into a pike for close combat.

Macaulay again states, "the firelock of the High-"lander was quite distinct from the weapon which he "used in close fight. He discharged his shot, threw "away his gun, and fell on with his sword. This was "the work of a moment. It took the regular mus-"keteer two or three minutes to alter his missile weapon "into a weapon with which he could encounter an "enemy hand to hand; and during these two or three "minutes the event of the battle of Killiecrankie had "been decided. Mackay therefore ordered all his "bayonets to be so formed that they might be screwed "upon the barrel without stopping it up, and that his "men might be able to receive a charge the very instant "after firing."

The socket bayonet was adopted from this time, and was in general use in 1703.

Anne.

A.D. 1702 to 1714.

In the reign of Queen Anne every infantry soldier was armed with a musket, bayonet, and sword, and the grenadier ceased to carry grenades.

George I.

A.D. 1714 to 1727.

In the reign of George I. no change appears to have taken place in the arms of the troops. Dragoons carried a carbine, bayonet, and sword.

George II.

A.D. 1727 to 1760.

The iron or steel ramrod was invented by the Prince of Dessau in Prussia, about 1741; this greatly increased the efficiency of the musket, and was an improvement on the scouring stick, which was very liable to be broken on service. Previous to this invention the corporals of the Prussian and Austrian infantry, were provided with spare iron ramrods in two parts, which, when required, were screwed together.

In the reign of George II. light companies were added to infantry regiments; in 1745 the men of battalion companies of infantry, and in 1746 of grenadier companies, ceased to carry swords. From this period the arms of the infantry soldier have been confined to the musket and bayonet.

George III.

A.D. 1760 to 1820.

In 1800 the light and heavy dragoons carried a sword and fusil; in 1808 the light dragoon had a carbine with a bayonet.

At the commencement of the present century the English musket with its ammunition was as follows:—

Weight of musket with bayonet .. 11 lb. 4 oz.
Do. bayonet .. .. 1 „ 2 „
Length of barrel of musket .. .. 3 ft. 3 in.
Diameter of bore of barrel ·753 in., or 14½ bullets to the pound.
Charge of powder 6 drs. F.G., with 3 flints to every 60 rounds.

There had been, at different periods, various methods of priming small firearms. Originally the priming was put into the pan from a flask containing a fine-grained powder called serpentine powder; in the early flint-lock musket this was rendered unnecessary, as, in loading, a portion of the charge passed through the vent into the pan, where it was prevented from escaping by the hammer; latterly, the top of the cartridge was bitten off, and the pan filled therefrom before loading, which was very unsafe.

The objections to the flint lock were that it did not entirely preserve the priming from wet, and that the flint failed sometimes to ignite the charge.

To remedy these imperfections, the Rev. Mr. Forsyth, in 1807, obtained a patent for priming with fulminating powder, which, when struck with any metal or hard substance, exploded. This fulminating powder at first consisted of chlorate of potash with sulphur and charcoal; it was, however, considered too corrosive, and was subsequently improved.

George IV.

No change in small arms took place during this reign. A.D. 1820 to 1830.

William IV.

In William IV.'s reign Mr. Forsyth's invention was A.D. 1830 to 1837. tested at Woolwich (1834) by firing 6000 rounds from six flint-lock muskets, and the same number from six percussion muskets, in all weathers; the result of this trial proved exceedingly favourable to the percussion principle; the shooting was more accurate; the recoil was less, the charge of powder having been reduced from 6 to 4½ drs.; the rapidity of firing was greater; and the number of miss-fires considerably reduced, being as 1 to 26 nearly in favour of the percussion system.

Victoria.

In consequence of the success mentioned in the foregoing paragraph, the flint lock in 1839 was altered to suit the percussion principle; this was easily accomplished, as the interior of the lock remained the same, by removing the hammer with the spring and pan, and replacing the cock which held the flint by a small conical-shaped hammer with a hollow to fit on the nipple when released by the trigger; this nipple is a small pillar screwed into the side of the barrel, with a hole through its centre communicating with the vent or touch-hole, to hold the copper cap containing the detonating composition, which now consisted of three parts of chlorate of potash, two of fulminate of mercury, and one of powdered glass.

In 1840 the Austrian army was supplied with the percussion musket, which does not appear to have been generally issued to the English army until 1842.

Percussion Musket, 1842.

In 1842 a new model musket on the percussion principle was adopted, with a block or back sight for 150 yards, its weight, &c., being as follows:—

Weight of musket and bayonet, 11 lbs. 6 oz.
Weight of bayonet, 1 lb. 8 oz.
Length of musket with bayonet fixed, 6 ft. 0 in.
Length without bayonet, 4 ft. $6\frac{3}{4}$ in.
Length of barrel, 3 ft. 3 in.
Size of bore, ·753 in., 14½ bullets to the lb.
Charge of powder, 4½ drs.

The bore of the English musket being larger than that of France, Belgium, Russia, and Austria, was considered an advantage, because their balls could be fired out of

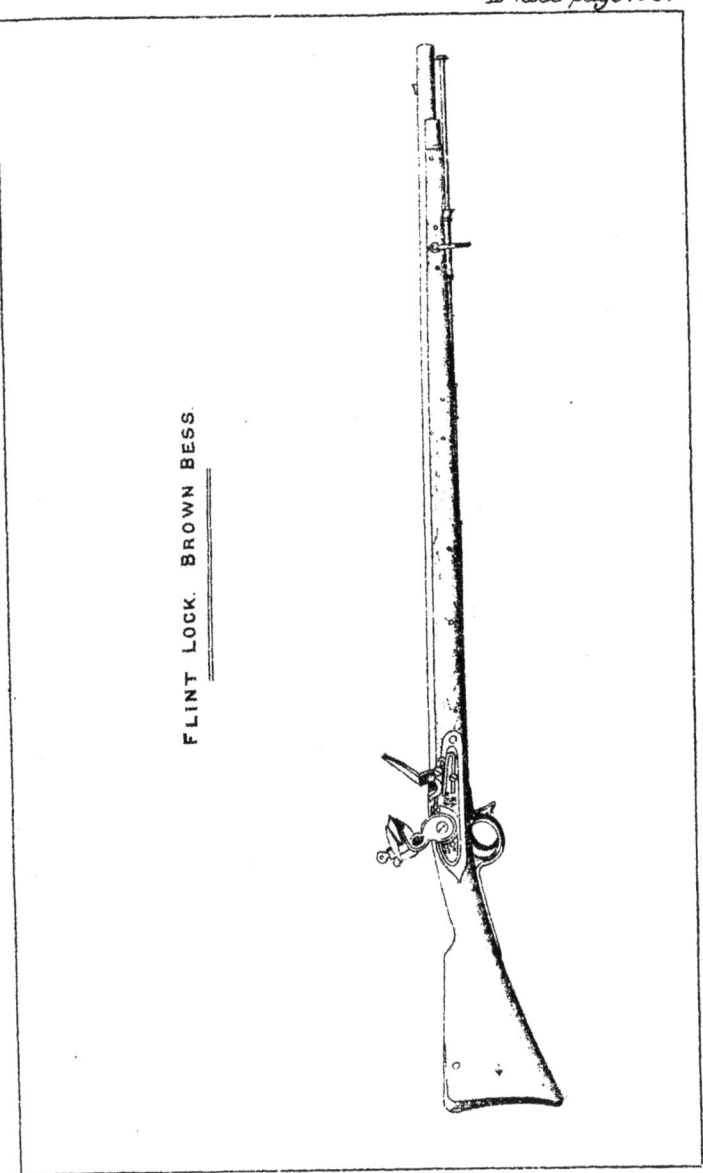

FLINT LOCK. BROWN BESS.

our barrels, whilst our balls could not be fired out of theirs. It was also thought that the greater weight of the English ball produced an increased range and momentum; this was, however, counteracted by the excess of windage.

The shooting powers of the percussion musket 1842 are shown in a report on "experimental musketry "firing" carried on by Captain McKerlie, of the Royal Engineers, at Chatham, in 1846, which concludes as follows:—

"It appears by these experiments that as a general "rule musketry fire should never be opened beyond 150 "yards, and certainly not exceeding 200 yards; at this "distance half the number of shots missed the target, "11 ft. 6 in., and at 150 yards a very large proportion also "missed; at 75 and 100 yards every shot struck the "target, 2 ft. wide; and had the deviation increased "simply as the distance, every shot ought to have struck "the target 6 feet wide at 200 yards; instead of this, "however, some were observed to pass several yards to "the right or left, some to fall 30 yards short, and others "to pass as much beyond, and the deviation increased in "a still greater degree as the range increased. It is only "then under peculiar circumstances, such as when it may "be desirable to bring a fire on field artillery, when there "are no other means of replying to it, that it ought ever "to be thought of using the musket at such distances as "400 yards."

The foregoing forms a true account of the value of the percussion musket 1842, which continued in use in our army until superseded partially in 1851 by the Minié rifle, and altogether by the Enfield rifle in 1855.

RIFLES.

A.D. 1498. The invention of rifling has been attributed to Gaspard Zoller, or Zollner, of Vienna, about the end of the 15th century.

The grooves were at first cut straight down the bore, for the purpose, it is supposed, cf receiving and decreasing the effect of the fouling. It also tended to increase the accuracy of shooting of the arm, inasmuch as the bullet was directed in a straight line down the barrel. The citizens of Leipzic used rifled barrels with straight grooves at target practice about this period.

A.D. 1520. About the year 1520, Koster, of Nuremberg, is said to have adopted the spiral form of grooving; whether from fancy, or from understanding the value of the change, does not appear at all certain.

Rifles were at first used for amusement, and were not employed in warfare until about the middle of the 17th century.

A snaphaunce rifled gun, 4 ft. 9 in. in length, of the time of Charles I., is to be found in Sir Samuel Meyrick's collection of arms.

In the official catalogue of the Tower armouries it is stated that "rifling barrels commenced about the be- "ginning of the 17th century," and that the earliest patent preserved in the Patent Office for rifling small arms is dated 24th June, 1635, which reads as follows:—" The " gunsmith undertakes to rifle, cutt out, and screwe barrels " as wide, or as close, or as deepe, or as shallowe, as shall " be required, and with great care."

A.D. 1610. In the Tower armouries may be seen a tricker wheel-lock rifled birding piece, dated about 1610;—a hunter's wheel-lock rifle, dated 1613, the barrel has seven grooves with double lines between the grooving;—a tricker flint-lock forest rifle, about 1630;—and a German wheel-lock rifle, dated 1797.

In 1680 each troop of Life Guards was supplied with eight rifled carbines. A.D. 1680.

Baker's Rifle.

In 1800 the 95th Regiment, now the Rifle Brigade, was armed with a rifle known by the name of "Baker's rifle," which weighed 9½ lbs. The barrel of this rifle was 2½ feet in length; it had 7 grooves, making a quarter turn in the length of the barrel, and its calibre was a 20 bore. A small wooden mallet was supplied with this rifle, to make the ball enter the barrel; this mallet was in use only a short time when it was withdrawn. This rifle was loaded with great difficulty. A.D. 1800.

The great objection to the use of the rifle in war was the difficulty experienced in loading it. To remedy this evil, M. Delvigne, a French infantry officer, in 1826, proposed to place at the bottom of the breech a small chamber having an abrupt connection with the bore (Fig. 1). The charge of powder nearly filled this chamber, and the ball, which was spherical in form and fitted the barrel loosely, rested on it and was forced into the grooves by several sharp strokes with a heavy rammer having a conical head, in order that it might receive a spiral motion during its projection from the barrel; this hard ramming also forced the ball into the chamber to the injury of the powder. A.D. 1826.

Fig. 1.

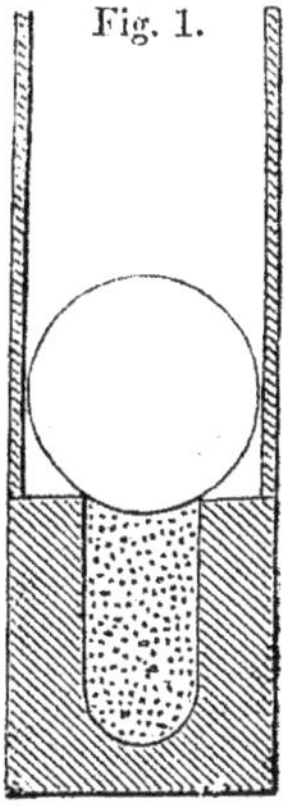

Although easy loading and increased accuracy in shooting (which at 600 yards was double that of the smooth-bore musket at 350 yards) resulted from this invention, it was soon abandoned, as it was found that the fouling increased so rapidly as to cause the powder, after a few shots had been fired, to project beyond the chamber, when the ball, resting on the powder instead of the chamber, was not so easily dilated into the grooves, but

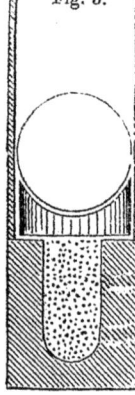

Fig. 2.

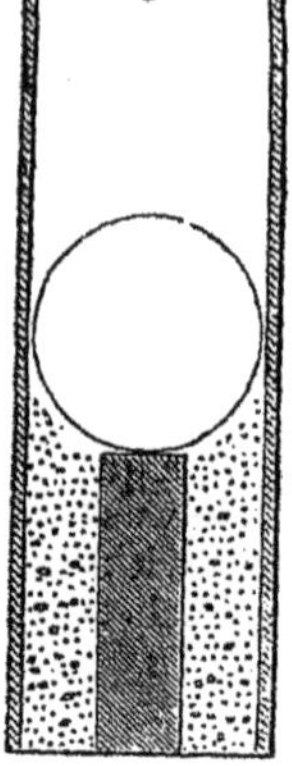

Fig. 3.

Fig. 4.

A.D. 1828.

A.D. 1833.

was,—by hard ramming to overcome the obstacle,—forced out of shape by being flattened in front, which caused irregularities in its flight.

In 1828, Colonel Thouvenin, of the French artillery, proposed a rifle on the tige principle. It consisted in substituting for the Delvigne chamber a small cylinder or pin of steel, fixed in the bottom of the bore, around which the powder lay, and on which the ball rested when loaded, thereby allowing the latter to be expanded more easily and without so much detriment to its shape (Fig. 2). The ball when in the barrel was quite firm, and could not be easily displaced by marching, or the ordinary movement of the rifle; but being spherical it received obliquely the impulse of the charge, and was consequently propelled with diminished force. The tige rifle was therefore not adopted at this time.

In 1833, Colonel Poncharra suggested placing a "sabot" of hard wood underneath the ball with a greased patch, which, resting on the offsets of the mouth of the chamber (Fig. 3), was prevented from entering it. The Delvigne-Poncharra rifle was objected to as a war weapon on account of the complicated nature of its ammunition, and the difficulty of procuring it in the field; besides which, the sabots frequently broke in loading, from the ramming necessary to expanding the bullet into the grooves.

Colonel Thierry, of the French artillery, about this time proposed a rifle from which cylindro-conical bullets, suggested by Delvigne, were to be fired; they were to be flat at the bottom,

To face page 201.

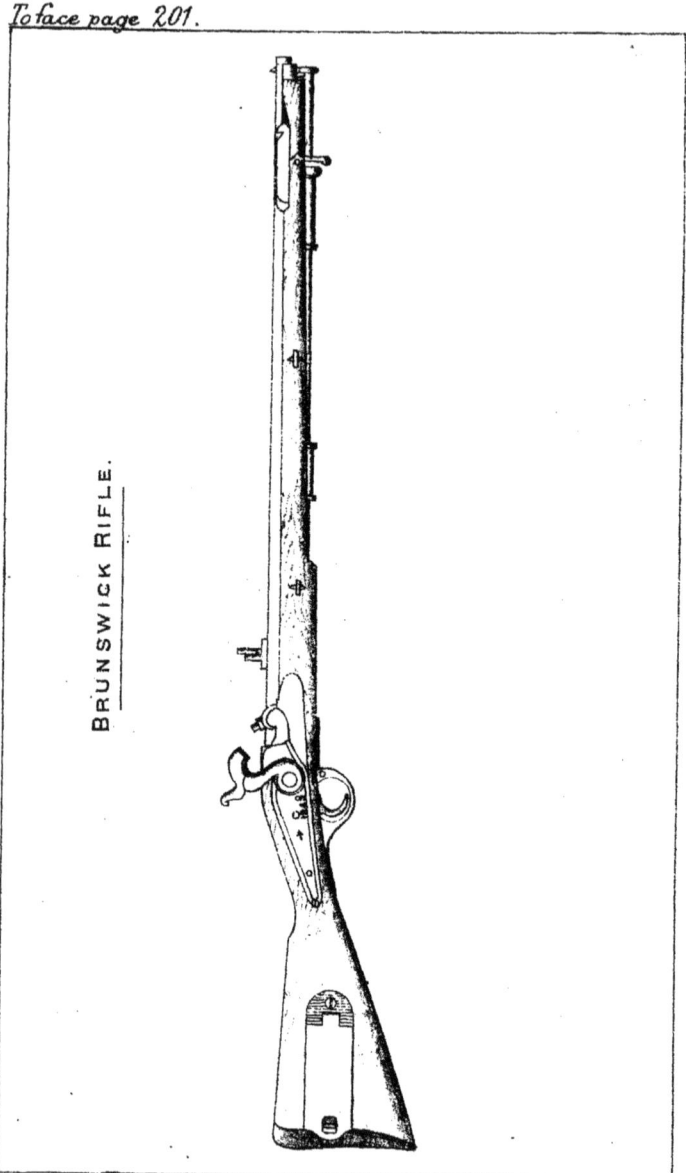

BRUNSWICK RIFLE.

Dangerfield, Lith 22, Bedford S.t Covent Garden. 6657.

cylindrical in the body, with a conical point (Fig. 4). This rifle was not found to answer with these projectiles.

Brunswick Rifle.

In William IV.'s reign the Brunswick rifle, with back action hook lock was introduced into the army; its weight with sword bayonet and scabbard was 11 lbs. 5½ ozs.; weight of barrel, 3 lbs. 14 ozs.; length of barrel, 2 ft. 6 in.; number of grooves, two, making one turn in the length of the barrel; weight of bullet (which was spherical and belted) (Fig. 5), 557 grs.; diameter, ·696 in.; charge of powder, 2½ drs.

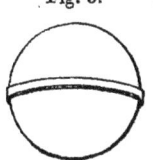

Fig. 5.   A.D. 1836.

This rifle, from the ball having a belt round it, with a patch to prevent its "stripping," i.e., passing out of the grooves, was found an inconvenient weapon, in consequence of the delay experienced in placing the belted ball properly in the grooves, without which loading was impossible. The rifle soon fouled, and its shooting beyond 400 yards was wild.

In 1836 Mr. Greener invented and submitted for trial at Tynemouth, under the authority of the Master General and Board of Ordnance, a bullet to expand by the action of the powder; it was shaped like an egg, having an opening at one end to receive a "taper plug, with a head like "a round-topped button, of a "composition of lead, tin, and "zinc" (Fig. 6); this plug, which was rather larger near the head than the opening, was driven home on the explosion of the powder, when the sides of the bullet were dilated, and forced into the grooves of the rifle, thereby stopping all windage, and increasing the accuracy of shooting as compared with the Government bullet. The Board of Ordnance rejected this invention on the ground of the bullet being a compound; in 1857, however, Mr. Greener was awarded 1000l. "for "the first public suggestion of the principle of expan-

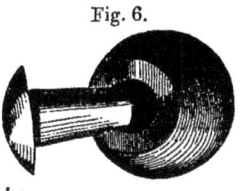

Fig. 6.

" sion, commonly called the Minié principle, for bullets,
" in 1836."

A.D. 1841.

Fig. 7.

Delvigne was the first of recent date in France to announce the fact, that elongated bullets, hollowed at the base, were expanded and forced into the grooves of the rifle by the gas evolved in the explosion of the powder, and in 1841 he obtained a patent for a bullet consisting of a cylinder terminated by a cone (Fig. 7).

A.D. 1844.

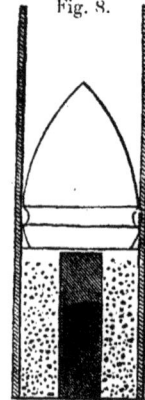

Fig. 8.

In 1844 Colonel Thouvenin's tige rifle was again brought forward to be tried with the elongated bullet already proposed by Delvigne and was adopted (Fig. 8). The size of the tige, stem, or pin, was such as to leave a sufficiently large space between the powder and the ball for the fouling accumulating in the barrel from 50 rounds.

The tige rifle was difficult to clean, a special instrument being required for the purpose; it appears to have been the first military arm in which an elongated projectile was successfully used, and to have been adopted in France as the arm for the Chasseurs.

A.D. 1847.

No practical result appears to have flowed from these discoveries until some time in 1847, when Captain Minié, an instructor of the school at Vincennes, suggested an iron cup (Fig. 9) being placed in a cavity at the base of the bullet which was found to be expanded thereby as well as, if not better than, the bullet Delvigne suggested, and which was used for the tige rifle.

Fig. 9.

Cup.

This discovery caused the manufacture of the tige or stem to be discontinued, and the Minié rifle (an ordinary rifle firing a Minié bullet) to become the favourite arm; and the smooth-bore musket was, by the simple operation of rifling, transformed into the long range rifle with which the Imperial Guard and some of the other troops of the line in France were armed.

After Captain Minié's suggestion of an iron cup in the base of the bullet, it was considered that a practical and definite solution of the principle of expansion had been obtained.

One of the early bullets of Captain Minié's principle was a cylindro-ogive in form, with a groove on its cylindrical portion intended to receive a greased patch; this groove having been dispensed with, it was found that the rifle lost much of its accuracy; it was therefore re-adopted, when it was discovered that any variation in the shape or position of the groove materially affected the shooting.

Captain Tamisier, another instructor of the school at Vincennes, after trying bullets of a cylindrical form of different lengths with conical points of various angles, concluded, that to increase the precision of elongated bullets, it was necessary to ascertain the means of giving them a point of resistance as far as possible behind their centre of gravity; he accordingly adopted the plan of rectifying the path of the bullet by creating, though the agency of grooves or cannelures at the posterior end, resistances which should act when its *axis did not coincide* with the direction of motion (Fig. 10). He tried to carry the centre of gravity of his bullet as far forward as possible, which compelled him to flatten the front of the projectile.

Fig. 10.

In the first elongated bullets made for the tige rifle, the centre of gravity being near the base, the rear end had a tendency to fall before the front; this was rectified by the cannelures.

Minié Rifle.

In 1851 a rifle musket of the Minié pattern was A.D. 1851. introduced into the English army; it was never generally issued, although used by our troops during the Caffre war in 1851, and in the Crimea, at the battles of the Alma and Inkerman; its weight, &c., was as follows:—

Weight of rifle musket with bayonet, 10 lbs. 8¾ oz.
Weight of barrel, 4 lbs. 10 oz.
Length of barrel, 3 ft. 3 in.
Diameter of bore, ·702 in.
Number of grooves 4, making 1 turn in 78 in.
Diameter of bullet, ·690 in.
Weight of bullet, 680 grains.
Windage, ·012 in.
Charge of powder, 2½ drs.
Sighted from 100 to 1000 yards.

Fig. 11.

Fig. 12.

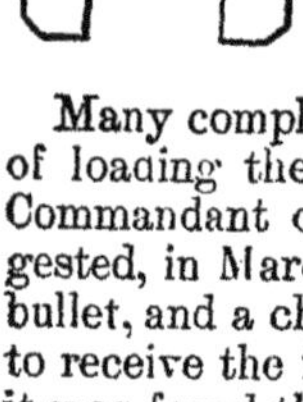

The form of bullet first used with the English Minié rifle was conoidal (Fig. 11). It soon became apparent that this form was defective, as there was little chance of the axis of the bullet coinciding with that of the barrel during its passage out; hence it was changed to a cylindro-conoidal form (Fig. 12), with an iron cup of nearly hemispherical form. These bullets were made up into cartridges, which had to be reversed by the hand (after pouring the powder into the barrel), to insert the bullet; the paper surrounding the cylindrical portion and base of the bullet was greased with a lubrication composed of five parts of tallow and one of beeswax; the paper above the point of the bullet and that forming the powder case was torn off before drawing the ramrod to place the projectile home on the powder.

Many complaints having been made of the difficulty of loading the Minié rifle with its regulation bullet, the Commandant of the School of Musketry, Hythe, suggested, in March 1854, a reduction in the diameter of the bullet, and a change in the form of the cavity at its base to receive the iron cup; these alterations were made, as it was found that the loading of the rifle was thereby rendered more easy, while, at the same time, the accuracy of its shooting was not in any way impaired.

A large number of percussion muskets, pattern 1842,

were converted into rifles by being grooved, and were issued to the Royal Marines, and made available for sea-service, whence the term "sea-service rifle;" the bullet was of the Minié pattern, its diameter was ·731 inch; weight 825 grains; and the charge of powder 3 drs.

In the early part of 1852 experiments were carried A.D. 1852. on at Enfield, by order of the late Viscount Hardinge, when Master-General of the Ordnance, to test the merits of different rifles submitted for trial by some of the principal gunmakers of England, with a view to ascertain the best description of fire-arm, combining lightness with efficiency, for military purposes.

Enfield Rifle.

In August 1852 two muskets were made at the Royal Enfield Manufactory in which were embodied the improvements and alterations suggested by the experience obtained during the course of the experiments referred to. The weight, &c., of these muskets, known afterwards as the Enfield 3-grooved rifle, "or rifle "musket pattern, 1853," was as follows:—

Weight of rifle musket, with bayonet, 9 lbs. 3 oz.
Length of barrel, 3 ft. 3 in.
Weight of ditto, 4 lbs. 1½ oz.
Diameter of bore, ·577 in.
Number of grooves, 3 having 1 turn in 78 inches.
Barrel secured to stock by three steel bands fastened by screws and breech nail.
Bayonet secured with locking ring.
Lock of swivel pattern.
Sights of Mr. Westley Richards' pattern capable of folding down either way. Fig. 13.
Charge, 2¼ drs.

A bullet of cylindro-conoidal form (Fig. 13), made up into cartridges and lubricated as for the Minié rifle, was adapted to these arms by Mr. Pritchett, for which he was awarded by Government 1000*l.*; the weight of this bullet was 530 grains; its diameter ·568, and windage ·009 in.

In December 1852 a trial of these muskets was made for the first time, at distances from 100 to 800 yards, when it was found that the shooting produced was equal in accuracy at the several distances to any hitherto obtained by the arms previously tried.

A.D. 1853.

In October 1853 the Enfield 3-grooved rifle was tried at Hythe in competition with the Minié, or rifle musket 1851, and Lancaster's smooth-bore elliptical rifle, with increasing spiral or gaining twist, freed at the breech. The Pritchett bullet was used with the Enfield and Lancaster rifles. The result of this trial was in favour of the Lancaster.

In December 1853 another trial was made between the Enfield and Lancaster rifles, when the former, on the whole, proved to be superior, the latter evincing a tendency to "strip," especially at the longer ranges.

A.D. 1854.

In January 1854 the Lancaster and Enfield rifles were again tried, the barrels of both arms, on this occasion, having been reduced from 3 ft. 3 in. to 2 ft. 6 in.; the result was a second time favourable to the Enfield system of rifling, and the stripping tendency of the Lancaster clearly established.

A further trial of the Enfield rifle took place in October and November 1854, by placing a certain number of these arms in the hands of non-commissioned officers and privates sent to the School of Musketry for instruction, and comparing the results of the individual shooting and file and volley firing, with those made in the same practices with the Minié rifle, pattern 1851, when the superiority of the Enfield rifle, pattern 1853, was confirmed, thus placing beyond a doubt its efficiency for military service over any arms that had yet been put into the hands of the infantry, combining as it did lightness and strength with increased accuracy of shooting.

A.D. 1855.

In 1855 the Enfield rifle was introduced into the English army; was used during the Crimean war, having there replaced the Minié rifle pattern 1851, and the Percussion musket 1842; and remained the general weapon of the entire infantry, until the introduction of breech-loaders. Short rifles of the same pattern, with barrels 2 ft. 9 in. long, and a sword bayonet, were supplied to the 60th and Rifle Brigade. About this time two small carbines, constructed on the same principle as the Enfield rifle, were introduced for the artillery and cavalry, also a rifled pistol.

In 1855 the Lancaster smooth-bore elliptical rifle, barrel 2 ft. 8 in. long, became the arm of the corps of Sappers and Miners, now the Royal Engineers.

Several improvements were made in the Enfield rifle after its first appearance, e.g.—

In 1854 a new back sight was adopted which combined the principles of Mr. Westley Richards and Mr. Lancaster with that of the Ordnance pattern 1851 fitted to the Minié rifle.

In Mr. Westley Richards' sight the flap can be put down on the barrel from or towards the muzzle; in Mr. Lancaster's the flap is protected by flanges; and in the Ordnance pattern the flap is kept in a perpendicular position by a spring.

In 1858 the grooves which were at first of uniform depth, were made progressive, being at the breech ·015 in. and at the muzzle ·005 in.

In 1860 all the parts of the rifle and lock were made to interchange, an incalculable advantage for a military arm, particularly in the field, and it was directed "that the army shall be equipped exclusively" with rifles of the interchangeable pattern.

Whilst the Pritchett bullet will shoot well from the Enfield rifle when the diameter of the former is ·568, and that of the latter ·577 in., no dependence can be placed on it when these conditions are not maintained, as was satisfactorily proved in a long course of experiments at the School of Musketry, Hythe, in 1855, Captain, now Colonel Fraser, Royal Artillery, being present. When it is considered that three-thousandths of an inch are allowed as a margin in boring the barrel, and one-thousandth in manufacturing the bullet, it will be seen that it is next to impossible to maintain the conditions mentioned. With a view therefore to correct any imperfections which might exist either in the diameter of bullet or bore of rifle, the cavity in the base of the bullet was altered, and an iron cup placed there as an auxiliary to expansion, on the strong recommendation of the late Lieutenant-General Hay.

To determine the best material and shape for the cup or plug, further experiments took place in 1855, which resulted in a new form of bullet, with a boxwood plug (Fig. 14), being recommended and adopted; the advantages claimed for it were:—

Fig. 14.

1st. Greater, more certain, and uniform expansion, leaving at the same time a sufficient margin to cover any trifling inaccuracy in diameter either of bore or bullet of rifle, caused by imperfect manufacture.

2nd. Great decrease of fouling, with corresponding facility of loading.

3rd. Increased accuracy of shooting.

In August 1857 it was directed that the lubricating mixture for the Enfield rifle was in future to consist of five parts of beeswax and one of tallow, instead of five parts of tallow and one of beeswax, and in April, 1859, in consequence of complaints of the difficulty experienced in loading this rifle during the Indian mutiny, the diameter of the bullet having enlarged from the incrustation of a white deposit, occasioned, it is said, by the acids of the fatty matter of the lubrication, an entire change of the ammunition for arms of the Enfield ·577 bore pattern was ordered, viz.:—

1st. The bullet to be ·55 in. in diameter and 1·09 in. in length, instead of ·568 in. in diameter and 1·05 in length.

2nd. The lubricating mixture to be beeswax, instead of beeswax and tallow.

3rd. The outer envelope or paper which contains the bullet to be fastened to the inner envelope or bag which contains the powder by a strip of gummed paper, instead of the two being twisted together beyond the stiff cylinder of the powder bag, to facilitate tearing off the end of the cartridge.

In 1858 a short rifle ·577 in. in diameter of bore, and having five progressive grooves with a turn in 4 ft., was made at Enfield for the Royal Navy to replace the sea service rifle pattern 1842. A similar rifle was supplied to the 60th Rifles, Rifle Brigade, and to serjeants of infantry of the line; it is a superior weapon, as regards accuracy of shooting, to either the long or short rifle of pattern 1853.

In 1854 Mr. Whitworth, the distinguished mechanist, was induced by the late Lord Hardinge, then General Commanding-in-Chief of the Army, to consider the subject of rifling; after a long series of experiments he adopted that system in which "the interior of the "barrel is hexagonal," and which, "instead "of consisting partly of non-effective lands, "and partly of grooves, consists of effective "rifling surfaces. The angular corners of "the hexagon are always rounded." *Vide* Fig. 15.

Fig. 15.

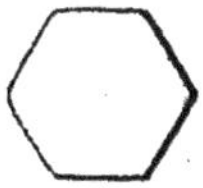

"For an ordinary military barrel 39 in. long" Mr. Whitworth "proposed a ·45-in. bore, with one turn in "20 ins.," which he considered the best for this length.

"Either cylindrical or hexagonal bullets may be used" with this rifle. "Supposing a bullet of a cylindrical "shape to be fired, when it begins to expand it is driven "into the recesses of the hexagon. It thus adapts itself "to the curves of the spiral, and the inclined sides of the "hexagon offering no direct resistance, expansion is "easily effected." *Vide* Fig. 16.

"While the ordinary grooved rifle depends upon the "expansion of the soft metal projectile, in the hexagonal "system rifling may be effected independently of expan-"sion, by making the projectile of the same shape as the "interior of the barrel (Fig. 17), in other words, by

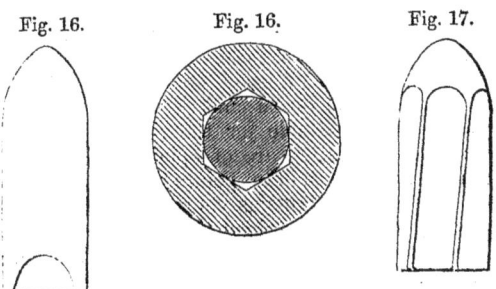

Fig. 16.　　Fig. 16.　　Fig. 17.

"having a mechanical fit between them. The projectile "may be used naked, and be made of metal of any degree "of hardness. The expansion principle may also be com-

"bined with an easy mechanical fit, so that a projectile
" of metal harder than lead, as an alloy of lead and tin,
" may be used, which, while it loads easily, will expand
" sufficiently to fill the bore, and give more than double.
" the penetration."

In April 1857 a trial of the Whitworth rifle against the Enfield rifle pattern 1853 took place at Hythe, in the presence of Lord Panmure, then Secretary of State for War, when the former proved greatly superior to the latter both in accuracy of shooting and penetration. It has since then been under trial before two committees at different times in competition with small bore rifles; the last committee, in their report of the 26th November, 1862, state in paragraph 69 that " the makers " of every small-bore rifle having any pretension to " special accuracy have copied to the letter the three " main elements of success adopted by Mr. Whitworth, " viz., diameter of bore, degree of spiral and large pro- " portion of rifling surface, it is not probable that any " further modifications or *quasi* improvements, that might " result from the question being now thrown open to the " gun trade would be attended with any practical ad- " vantage." The result of this trial will be best conveyed in the words of the committee's report, par. 68, viz., " They think it only just to Mr. Whitworth to " acknowledge the relative superiority of his small bore " rifle even as a military weapon, over all the other rifles " of similar calibre that have been under trial," viz., the Enfield, Lancaster, and Westley-Richards' breech loader ; and again, in par. 70, " With the exception of the defect " already noticed as to wear, and the difficulty of obtain- " ing ammunition suitable for the rifle as well as the " service, the Committee are of opinion that the Whit- " worth rifle, taking all other points into consideration, is " superior to all other arms as yet produced, and that this " superiority would be retained if Mr. Whitworth could " ensure all the arms being made with equal mechanical " perfection."

It is worthy of record that the first meeting of the National Rifle Association at Wimbledon, on the 1st July, 1860, was opened by Her Majesty Queen Victoria firing the first shot from a Whitworth rifle rest at 400 yards, the bullet hitting within 1½ inches of the centre of the target; and that the Queen's prize of 250*l*. was shot for yearly (1865-66 and 67 excepted) at the said meeting with the Whitworth M.L. rifle, until superseded by the Martini-Henry rifle in 1871.

Between 1857 and 1861 four breech-loading carbines were introduced for experimental use in the cavalry, viz., Sharp's, Terry's, Green's, and Westley-Richards'.

In July 1861 a new back-sight for the naval rifle, pattern 1858, and short rifle, pattern 1860, was introduced, and the fore-sight was ordered to be made of cast steel, and in November 1861 a new back-sight for the Enfield rifles, pattern 1853, graduated up to 1000 yards instead of 900.

In December 1861 a carbine with five grooves and pitch of one turn in four feet was introduced for the Royal Artillery; also a pistol of reduced weight for the Cavalry; length of barrel, 8 inches; calibre, 0·577 inches; weight, about 2 lb. 10½ oz.

In November 1863 Metford's explosive bullet was introduced, but in consequence of the decision of an international convention held at St. Petersburgh in 1868, that no explosive projectiles weighing less than 400 grammes (about 14 oz.) should be used in warfare, this bullet was declared obsolete in March 1869.

In December 1863 plugs of baked clay were adopted for the hollow in the base of the elongated bullets instead of boxwood, in consequence of the difficulty of procuring the requisite supplies of the latter.

In December 1863 a pattern Whitworth rifle was approved to guide a supply of 8000 ordered to be made at Enfield; calibre across angles, 0·4895 in.; sides, 0·4495.

In June 1864 a committee of officers was ordered to consider and report on the expediency of introducing breech-loading arms for general adoption by the British Army, who, after a very few sittings, unanimously recommended that the system should be at once introduced, and the Secretary for War invited the various gunsmiths and manufacturers of fire-arms to send in to the Ordnance Select Committee patterns of the modes in which they might propose to convert the existing stock of Enfield rifles, pattern 1853. Nearly 50 different methods of conversion were proposed, the great majority of which were disapproved of on account of their requiring the stock to be materially altered or cut away; and the Committee, after most laborious and protracted experiments, recommended the plan proposed by Mr. Jacob Snider.

The rifles converted on this plan did not at first appear to produce accuracy in shooting at all equal to that of the unconverted arms, but Colonel Boxer, R.A., having devoted much time and attention to the subject, invented a cartridge for them which rendered their shooting at least equal if not superior to that of the muzzle-loading arm.

In the early part of 1866 Lord de Grey, then Secretary of State for War, gave orders for the conversion of a considerable number of the Enfield rifles into breech-loaders on the Snider principle. A number of these rifles were sent for experiment to the Schools of Musketry at Hythe and Fleetwood in September 1866. The shooting with those sent to Hythe with the first supply of ammunition furnished not having proved satisfactory, Colonel Boxer again turned his attention to the construction of the cartridges, and with his later ammunition the results were remarkably good, and the number of miss-fires much less than with the muzzle-loaders.

The whole of the Enfield rifles available were eventually converted on this principle, and the store of arms suitable for conversion having been exhausted before the question as to the best arm for the future was settled, a number of *new* arms on the Snider principle were also made. The principal points in which these rifles differed from the converted arms were that steel was used for the barrels instead of iron, and a locking bolt was added to the breech-block.

On the 30th October, 1866, the Lancaster oval-bore rifles of the Royal Engineers were ordered to be converted on the Snider principle.

In May 1867 the cavalry carbine, pattern 1861, and the artillery carbine, pattern 1861, were ordered to be converted on the Snider principle.

In August 1867 the naval rifle, pattern 1858, was ordered to be converted on the Snider principle.

The under-mentioned forces still have Snider arms, viz., Volunteers, Yeomanry, Royal Irish Constabulary, and some native regiments in India.

The object of providing the army with an efficient breech-loader by the conversion of the existing muzzle-loading rifles having been attained by the adoption of the Snider system, attention was at once turned to the question of procuring the best weapon to be adopted for future manufacture.

An advertisement was issued from the War Office in October 1866, inviting proposals, and a Special Committee was appointed to consider and report upon those submitted.

About 120 arms and 40 descriptions of ammunition were sent in, and, after careful examination, followed by trials of certain selected arms, the Committee reported that no arm submitted possessed, in their opinion, sufficient merit to render its adoption into the service advisable.

In December 1867 the Committee were directed to extend their inquiries, with a view to deciding upon the arm they would recommend for adoption in the service.

Forty-five additional arms were sent in while the Committee were pursu ng their inquiry. In February 1869 they reported, after careful and elaborate trials, recommending a combination of the breech mechanism submitted by Mr. Martini, with Mr. Henry's barrel, the arm to be called the " Martini-Henry," the ammunition to be made up in " Boxer " cases, a bullet of 480 grains being used, and wax lubrication applied in the form of a wad in rear of it, according to a plan proposed by Mr. Henry.

Among the arms which the Committee had before them were six systems of repeating rifles; of these they preferred the " Winchester," but even that they considered too complicated, and so liable to injury as not to be calculated to withstand the wear and tear of service.

In November 1869 200 rifles of the description recommended by the Committee, with a supply of ammunition, were issued to various stations at home and abroad, and to the Royal Navy, for trial by the troops and seamen.

Meantime the subject of overcoming the disadvantages of length and slenderness of the ammunition proposed for the new rifle had been under consideration, and trials had been made with arms having the chamber enlarged to suit cartridges of a "bottle" shape.

A Committee which had been appointed to report upon this and other points connected with ammunition recommended, in March 1870, the adoption of a short chamber cartridge, and a rifle with a short chamber and short breech-action. 22 arms of this pattern were issued for trial in October 1870.

A new Committee was appointed in May 1870, to consider reports connected with the Martini-Henry rifle received from time to time. They finally reported in February 1871. They had made a careful examination of the whole of the reports received, and had taken the evidence of certain eminent civil engineers and other experts on the subject of the mechanical construction of the breech-action. This was, in the Committee's opinion, conclusive as to the soundness of the mechanical principles involved. They expressed the opinion that the short-actioned Martini-Henry rifle was admirably adapted for a military arm, and they unanimously recommended its adoption into the two services, together with the short chamber Boxer-Henry ammunition. His Royal Highness the Field Marshal Commanding-in-Chief concurred, and in April 1871 the arm was definitely adopted.

INDEX.

A.

	PAGE
Accidents with bolt actions	52
Advantages of breech-loading arms	50
,, of flat trajectories	23
Albini Braendlin rifle, Belgium	80
Ammunition, small arms	124
Amount of twist necessary for a rifle can only be definitely determined by experiment	14
Angle of descent	16
,, of elevation	16
,, of elevation for different ranges (M.H. and Snider rifles)	35
,, of spiral	10
Angular velocity of a bullet	13
Arms in a general sense	156
,, Ancient Britons	157
,, Roman Period	159
,, Saxon Period	160
,, Norman Period	160
,, William I.	161
,, ,, II.	161
,, Henry I.	161
,, Stephen	161
,, Henry II.	161
,, Richard I.	162
,, John	165
,, Henry III.	165
,, Edward I.	166
,, ,, II.	167
,, ,, III.	167
,, Richard II.	169
,, Henry IV.	169
,, ,, V.	169
,, ,, VI.	171
,, Edward IV.	173
,, ,, V.	174
,, Richard III.	174
,, Henry VII.	174

INDEX.

	PAGE
Arms, Henry VIII.	176
,, Edward VI.	181
,, Mary	181
,, Elizabeth	181
,, James I.	184
,, Charles I.	188
,, Cromwell	189
,, Charles II.	189
,, James II.	192
,, William and Mary	192
,, Anne	194
,, George I.	194
,, ,, II.	194
,, ,, III.	194
,, ,, IV.	195
,, William IV.	195
,, Victoria	196
,, interchangeable	15
Arms with short barrels have a range due to "jump"	17
Artillery carbines	65, 98
Axis of bullet, position preserved by during flight	32
,, of rotation defined	9
,, of the bore	16

B.

Baker's rifle	199
Barrels, browning of	71
,, processes of manufacture	67
Bashforth adopts the cubic law	27
Bashforth's experiments	28
,, general Tables, with examples	135
Bayonet	189
,, introduced	189
,, M.H. "long"	109
,, pattern 1853 for Snider long rifle	109
,, sword	109
Beaumont rifle, Holland	58
Berdan, No. 2 rifle, Russia	61
Block system, varied forms	52
Blueing components	76
Body, M.H. rifle, manufacture of	72
Bolt system most in favour on the Continent	52
,, ,, objections to	52
Bows and arrows	156
Breech-loading action good, objects to be attained in	51

INDEX.

	PAGE
Breech-loaders, advantages of	50
,, block system	62
,, bolt ,,	53
,, invention of, in 15th century	50
Brunswick rifle	201
Bullet, good sectional density necessary for	125
,, explosive, Metford	211
,, the longer in calibres the greater the twist of rifling necessary	14
,, M.H. composition of	122, 132
,, papering, effect of	15, 133
,, Pritchett	205, 207
Bullets, expanding, of Delvigne	202
,, lead as a material for	122
,, of equal weight, that with least diameter most favourable for penetration	37
Butts, long and short	15
,, principal processes in manufacture	66

C.

Calibre defined	9
,, the effect of diminishing in a rifle	20
Calibres of bullets	42
Carbine introduced	181
,, M.H. artillery	65, 98
,, M.H. cavalry	65, 98
,, Snider, artillery	98, 212
,, ,, cavalry	98, 212
Cartridge, blank	132
,, buckshot	132
,, cases, qualities necessary for	126
,, ,, of rolled sheet brass	126
,, ,, solid drawn	126
,, central fire	127
,, chief points to be considered with respect to	124
,, consuming	52
,, difficult to explode *en masse*	132
,, Enfield pistol	134
,, first used	187
,, form of, effect on recoil	45
,, M.H. carbine	133
,, M.H. description of	132
,, rimfire	127
,, Snider, description of	130
,, weight of, important to reduce	130

INDEX.

	PAGE
Case hardening components	76
Cavalry, dangerous zone for	23
Central fire cartridge, advantages of	127
Chassepot rifle, France	55
Claymore, staff serjeants of Highland regiments	106
Clubs	156
Conical cartridge case easy to extract	128
Cross bow, invention of	161

D.

Dangerous zones for cavalry and infantry	23
Deeley Edge breech-loading rifles	81
Deep and angular grooves increase fouling	15
Definition of terms in connection with small arms	7
Density and humidity of the atmosphere, effect on flight of bullet	39
Deviation, lateral, of a bullet	18
Diagrams of the trajectories of Snider and M.H. rifles	36
Dirk, Highland, drummers and band	107
Drift	14
,, effect of	14
Dungeness, musketry experiments carried on at	36

E.

Effect of density and humidity of the atmosphere on the flight of bullet	33
E.C. powder, said to give less recoil than black	45
Elevation, angle of, defined	16
,, ,, for different ranges	35
Energy	24
,, of a bullet	24
,, ,, at the muzzle is equal to the work done upon it in the bore by the pressure of the powder gas	25
,, of the M.H. bullet at the muzzle	25
,, penetrative	37
,, per inch of circumference of a bullet	25, 38
,, of recoil, how obtained	43
,, ,, of different rifles	44
,, ,, how reduced	45
Enfield revolver pistol	95
,, rifle	205
,, rifles converted to Snider	212

INDEX.

	PAGE
Experiments to determine the form of head of bullet which offers least resistance to the air	28
,, to test the penetration of bullets	39, 40
Explosives, quick, recoil may be absorbed by stock	45

F.

Farquharson, Metford rifle	83
Field rifle	83
Figure of merit of rifles	101
Fire arms first introduced	168
Firing at objects at a high and low level	34
,, at moving objects	35
Flat trajectory, advantages of	23
Flight of rifle bullets, problems on	135
Flintlock, first introduced	189
Fluctuations in resistances due to different velocities	27
Foil, fencing	108
Force defined	7
,, different forms of which act on a bullet during its flight	7
Form of cartridge case, its effect on recoil	45
,, of trajectory of a rifle bullet important to know	35
Fouling effect on recoil	43
,, increased by an increase of charge	125
,, ,, damp powder	15
,, of the barrel	15
Fraser rifle	84
Fulminating powder first used for priming in 1807 by Rev. Mr. Forsyth	195

G.

Galileo first to consider the path of a bullet to be a parabola	29
Glazing retards ignition of gunpowder	113
Gras rifle, France	59
Greatest velocity of recoil, when attained	45
Greener suggests principle of expansion for rifle bullets	201
Grooves	9
,, deep and angular increase fouling and leading	15
,, of modern rifles always shallow	50
,, of progressive depth	9
,, straight	198
,, with uniform twist	10

INDEX.

	PAGE
Grooves with increasing or gaining twist	10
,, with right or left handed twist	15
Gunpowder, advantages and disadvantages of	112
,, amount of charge	115
,, amount of space occupied by charge	114
,, composition of	111
,, density of	113
,, effect of air-space on pressure	114
,, ,, of length of barrel on	114
,, ,, of windage	115
,, explosive action of	111
,, fine grain, more rapid ignition, and combustion with small charges	114
,, first manufactured in England	168
,, force of	111
,, ,, of, how influenced	112
,, glazing of	118
,, hardness of	113
,, hygrometric test	119
,, importance of keeping in a dry place	120
,, objects to be attained with	115
,, outline of manufacture	116
,, pistol	118
,, proportion of moisture in	113
,, ,, of the ingredients	113
,, quality of the ingredients	112
,, R.F.G.	117
,, R.F.G^2	117
,, rate of combustion	114
,, ,, of ignition	114
,, size of grains	114
,, ,, shape, and colour of grains	119
,, specification for	118
,, the circumstances which influence the force of	112
,, theoretic work of	112
,, velocity imparted to bullet by	120

H.

Hand gun first used	171
Heights of trajectory	35, 36
Hélie, experiments of	26
Henvy rifling	48
,, magazine rifle	91
Hilt, sheet-steel, introduced in 1864	103

INDEX.

	PAGE
History of small arms	156
Hole made by bullet always circular	33
Hotchkiss' magazine rifle	92
Hutton, experiments of	26

I.

Increasing twist unsuitable for military arm	10
Infantry, dangerous zone for	23
Ingram rifle	84
Interchangeable arms	15

K.

Kropatschek magazine rifle	93

L.

Lancaster rifle	206
Lands	9
Lance, service	108
,, practice	108
,, old pattern	108
Lapping	10
Lateral deviation	18
Lead as a material for bullets	37, 122
,, pure, necessary for Snider bullets	123
Leading of the barrel	15
Lead-cutter	108
Lee magazine rifle	94
Lengths of different bullets in calibres	42
,, of different bullets in inches	42
,, of rifles	98
Light bullet with high velocity may have as great momentum as heavy bullet with low velocity	9
Limits not to be exceeded in diminishing the bore and lengthening the bullet	21
Linear velocity of rotation	12
Line of fire	16
,, of sight	16
Long butts	15
Loss of velocity due to the resistance of the air	18

M.

	PAGE
Magazine rifles, advantages and disadvantages of	89
,, ,, classified	89
Magazines, rules respecting ventilation of	120
Manner of holding a rifle, its influence on recoil	45
Manufacture of Martini-Henry rifle	65
,, of swords	102
Martini-Henry rifle introduced	213
,, ,, shoots higher from fixed rest than from the shoulder	17
,, carbines	65
Match rifles generally made heavier than military	43
Mauser rifle, Germany	56
Maximum effective range of Martini-Henry rifle	36
Matchlock introduced	174
Material of which the parts of M.H. rifle are made	75
Metford rifling	81
Military rifles, patterns used in different countries. Table I	98
,, ,, lengths and weights of. Table II	98
,, ,, velocity, charge, calibre, &c. Table III	99
,, ,, trajectories of bullets. Table IV	100
,, ,, times of flight of bullets. Table V	101
,, ,, figures of merit of. Table VI	101
Minié rifle	203
,, suggests an iron cup for the expansion of bullets	202
Momenta of bodies compared	9
Momentum	8
Motion of translation, and rotation of a bullet fired from a rifle	11
Much recoil unfavourable to good shooting	45
Musket first introduced	180
Muzzle-velocity of bullet, its effect on recoil	45
,, ,, bullets	44
,, ,, high, desirable	21

N.

Naval cutlass	107
Needle-gun	53

O.

Objects at a high and low level, firing at	34
,, to be attained in a good breech-loading action	51
Objections to bolt systems	52

INDEX.

P.

	PAGE
Peabody-Martini rifle	77
Peabody rifle, America	62
Penetrative energy of bullets	38
Penetration for, velocity more important than weight	36
,, increased by rotation	36
,, results of experiments on steel plates	39
Percussion musket introduced	196
,, ,, shooting powers of	197
Pistol first introduced	177
,, powder	118
,, revolver, Enfield	95
Plane of sight	16
Point blank	16
,, ,, range	16
,, ,, ,, of a gun, how obtained	17
Position preserved by axis of elongated bullet during its flight	32
Powder charge, weight of, how regulated	125
,, fulminating, first used for priming in 1807	195
Problems on the flight of rifle bullets	135
Prussians first to see the advantages to be gained by breech-loaders	53

Q.

Quick, explosives with, some of recoil may be absorbed in compressing stock	45

R.

	PAGE
Range	16
,, how obtained	21, 22
,, maximum theoretically obtained at 45° in practice, owing to resistance of air about 33°	31
,, to obtain with little elevation, importance of	22
Ranging power of a bullet proportional to $\frac{w}{d^2}$	19
Ratchet rifling	49
Recoil	42
,, caused by Schultz and E.C. Powder	45
,, energy of	45
,, energy of, how reduced	45

INDEX.

	PAGE
Recoil estimated by springs, &c., unreliable	45
,, form of cartridge case, its effect on	45
,, methods of registering amount of	45
,, on what it depends	42
,, velocity of	43
Regular soldiers first appointed	165
Remaining velocity	8
Remington rifle	79
Repeating rifles	88
Resistance, fluctuations of	27
,, of the air	18, 31
,, of the air affects the time of flight of a bullet	31
,, of the air to a flat head the greatest	29
Retardation	18
,, on what it depends	18
,, proportional to $\dfrac{d^2}{w}$	19
Revolvers	95
Rifle, Baker	199
,, Brunswick	201
,, Enfield	205
,, Minié	203
,, Remington, Spain, Norway, Sweden, Denmark, Egypt	79
,, shooting at high elevations above sea level	34
,, Tige	200
,, Whitworth	209, 210, 211
Rifles, early, difficult to load	199
,, Enfield, converted to Snider	212
,, figure of merit of. Table VI	101
,, heights of trajectory of. Table IV	100
,, lengths and weights of. Table II	98
,, patterns used in different countries. Table I	98
,, velocities of bullets of. Table III	99
,, times of flight of bullets. Table V	101
Rigby B.L. rifles	85
Rigby-Banks action	86
Rifling	47
,, different systems of	47
,, Enfield, 1853	47
,, Henry	49
,, invention of, to whom attributed	198
,, Lancaster	206
,, ratchet	49
,, Snider	47
,, the simpler the better	50

INDEX.

	PAGE
Rifling to determine the right or left edge of a groove	50
,, Whitworth	48
Rimfire cartridge	127
Robins first to demonstrate the effect of the resistance of the air	26
Rotation, axis of..	9
,, of bullet increases penetration	36
,, of earth unnecessary to consider	33

S.

Scabbard, solid wood lining for, introduced in 1864..	103
Schultz powder said to give less recoil than black	45
Sectional density..	19
,, ,, how expressed	19
Sergeant-at-Arms, corps of, first appointed	165
Short barrels have probably a range due to the "jump"	17
,, butts	15
Sighting M.H. carbines..	65
,, ,, rifles	65
,, Snider carbines	78
,, ,, rifle	78
Small-arm ammunition ..	124
Small arms, history of ..	156
,, bores	16
Snider action introduced	212
,, cartridge, description of	130
,, rifle	77
,, ,, sighted to ..	78
Spears	156
Spencer magazine rifle ..	90
Springfield rifle, United States..	81
Stocks, defects in	66
Striking velocity..	8
Stripping..	15
Sword bayonets ..	109
,, ,, M.H. carbine	109
,, cavalry pattern, 1853 and 1864	103
,, ,, ,, 1882, "long and short"	104
,, drummers and band of the line	107
,, ,, ,, of rifle regiments	107
,, household cavalry, "long and short"..	105
,, pioneer sawback..	107
,, practice ..	108

(S.A.)

INDEX.

	PAGE
Swords, service	102
,, staff sergeants of the line	106
,, ,, ,, of rifles	106
,, ,, ,, of artillery	106
,, ,, ,, of engineers	106
Swords, manufacture of	102
,, quality of, how tested	103

T.

Table comparing weight of rifle and 70 rounds of ammunition in British and foreign armies	130
,, giving lengths of bullets fired from various military rifle	42
,, giving particulars as to various military cartridges	127, 129
,, M giving heights of trajectory of M.H. rifle	36
,, of mechanism, proportion of weight of powder to weight of bullet, weight of one cartridge	98
,, of times of flight and angles of elevation of M.H. and Snider rifles and carbines	35, 36
,, showing recoil of military rifles	44
,, showing relation between charge and muzzle velocity	99
,, of the $\frac{d^2}{w}$ of different military bullets	21, 99
,, of penetrative energy of bullets	88
Tempering components	76
Terminal velocity	8
Thicknesses of different substances proof against bullets	41
The longer the bullet the greater must be the velocity of rotation	14
Tige rifle	200
Time of flight longer in the air than in a vacuum	31
,, ,, of a bullet and form of trajectory important to know	35
Trajectory always described by centre of a gravity of bullet.	32
,, cause of being a curved line	31
,, defined	21
,, flat	21
,, general form of, established	31
,, how modified by the resistance of the air	31
,, of the M.H. and Snider rifles and carbines	36
Trajectories, approximate method of finding	138
Tranter's revolver	96
Turner B.L. rifle	87
Twist, increasing, unsuitable for military arm	10
,, of rifling	10

INDEX.

	PAGE
Twist of rifling, how estimated	11
,, ,, best expressed in calibres	11
,, uniform	10

U.

Uniform twist	10
,, velocity	7

V.

Vacuo, in a, no rotation would be necessary for a bullet	31
Values of the $\frac{d^2}{w}$ of different bullets	21, 99
Velocity	7
,, greatest, of recoil	45
,, loss of, due to the resistance of the air	18
,, muzzle, how obtained	134
,, of a bullet more important than weight for penetration	36
,, of recoil	43
,, of rotation	11
,, of translation	11
,, remaining	8
,, retarded and accelerated	8
,, striking	8
,, terminal	8
,, uniform and variable	7
,, ,, how measured	8
,, variable, how measured	8
Ventilation of magazines, rules to be attended to	120
Vetterli magazine rifle	92
,, rifle, Italy	60

W.

Wads	128
,, and lubrication	128
,, inferior, effect on fouling	128
,, object of	128
,, table of those used with various military rifles	129
,, wax	129
Wax, a better lubricant than grease	129

INDEX.

	PAGE
Webley's revolver	97
Webley Wyley B.L. rifles	88
Weight of bullet, effect on recoil	42
" of bullets must not be too great	124
" of powder	125
" of rifle, effect on recoil	42
Werndl rifle, Austria	78
Wheel Lock	178
Whitworth rifling	48
" rifle	209
Winchester magazine rifle	91
Wind, velocity and direction of, influencing the motion of a bullet	7
Windage	9
" cause of inaccuracy with muzzle-loading smooth-bores	9
" defined	9
" how measured	9
Work	23
" done by the powder on the M.H. bullet	24
" how expressed	23

Y.

Yeomen of the Guard first appointed 175

TRAJECTOR[IES]
·45" & ·577" [...]

SCALE. { HEI[GHT]
         RAN[GE]

Calculated by Maj. Mc Clintock, R.A. Assist^t Sup^t
from Mr Bashforths amended tables.
Sept 1881.

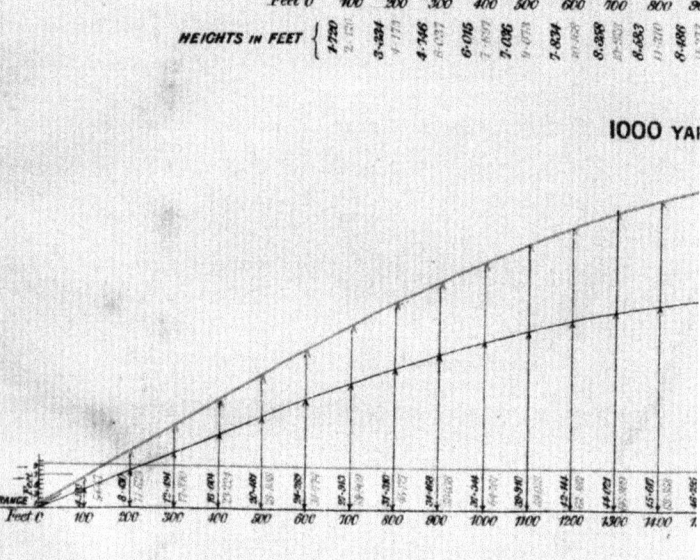

IES, *RIFLE.*

ORE OF BARREL.

HT .1"—1 FOOT
E .01"—1 FOOT

BORE	POWDER	BULLET	MUZZLE VELOCITY	$\dfrac{d^2}{W}$	SYSTEM OF RIFLING
0·45	85 grains	480 grains	1315 ft p. second	2·953	Henry.
0·577	70 " "	480 " "	1240 " "	4·855	Enfield.

$$g = 32.2$$

Cavalry height.
Infantry height.

RDS RANGE.

·577" bore

·45" bore

S^d H. T. Arbuthnot,
Col^l Sup^t
Royal Small Arms Factory
Enfield Lock.

TRAJECTORI
45" & ·577" /
SCALE. { HEIG
         { RANG

*Calculated by Maj. M! Clintock R.A. Assist Sup!
from M! Bashforths amended tables
Sep! 1881.*

500 YARDS

1000 YARDS RANGE.

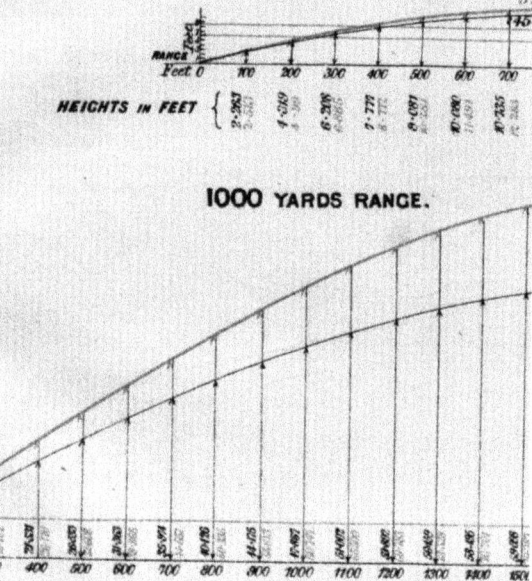

ES, CARBINE.
ORE OF BARREL.

·1" = 1 FOOT
·01" = 1 FOOT

BORE	POWDER	BULLET	MUZZLE VELOCITY	$\frac{d^2}{W}$	SYSTEM OF RIFLING
0·45"	70 grains	410 grains	1135 f.p. second	3·457	Henry
0·577	70 " "	480 " "	1120 " "	4·855	Enfield

$g = 32·2$

RANGE.

Cavalry height.
Infantry height.

·577 bore

·45 bore

Cavalry height.
Infantry height.

S.^d H. T. Arbuthnot,
Col.^l Sup.^t
Royal Small Arms Factory
Enfield Lock.

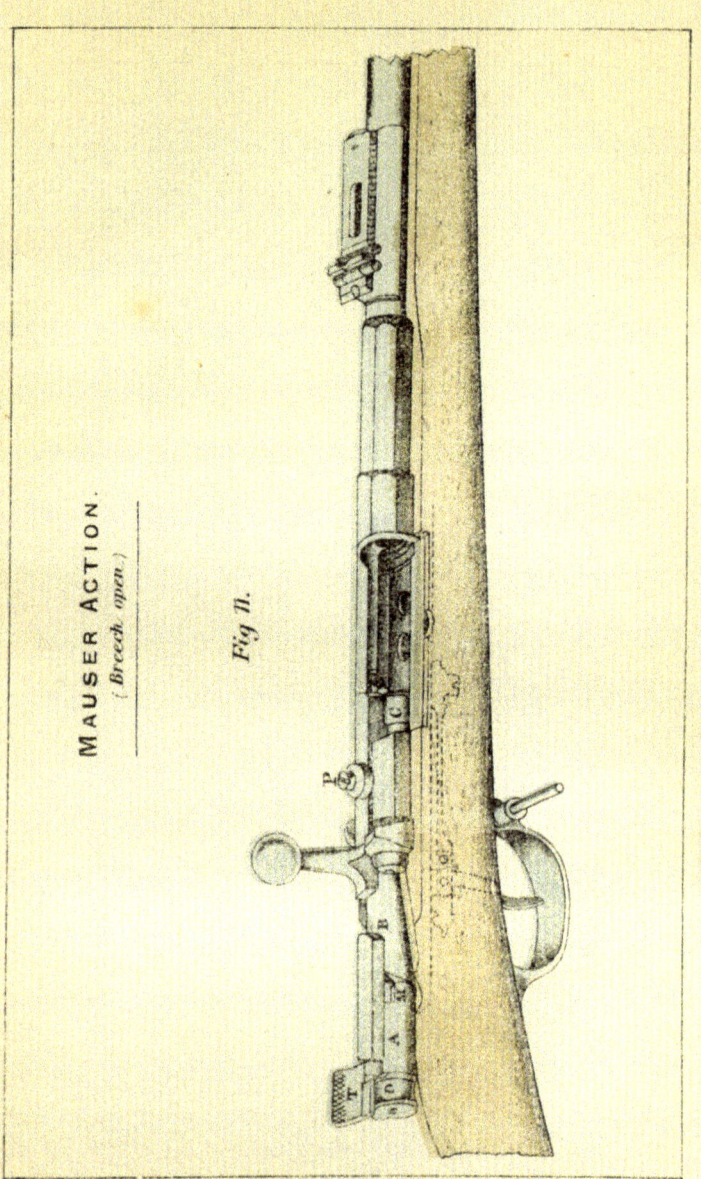

MAUSER ACTION.
(Breech open.)

Fig. II.

DANGERFIELD, LITH 22, BEDFORD ST COVENT GARDEN. 6657.

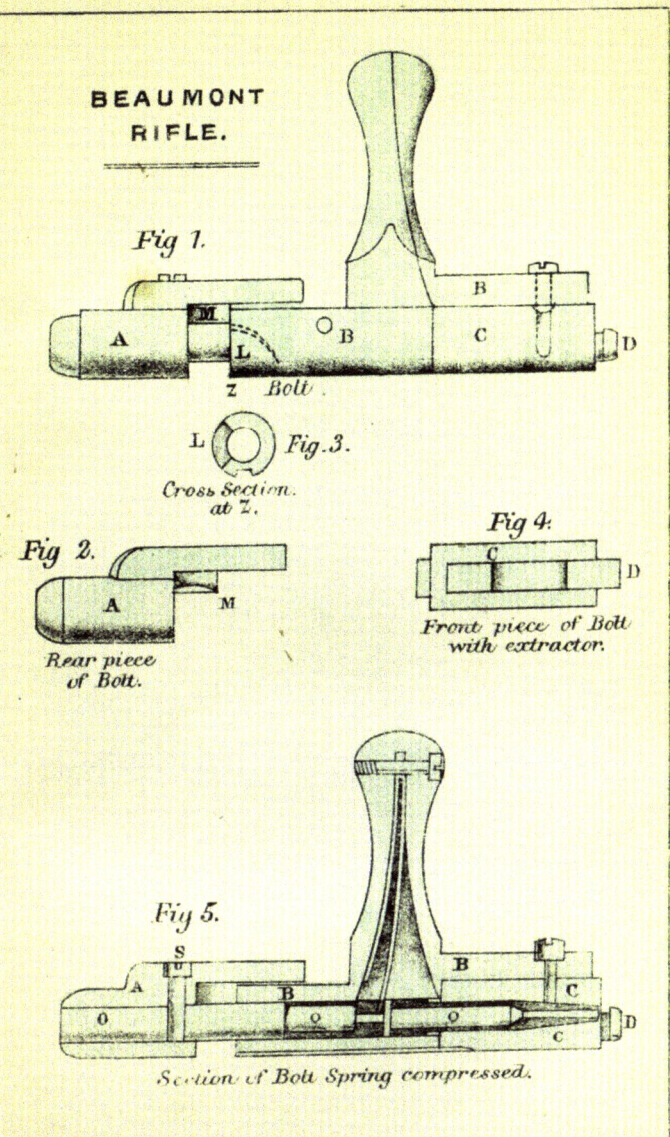

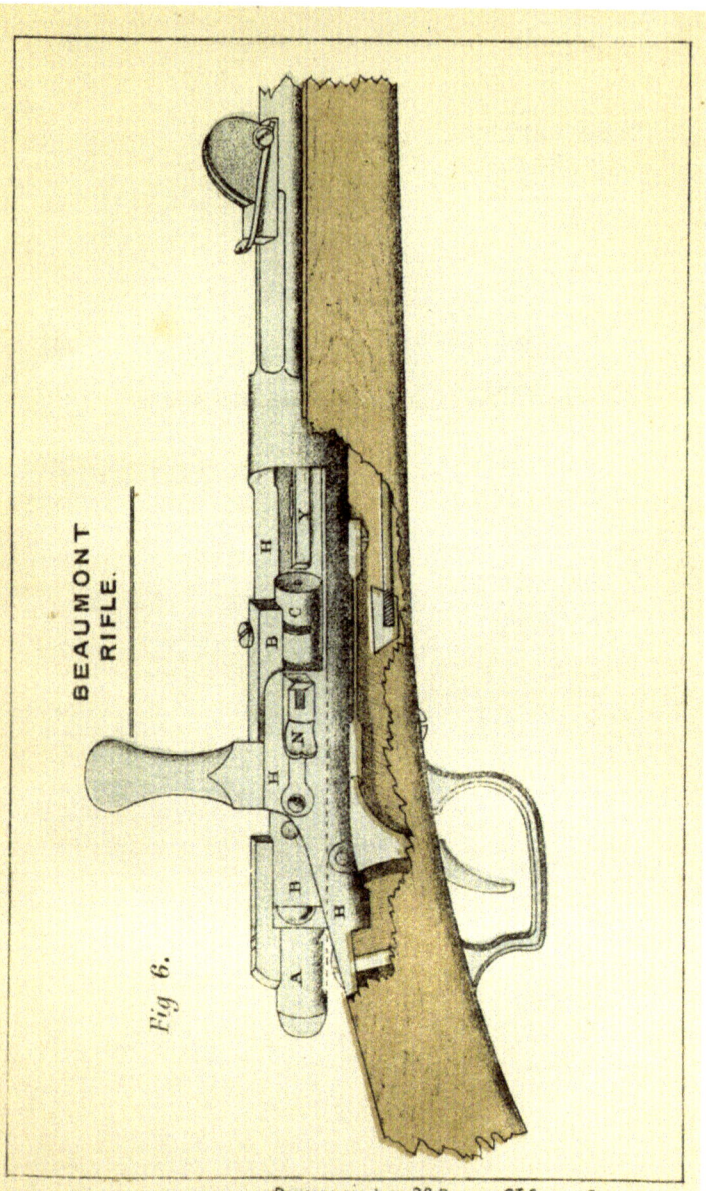

Fig 6.

BEAUMONT RIFLE.

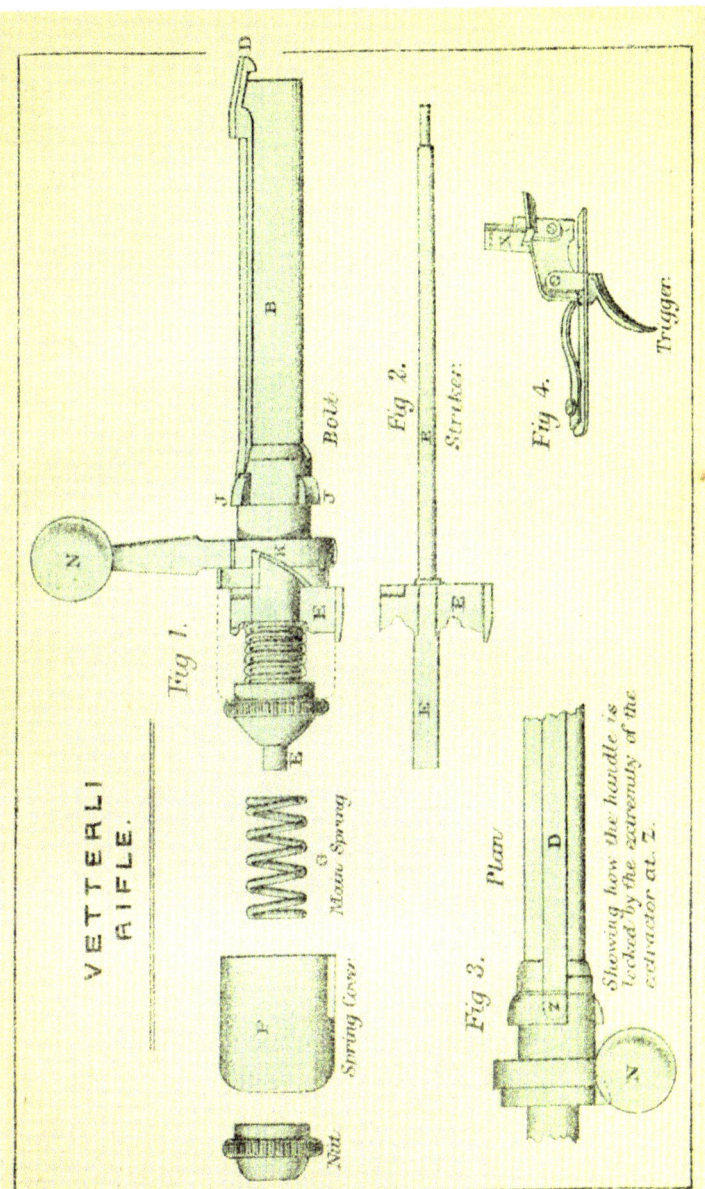

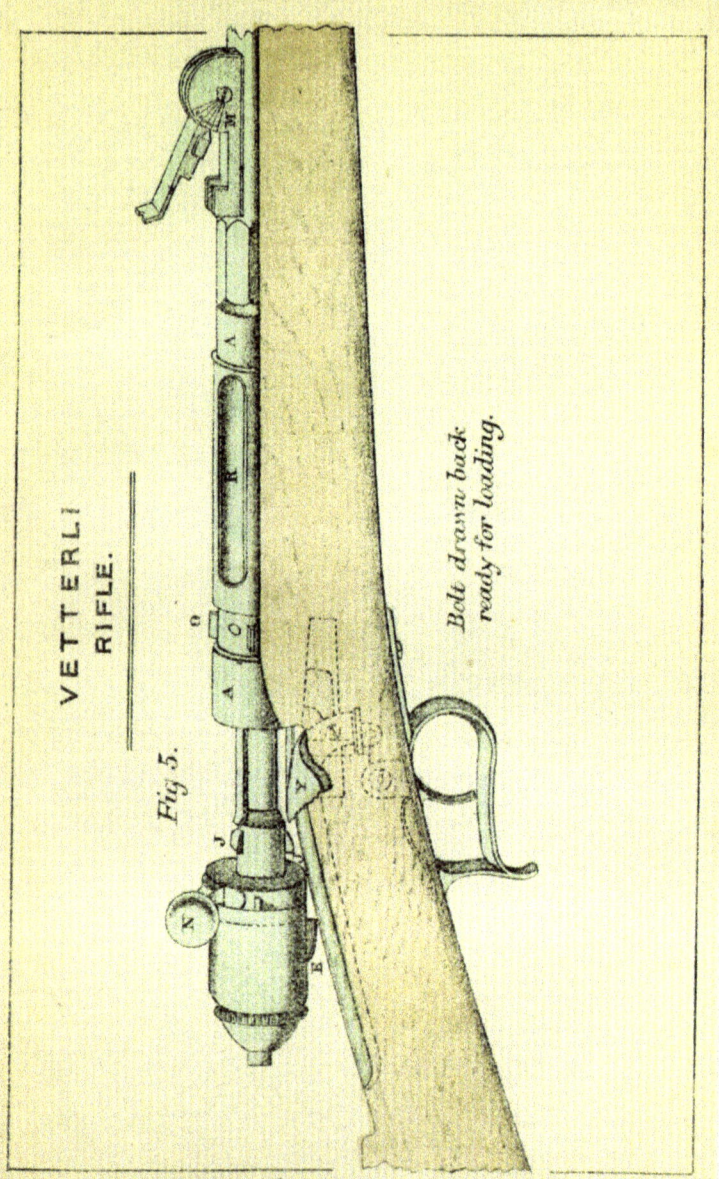

VETTERLI RIFLE.

Fig 5.

Bolt drawn back ready for loading.

SPRINGFIELD RIFLE.

Fig 2.

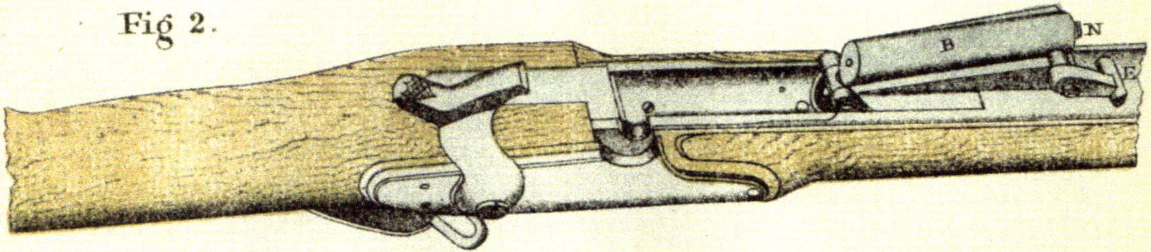

Original Pattern.

DANGERFIELD. LITH. 22. BEDFORD S^T. COVENT GARDEN. 6657.

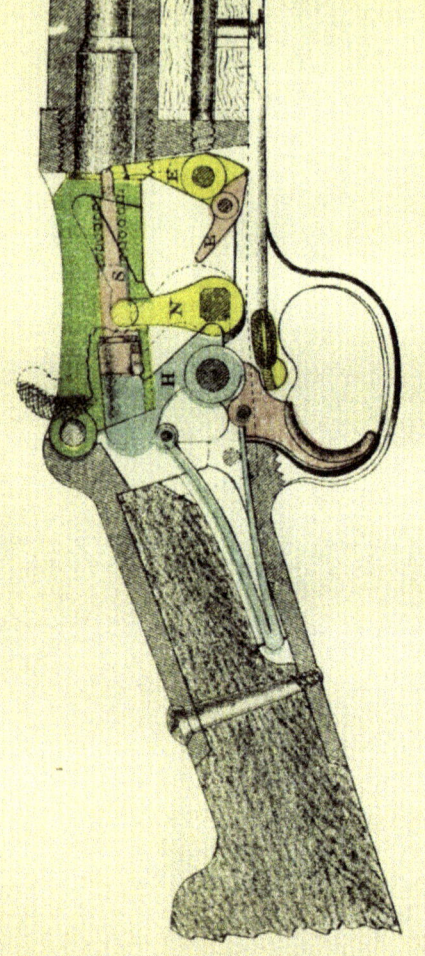

FIELD RIFLE.

Action for the Military arm.

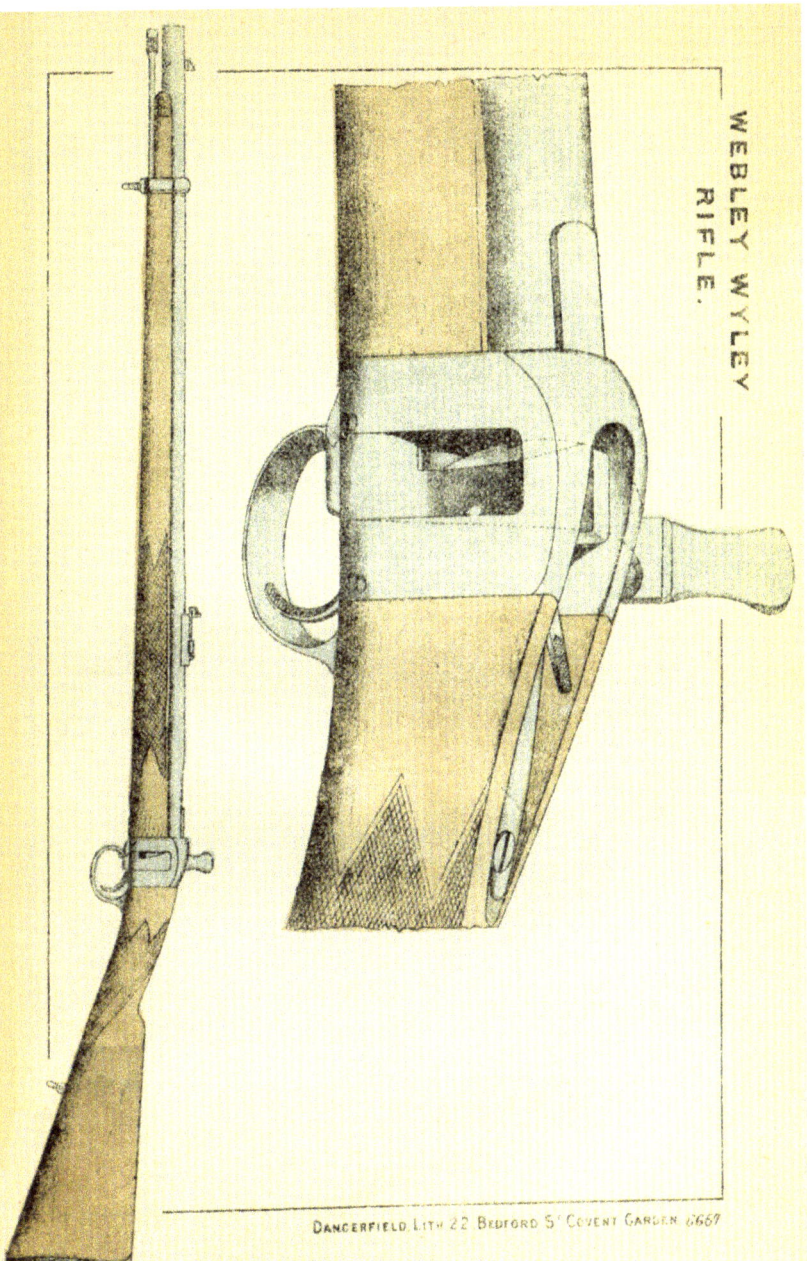

WEBLEY WYLEY RIFLE.

DANCERFIELD LITH 22 BEDFORD ST COVENT GARDEN

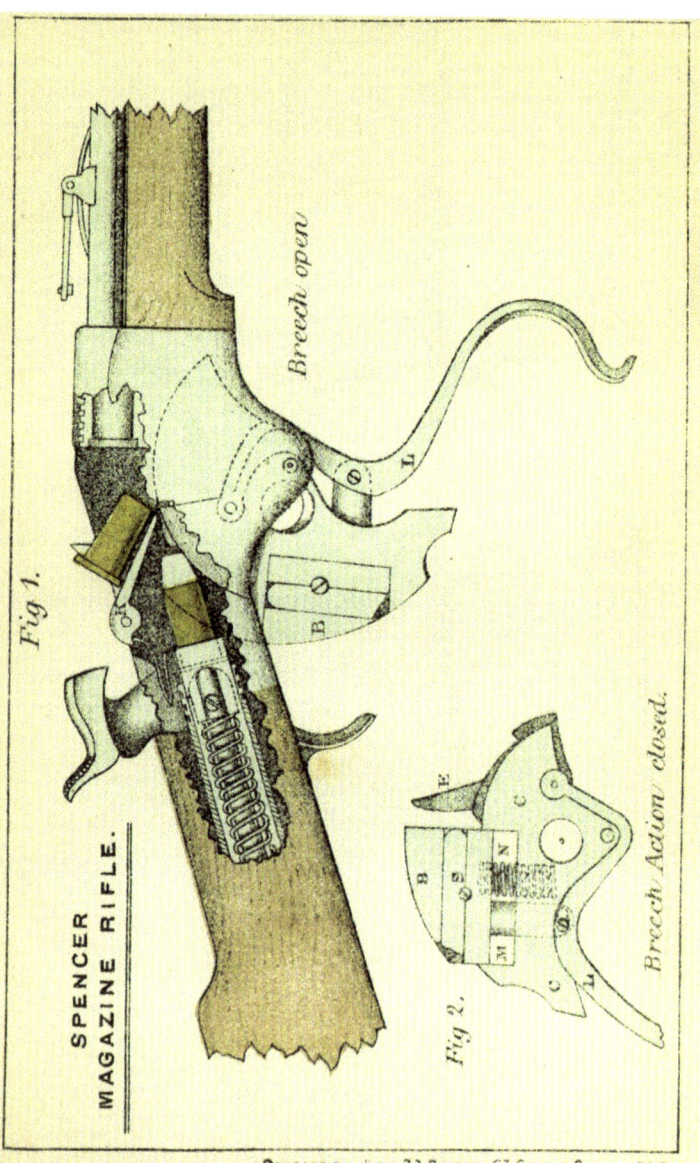

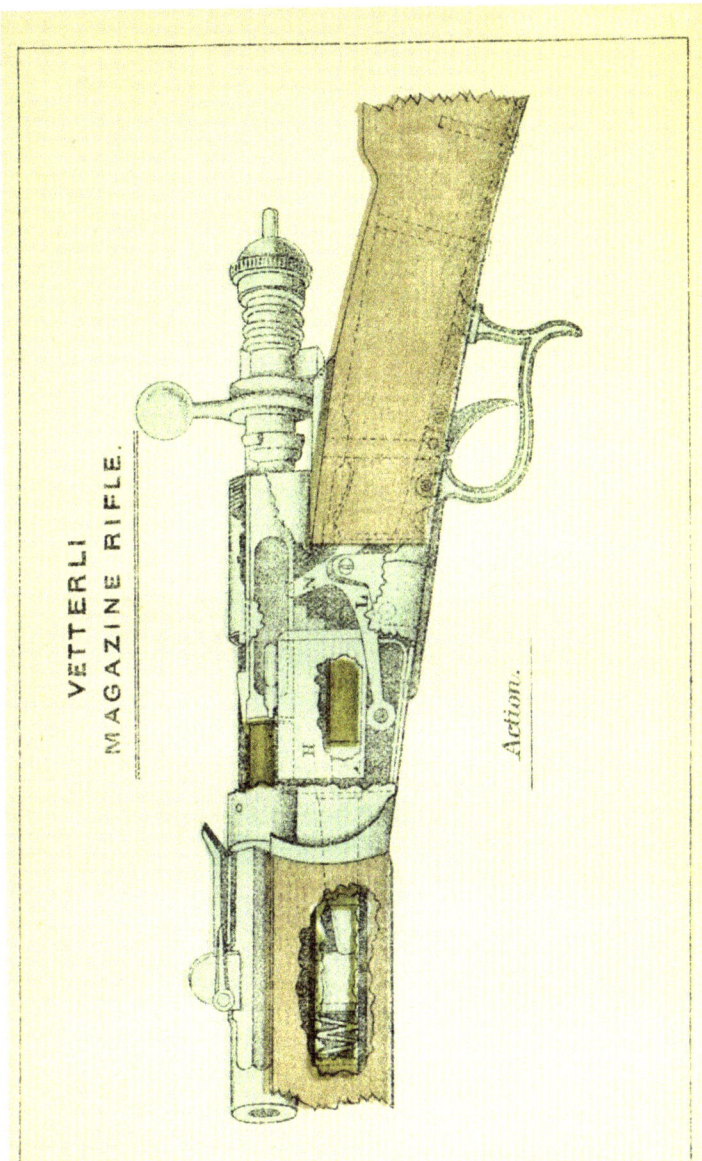

VETTERLI MAGAZINE RIFLE.

Action.

www.ingramcontent.com/pod-product-compliance
Ingram Content Group UK Ltd.
Pitfield, Milton Keynes, MK11 3LW, UK
UKHW022121230426
12048UKWH00011BA/640